FORGING THE PRAIRIE WEST

FORGING THE PRAIRIE WEST

John Herd Thompson

The

Illustrated

History

of

Canada

OXFORD
UNIVERSITY PRESS

OXFORD
UNIVERSITY PRESS

70 Wynford Drive Don Mills Ontario M3C 1J9
www.oup.com/ca

Oxford University Press is a department of the University of Oxford.
It furthers the University's objective of excellence in research, scholarship,
and education by publishing worldwide in

Oxford   New York
Auckland   Cape Town   Dar es Salaam   Hong Kong   Karachi
Kuala Lumpur   Madrid   Melbourne   Mexico City   Nairobi
New Delhi   Shanghai   Taipei   Toronto

With offices in

Argentina   Austria   Brazil   Chile   Czech Republic   France   Greece
Guatemala   Hungary   Italy   Japan   Poland   Portugal   Singapore
South Korea   Switzerland   Thailand   Turkey   Ukraine   Vietnam

Oxford is a trade mark of Oxford University Press

Canadian Cataloguing in Publication Data

Thompson, John Herd, 1946–
    Forging the Prairie West

(The illustrated history of Canada)
Includes bibliographical references and index.
ISBN-10: 0-19-541049-1
ISBN-13: 978-0-19-541049-5

1. Prairie Provinces – History. I. Title II. Series.

FC3237.T45 1998   971.2   C98-930126-5
F1060.T45 1998

'Buffalo Hunt on the Prairies' by Henry Hine (1847). Photo courtesy of the Royal
Ontario Museum Sigmund Samuel Collection © ROM.

4 5 6 7 — 09 08 07
This book is printed on permanent (acid-free) paper ∞.
Printed in Canada

To my aunt, Tillie Lennerton, and the memory of my uncle, Clyde Lennerton, Manitobans who endured more than six decades of Prairie winters

TABLE OF CONTENTS

MAPS

ABBREVIATIONS

Glenbow: The Glenbow-Alberta Institute, Calgary

NAC: National Archives of Canada, Ottawa

PAA: Provincial Archives of Alberta, Edmonton

PAM: Provincial Archives of Manitoba, Winnipeg

ROM: Royal Ontario Museum, Toronto

SAB: Saskatchewan Archives Board, Regina

WCPI: Western Canada Pictorial Index

INTRODUCTION

Imag(in)ing a Region

Contemporary Canadians routinely think about their country as a segmented sequence of regions. When Oxford University Press convened six historians to plan this series, we did not pause to discuss, let alone to examine seriously, the fundamental assumption underlying these books: that six regional histories were the appropriate way to represent Canada's past. Canadian historians no longer seriously question the legitimacy of the 'limited identity' of region.[1] But as Patricia Limerick points out, 'regions are much more the creation of human thought and behavior than they are products of nature'.[2] The region that is the subject of this book is a creation of the very recent historic past. The Native people and European traders who knew intimately the forests, park belt, and grasslands of the geographical area would have found the concept of 'the Prairie provinces' meaningless. When Canada bought the western interior north of the forty-ninth parallel from the Hudson's Bay Company in 1869, the Canadians who moved west brought with them a transcontinental vision of a Canada *a mari usque ad mare*—from Atlantic to Pacific; to the extent that these women and men had any overarching purpose beyond building new

lives for themselves, it was to extend their nation-state, not to build a group of provinces and a region. The process of constructing the Prairie West as a cultural region—what historian Richard Allen called 'A Region of the Mind'—was slow. A sense of regional consciousness developed only gradually, and only in the last two decades of the twentieth century has this regional identity been honed to such anguished perfection that it co-exists, uneasily, with the nationalist aspirations of the nineteenth century.

Thus any history of the Canadian Prairies must be a book about the myths of the people who shaped a prairie regional identity and through it shaped the Prairie West. 'Myth' in this context is not the opposite of fact, something that stands in contrast to reality. A myth is a story that through persistent repetition comes to symbolize a society's beliefs about itself: where it came from, where it has been, and where it might be going. Because the concept of 'the Canadian Prairies' was the creation of European colonizers and their descendants, that designation itself makes this a book about their myths and chronologically bounded by their presence. Just as Richard White explains of the United States, however, 'there is not and never has been a single myth, a single imagined West. Myths . . . are constantly in competition just as various groups within the West were always in competition.'³ In this book I've tried to encompass as many of the diverse myths of the Canadian Prairie West as 70,000 words and 166 images will allow.

Because this is an illustrated history, additional words about the images are required. To make this a book that would be something more than 'The Canadian Prairies in Pictures', I started with three broad objectives. First, I would take full advantage of images as historical documents. I would 'read' the thousands of pictures that I consulted as carefully as I would read a diary, a letter, or the record of a parliamentary debate, and I would use the pictures not simply to ornament a written text but as sources to construct history. Reflecting an academic historian's fetishism about primary sources, I resolved to consider only 'factual' images 'authentic' to the historical events that they depicted: no 1920s drawings of Selkirk colonists from C.W. Jeffreys' *Picture Gallery of Canadian History*, or 1940s Franklin Arbuckle paintings such as 'Anthony Henday enters a Blackfoot Camp, 1754'. My second objective was to choose images representing the cultural diversities of the Prairie West, the 'limited identities' of gender, ethnicity, and class, as well as the identity of region. Third, to the greatest extent possible, the images would be original, never before reproduced.

I have completely achieved none of these (I now realize) naive and partially contradictory objectives, but the attempt has taught me many things. Learning to use images as historical evidence proved the most rewarding of my three endeavours. Through their writings and by generously sharing their time, many archivists patiently taught me that not one of the images that I examined was an objective fact: like any written document, each image had been created by a particular person, with a particular point of view, for a particular purpose. Like any written document, each image would yield meaning only with interpretation. Each image had to be subjected to the same rigorous questioning that a historian would apply to a written source: who created it? when was it created? and for what purpose?⁴

Historians of images also explained that photographs do not necessarily tell greater truths than sketches or paintings. Precisely because they seem to provide incontrovertible proof, photographs can actually distort reality more effectively than either documentary art or the written word. The first edition of *The Art of Retouching* appeared in 1880, and literally hundreds of celebrated 'candid' photographs have in fact been carefully stage-managed. Captain Ivor Castle's frequently reproduced photos of Canadian soldiers in the First World War leaping enthusiastically from the trenches to launch an attack were staged in training far behind the front line. Charitably, these photographs could be described as 're-enactments'; uncharitably, they are simply fakes. 'Photographs may not lie,' the American photographer Lewis Hine liked to say, but 'liars may photograph.'⁵

Hine's aphorism also has a deeper, subtler meaning. However honest the photographer may be, photography by its very nature takes its subjects out of their context and manipulates their meaning through the choice of viewpoint, lighting, and composition.⁶ Lest we become indignant at such deception, we should remember that most of the photographers upon whom historians rely have been primarily businesspersons and only secondarily artists; faithfully documenting reality for the benefit of future generations was not their concern. As Lilly Koltun has pointed out, the origins of nineteenth-century photography were purely commercial: 'no professional photograph . . . was ever taken . . . without visualizing a direct commercial or practical application for the image or without considering the popular preference in subject matter and effect.' Like artists who had to please their patrons, photographers produced images that would tempt a client to buy. Canada's most successful nineteenth-century photographer, William Notman, forced a 'house style' upon his employees, squeezing 'reality into a mould rather than flexibly "mirroring" it', so that their photographs showed 'almost exclusively posed and self-consciously constructed images. . . .'[7]

These lessons helped me to overcome my false certainty that only images from the same period as the events they depicted were of real use to historians. Understood in an interpretive context, a C.W. Jeffreys sketch could inform the understanding of history that I wanted to convey—even if it told me more about the period in which it was created than the one it portrayed. Nevertheless, for my own vaguely defined aesthetic reasons, I continued to resist Franklin Arbuckle's work.

My second goal, to visually represent the diverse 'limited identities' of the Prairie West, proved frustratingly elusive. Images of ethnic and racial diversity abound, but the men, women, and children of the exotic 'other' race or ethnicity were depicted almost exclusively through the eyes of British-Canadian painters and photographers. Native people, for example, appear frequently among the images that follow, but only as they were represented by painters and photographers who were overwhelmingly non-Native. Gender presents similar problems. Most images of the Prairie West have been created by men, and almost half of all the images reproduced here depict men alone; a mere dozen depict only women. In most of the pictures showing both men and women, it is the men who are doing while the women watch or assist. These images reflect socially defined gender roles rather than 'reality': just as the white men who painted Aboriginal people were more interested in the hunt than in the processing of the buffalo hides, male photographers paid more attention to the public sphere of men than the private one of women. In the same way, when members of the élite created images of working-class people, they tended to produce stylized portraits of 'a class frozen at work, at play, or on parade', imposing an 'inevitable passivity' on working-class experience.[8] Rather than reject these imperfect images of ethnicity, gender, and class, however, historians must search for meaning in the things that are implicit and unspoken, just as they would do with written sources.

If my goal of representativeness was difficult to achieve, my ambition of absolute originality proved to be a fantasy. Remarkably few never-before-reproduced images were waiting to be 'discovered' in any of the nine archives that I visited: the National Archives of Canada, the Library of Congress, the Western Canada Pictorial Index, the Provincial Archives of Manitoba and Alberta, the Saskatchewan Archives Board, the City of Edmonton Archives, and the Glenbow-Alberta Archives. Some historical periods produced fewer images than others. The two centuries discussed in chapters two and three, for obvious reasons, left the most fragmentary visual account. But gaps appear in later periods as well: there are surprisingly few images of the 1930s, for example. And in all periods there have been subjects that, for one reason or another, were seldom sketched, painted, or photographed: leaving out previously published images would have meant leaving out those subjects.

Thus only about a third of the images in this book have, as far as I am able to tell, never been published. The others have appeared at least once, several many times. Douglas Cass of the Glenbow estimates that every image in the Institute's catalogue has been published at least half a dozen times. I hope that the necessity of including previously published images will prove to be a virtue. In the past, some of them have been used out of context, or inventively misrepresented; the histories of those misrepresentations should themselves be part of the visual history of the Canadian Prairie West. Other images—Paul Kane paintings, the Hind expedition camped in front of a canoe, strikers tipping a Winnipeg streetcar—have been chosen expressly because they are so familiar as to have become near-iconic, and it is in that framework that they are discussed. The captions relating the images to the narrative are intended to encourage readers to look for new meanings in familiar pictures.

This introduction would not be complete without expressions of gratitude. Dedicated archivist-historians have helped me as they have helped many others: Johwanna Alleyne, Elizabeth Blight, Jim Burant, Douglas Cass, Lynne Champagne, Tonia Fanella, June Honey, Dennis Hydak, Tim Novak, and Keith Wilson merit special thanks. Lilly Koltun, Andrea Kunard, and Brock Silversides, three archivist-historians I never met, deserve individual acknowledgement in addition to the note references to their written work. Bill Brennan shared the knowledge he gained writing two fine books about Regina. Paige Raibmon, a gifted young historian, was kind enough to read and comment on the manuscript, as did Heather McAsh, and an anonymous reader saved me from mistakes of fact and emphasis. Gerry Friesen went well beyond the call of collegiality in helping identify images. My autumnal colleagues in the department of History and Classics at the University of Alberta provided both practical assistance and a congenial working atmosphere when the manuscript was in its final stages: Gerhard Ens, Paul Voisey, David Mills, Rod Macleod, and Frances Swyripa. Sally Livingston, my wonderful editor, clarified and enlivened my prose. Finally, I thank Mark, Anne, and Katrin Thompson for their patient endurance as son, daughter, and wife to a man who lives in so many pasts.

CHAPTER ONE

'Ever . . . useless to cultivating man'

$\mathcal{W}$hat criteria make a particular portion of the earth a region? 'There are no "natural" regions,' William Westfall points out; 'the land is divided into formal regions only as abstract criteria are applied to it.'[1] If distinct physical geographic boundaries are a critical test of a region, the Canadian Prairie West must fail. Only one side of the huge quadrilateral that encloses Manitoba, Saskatchewan, and Alberta has any physiographic reality: the west, where the peaks of the Rocky Mountains describe a barrier between the western interior of the continent and the Pacific slope. On the south, east, and north it was politics, not physical geography, that drew the lines. The forty-ninth parallel, which partitions the Prairie provinces of the Dominion of Canada from the Plains states of the American republic, was traced in 1818 by British and American diplomats who had never set foot there. The sixtieth parallel, which separates the modern provinces from the territories to the north, was drawn in 1905 when Wilfrid Laurier's Liberal government invented Alberta and Saskatchewan. Robert Borden's Conservative government extended that line eastward to Hudson Bay in 1912, after

Manitobans demanded a piece of the North of their own. The crooked line that defines the eastern boundary of the Prairie West and gives Manitoba its distinctive keystone shape appeared that same year, ending three decades of interprovincial arguments about where Ontario ended and the Prairie West began.

Physically, the 1.95 million square kilometres of the three Prairie provinces—20 per cent of Canada's area—are extraordinarily diverse. Geographer John Warkentin warns that the very term 'Prairie provinces' 'is quite inappropriate and has misled many people about the character of the land'. Actual 'prairies'—level or undulating treeless grasslands—are in fact a geographic sub-region within the Prairie West, and three-fifths of the region has none of the characteristics of a prairie. Millennia before cartographers sketched the three provinces, retreating glaciers carved two very dissimilar landforms across what would become Manitoba, Saskatchewan, and Alberta. To the south and west an interior plain spreads from the Red River Valley towards the Rocky Mountains; north and east of this plain runs the rugged Canadian Shield of Precambrian rock, the area that Native people and European traders called 'the Stony Country'. These two landforms, the interior plains and the Shield, are so different that *The Canadian Encyclopedia* uses Saskatchewan's Big Muddy Valley and the Shield near Flin Flon, Manitoba, to illustrate 'the enormous variety among Canada's geological regions'.[2]

The Big Muddy Valley also embodies the striking physiographic variation found within the interior plain itself. From an elevation of 300 metres at its eastern edge, the interior plain rises in a series of steps to a height of 1,200 metres at the foot of the Rocky Mountains. Dr James Hector, the geologist who accompanied Captain John Palliser across the western interior in 1857, reported that 'three boldly marked levels . . . of different mineral composition as well as geographical distribution' intersected the plain between the Red River and the Rocky Mountains. The 'first prairie level, . . . the wide flat plain upon which the Red River Settlement is situated' he attributed to 'a time when Lake Winepeg [sic] covered a much more extensive area than it at present occupies.' This Manitoba Plain ends in lines of hills—the western shore of the ancient lake—that demarcate the Saskatchewan Plain, Hector's 'second prairie level'. Midway across what became the province of Saskatchewan, the 'irregularly disposed ridges and cones of very coarse drift' of the Missouri Coteau begin the Alberta Plain, which runs west to the foothills of the Rockies. Hector and his colleagues 'did not traverse this level at all' in 1857; the Scottish scientist described it second-hand from the stories of 'La Grande Prairie' recounted to him by the Métis hunters who fed and guided Palliser's party.[3]

In the past, the flora of the Canadian prairies varied as much as the physiography. Until the European presence reshaped the landscape in the second half of the nineteenth century, prairie—grassland with perennial grasses, forbs (non-grass plants), and small shrubs—covered the southern triangle of the interior plain. But the term 'prairie' masked a diverse set of vegetation sub-regions. In the driest of these sub-regions, in what is now southwestern Saskatchewan and southeastern Alberta, hardy drought-resistant grasses populated the short-grass prairie. In the more humid 'mixed prairie' that encircled it, these same grasses were joined by taller species, like northern wheat grass. Only the southeastern corner of the interior plain, in what is now Manitoba, received enough precipitation to create what botanists consider 'true prairie', with big bluestem and porcupine grass growing past a man's shoulders. As the interior plain moves northward, groves of poplar and scrub oak (universally called 'bluffs' by English-speaking prairie-dwellers) interrupt the prairie, coming together to create a crescent known as the 'park belt' that overlaps the intersection between the prairie and the taiga, the boreal forest of the Canadian Shield. As this coniferous forest of spruce and pine descends to the shores of Hudson Bay, the inland ocean of the Canadian prairies, it gives way to what Native people called 'the Land of Little Sticks'—a subarctic region of stunted spruce and lichens.

The northwestern interior's great distance from Europe, and the difficulty of travel across the Shield, insulated it from integration into a European economic system for two centuries. But when French and English traders arrived

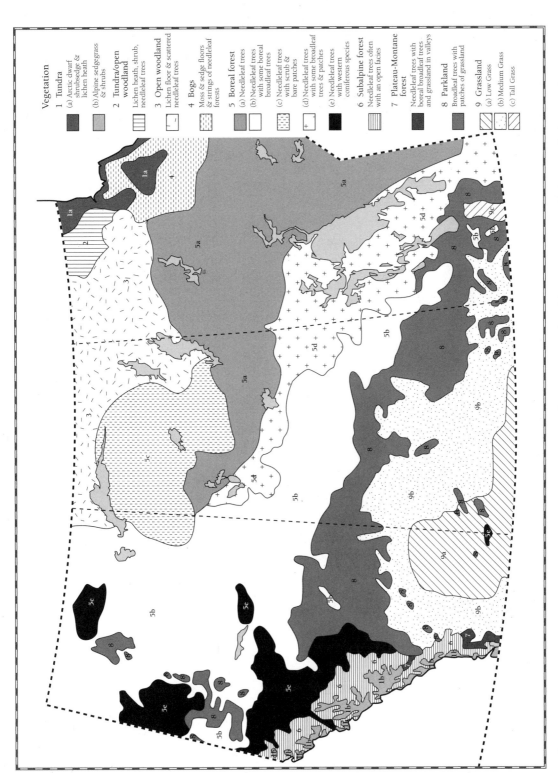

Vegetation regions of the Prairie West. Source: Thomas R. Weir and Geoffrey Matthews, *Atlas of the Prairie Provinces* (Toronto: Oxford University Press Canada, 1971), p. 2.

Vegetation

1 Tundra
(a) Arctic dwarf shrubsedge & lichen heath
(b) Alpine sedgegrass & shrubs

2 Tundra/open woodland
Lichen heath, shrub, needleleaf trees

3 Open woodland
Lichen floor & scattered needleleaf trees

4 Bogs
Moss & sedge floors & strings of needleleaf forests

5 Boreal forest
(a) Needleleaf trees
(b) Needleleaf trees with some boreal broadleaf trees
(c) Needleleaf trees with scrub & bare patches
(d) Needleleaf trees with some broadleaf trees & patches
(e) Needleleaf trees with western coniferous species

6 Subalpine forest
Needleleaf trees often with an open facies

7 Plateau-Montane forest
Needleleaf trees with boreal broadleaf trees and grassland in valleys

8 Parkland
Broadleaf trees with patches of grassland

9 Grassland
(a) Low Grass
(b) Medium Grass
(c) Tall Grass

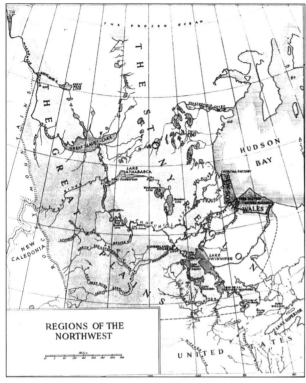

'Regions of the Northwest', Map 2 in Eric Ross, *Beyond the River and the Bay: Some Observations on the State of the Canadian Northwest in 1811* (Toronto: University of Toronto Press, 1970). Eric Ross used the accounts written by North West Company and Hudson's Bay Company traders to create a fictional 1811 guidebook providing 'the Intending Settler with an Intimate Knowledge of That Country'. He also invented an imaginary Scotsman, Ian Alexander Bell Robertson, to be the book's author. This map uses the traders' actual descriptive names for the geographic sub-regions. Ross's Canadian patriotism got the better of him, however: the forty-ninth parallel shown here was not negotiated as the boundary between the territories claimed by Britain and the United States until 1818, seven years after the year that this map is supposed to depict.

in the eighteenth century, they learned from the local Native people the river and lake routes that made summer transportation within the region relatively simple. Three some-

times turbulent rivers, called by the English the Hayes, the Nelson, and the Churchill, could take them south and west from Hudson Bay across the Shield. The Hayes and the Nelson both entered an immense lake that the Cree called *win-nipi*—'murky waters'. From *win-nipi* a canoe could turn directly west into the Saskatchewan River system or head south into the Red River and join the Assiniboine River as it meandered west through the prairie and into the park belt. Either the Churchill River or a second branch of the Hayes provided a third route west, which then led north again on the Athabasca River to Lake Athabasca and the valley of the Peace River.

The climate of the northwestern interior required greater adaptations from Europeans than did the transportation routes, and these adaptations too they learned from the Native people. Climate varies over time, but the Canadian prairies have been cold and dry for forty centuries. Before Canadians labelled the region the Prairie West, they more appropriately called it the 'North West': its southern boundary, the forty-ninth parallel, was to the north of agricultural settlement in the rest of nineteenth-century Canada. Mean temperatures in January approach -20°C in southern Manitoba and Saskatchewan; the Chinook winds warm southern Alberta only to -12°C. The abundant sunshine (over 2,200 hours annually) falls for much of the year on frozen ground: the length of the frost-free season varies within the region from about 100 to about 150 consecutive days, and can vary substantially from year to year in any specific location. Since cold air holds less moisture than warm air, precipitation levels are (to use meteorologists' terms) at best 'sub-humid' and at

Short-grass prairie near Swift Current, Saskatchewan. Bill Brooks/Masterfile.

The Canadian Shield near Flin Flon, Manitoba. Comstock Photofiles Limited.

Big Muddy Valley, Saskatchewan. Comstock Photofile Limited.

worst 'semi-arid'. No place in the Prairie West gets much more than 500 millimetres of rain and snowfall annually, and the southern prairies get as little as 250 mm. Nor can this precipitation be depended upon from year to year: meteorologists calculate that there have been droughts—periods of at least five years with less than 60 per cent of average rainfall— thirteen times over the past seven centuries. A seemingly ceaseless wind exacerbates summer dryness and whips winter snow into life-threatening blizzards. Writing in the 1930s, the poet Anne Marriott called it 'The Wind, Our Enemy'.

Violent, unpredictable change and the relentless wind are the only constants about the prairie climate. On 10 December 1797, in what is now southwestern Manitoba, the North West Company's David Thompson awoke to bright sunshine and bitter cold of minus 20 degrees Fahrenheit (-29°C). Two hours later 'a heavy Gale, with high drift and dark weather' lashed his party as it crossed the Souris River Valley. By noon, 'a perfect Storm' of blinding snow made it impossible for Thompson to read his compass. A southerly wind turned the snow to 'showers of rain' in mid-afternoon; the great map-maker found wooded shelter only because, 'thank good Providence, my face struck against some Oak saplings'. His men threw their tent over the oaks to shelter themselves from the 'hail and sleet', huddled together, and 'all thanked the Almighty for our preservation'. 'In little more than twelve hours a difference of temperature of fifty-six degrees [Fahrenheit],' Thompson recorded with awe. 'I had weathered many a hard gale, but this was the most distressing day I had ever seen.'[4]

Until the mid-nineteenth century, European visitors chronicled the profuse animals and birds with wonder. The lush pelts of the beaver, marten, and muskrat had attracted men like Thompson to the western interior of North America, but it was the abundance of game animals that seized their hunters' imaginations. Cranes, herons, geese, and ducks bred in pot-holes and sloughs on the prairie and on the lakes of the Shield; prairie chicken, ruffed grouse, and spruce grouse could be found on prairie, park belt, and Shield. The prairie was thick with elk, mule deer, and pronghorn antelope; bighorn sheep wandered east from the Rockies to graze in the foothills. Amazed Europeans exhausted their stores of adjectives to describe the millions of plains bison, herds too vast to see across. 'We were never out of sight of . . . astonishing numbers of these animals,' wrote the artist Paul Kane of a journey across the park belt in 1848. 'We had not found it necessary to go a step out of our direct course to find more than we required for our use.' Like Kane and his party, other predators too prospered on the large ungulates; in 1754 Hudson's Bay trader Anthony Henday reported 'wolves without numbers', and bears, both grizzly and black, hunted from the Red River west to the Rockies. Smaller predators—coyotes, foxes, and hawks—made do with grouse and ground squirrels.[5]

Captain William Butler (1838–1910), a British officer who travelled west to the mountains and north to Lake Athabasca, told spellbound readers of a pristine wilderness in books that he called *The Great Lone Land* (1872) and *The Wild North Land* (1873). In the 'complete absence of history', the plains and the Shield of the northwestern interior were 'the world as it had taken shape and form from the hands of the Creator'; 'the roll of the passing centuries disturbed not its slumber.'[6] But Butler's depiction of a never-changing natural environment was a romantic exaggeration: climate, fire, wildlife, and human beings were constantly reshaping the 'natural' landscape even as he described it. The environment of the western interior was not pristine, frozen in time, but in constant flux. On the grasslands, the annual migration of millions of buffalo fertilized, compacted, and eroded the soil, fouled the waters, and uprooted trees. Fires, some started by lightning and others deliberately set by Native people, destroyed small trees and rejuvenated the forbs and perennial grasses, which grew more rapidly on burned-over prairie. In fact, fire had pushed the southern boundary of the park belt farther north as the centuries passed.[7]

Until the mid-nineteenth century, however, all but an eccentric handful of the few Europeans who saw the northwestern interior of North America agreed that it would remain a wilderness. The artist George Catlin concluded that 'this strip of country, which extends from the province of Mexico to Lake Winnipeg on the North, . . . is, and ever must be, useless to cultivating man.' The region had surely been, wrote David Thompson, 'given by Providence to the Red Men for ever, as the wilds and sands of Africa are given to the Arabians'.[8]

CHAPTER TWO

Cultures in Contact:
1670–1821

When James W. St. G. Walker examined 'The Indian in Canadian Historical Writing' in 1971, he discovered 'a picture of the Indian as a human being [that] is confusing, contradictory and incomplete'. In general histories, Native people appeared briefly in the section on Canada's formidable geography, as if Aboriginal societies were another natural obstacle for Europeans to overcome, like the Canadian Shield, the harsh winters, or the black flies. The First Nations who received the most attention were those who presented the most formidable military obstacles: in Central Canada the Iroquois, and in the Prairie West the Blackfoot. Euro-Canadian historians described Native people either as brutal 'savages' who 'massacred' European colonizers, or, if they were more sympathetic, as child-like 'noble savages'. Seen as occupying a lower rung on the human evolutionary ladder, Native societies were portrayed as static and unchanging, frozen in a stone age. Native people were ascribed no motivations of their own save 'primitive' urges; without agency, they merely reacted to the initiatives of European explorers and traders. Once the explorers and traders left the scene, the Native people too vanished from the history books.[1]

This 'old' version of Native history, writes Bruce G. Trigger, helped Euro-Canadians to 'create a myth of the past that reflected their prejudices against native peoples and justified their mission of supplanting them'. Since the 1960s, archaeologists have amassed evidence that pre-contact Native societies were not static, but adapted to changing circumstances just as all human societies did, sometimes with remarkable rapidity. 'New' historians like Trigger, Jennifer S.H. Brown, Toby Morantz, Olive Patricia Dickason, and Arthur J. Ray have reinterpreted the documentary record left by European traders, missionaries, and officials to reshape our understanding of post-contact Native history, and have presented us with a story of Native-white relations that is more complex and less comfortable.[2]

To write of 'Native peoples of the Canadian prairies' in the period before the arrival of Europeans, however, would be to impose our Euro-Canadian present upon the Aboriginal past, for the recent political boundaries of the Prairie provinces had no meaning to the people who made their lives on those lands for millennia before any European had crossed the Atlantic. Precisely where those first people came from and when they arrived are questions that will never have definite answers. The most widely accepted theory is that they migrated to North America from Asia over the Bering Strait across a northern land bridge that no longer exists; but in fact there is surprisingly little archaeological evidence to support this assertion. Most of the creation myths of the First Nations reject the migration hypothesis and insist that their ancestors inhabited this continent from time immemorial. In the Lakota Sioux account, for example, 'the first man sprang from the soil in the midst of the great plains. . . . From this man sprang the Lakota nation and . . . our people have been born and died on this plain; and no people have shared it with us until the coming of the European.'[3] We do know for certain that people have lived in the western interior of North America for a very long time: at least 17,000 years, and possibly as many as 60,000.

Scholars also dispute the numbers of Native people who lived in the Americas before Europeans arrived. The consensus, according to Olive Dickason, is that each region was inhabited 'in large part to the carrying capacities of the land for the ways of life that were being followed'.[4] Given the climate and topography of the northern plains and the boreal forest of the Shield, their carrying capacity was likely quite low. Thus the people who lived there were probably few and widely dispersed: a population estimate of 30,000 stands midway between the high and low speculations.

These 30,000 people were hunters and gatherers who moved seasonally within defined territories in search of game. Their cultures differed considerably, and the boundaries between cultural groups shifted constantly over the hundreds of centuries of Native history. In AD 1600, five groups of Native people lived in or adjacent to what would eventually become the Canadian Prairie West. They spoke five different languages from three distinct linguistic families: Athapaskan, Algonkian, and Siouian. These linguistic families are as dissimilar, linguists suggest, as German and Chinese; and within each one, the languages differ as much as English and Dutch.

The 4,000 Chipewyan who lived in the boreal forest west of Hudson Bay were Athapaskan-speakers. The name Chipewyan came from their enemies the Cree and meant 'pointed skin', a reference to the tails the Chipewyan left on the furs they made into garments. They called themselves the Dene, which in their own language means 'people'. Chipewyan bands, seldom numbering more than fifty, moved north onto the tundra to hunt caribou with bows and spears, and returned to the forests to fish with nets and hooks and lines, to hunt moose and bear, and to snare rabbits and beaver. Their mobile lives meant that the Chipewyan amassed no possessions they could not carry with them.

To the south and east, some 5,000 Algonkian-speaking Cree spread across a broad territory from north of Lake Superior to Hudson Bay and west to the Saskatchewan River. Family-based Cree bands journeyed by birchbark canoe in summer and by toboggan and snowshoe in winter to hunt moose and woodland caribou, to snare ducks and geese, and to fish with nets and spears. In summer, groups of individual bands pitched their tents together for ceremonies and celebrations.

About 5,000 Ojibwa (sometimes called Chippewa) lived south of the Cree along the north shore of Lake Superior. They moved west into the region that would eventually become the Prairie provinces only in the seventeenth century. Like the Cree, the Ojibwa spoke an Algonkian language. But they had access to more abundant hunting and fishing grounds, which enabled them to establish a semi-sedentary culture, with village populations of perhaps more than 200. Dwellings in these villages were usually rectangular birchbark structures large enough to hold several families, but the Ojibwa also used tipis when they moved to hunt or fish. Although they grew no crops, they harvested wild rice each autumn.[5]

On the plains to the west and south lived 4,500 Siouian-speaking Assiniboine and 9,000 Algonkian-speaking Peigan, Blood, and Siksikaw—the last three making up the Blackfoot Confederacy. They knew how to cultivate plants for food, and tilled fields to grow corn until about AD 900, when they abandoned horticulture, probably because of recurring cycles of drought. The decision not to farm was a reasonable response to the dry plains environment. Agriculture involved long hours of hard work, all of which had to be done by hand, and the immense herds of buffalo that moved north and south each year between ranges on the plains and parkland would have trampled or devoured any crops that stood in their paths.[6] In addition, prior to the European invasion, the Native peoples of North America had no domesticated animals except the dog, which the plains hunters used as a pack animal or to drag a travois. And North America lacked the large mammals—horses, cattle, sheep,

goats, pigs—that were suitable candidates for domestication on other continents.

Instead of farming, the plains peoples made the buffalo the staple of their economies. They hunted these dangerous animals—a half-tonne buffalo could charge at 50 kmh—with great skill. 'They have invented so many methods for the destruction of these animals,' wrote a European trader in 1794, 'that they stand in no need of ammunition [for firearms] to provide a sufficiency. . . .'[7] In summer individual hunters disguised beneath buffalo hides would stalk stragglers from a herd until they got close enough for a good bow shot; in winter they used snowshoes to pursue animals struggling through drifts up to their bellies. The Assiniboine drove small herds into 'pounds', enclosures built by driving stakes among the trees of a bluff, where they could be shot at close quarters. Blackfoot bands efficiently slaughtered hundreds of buffalo by stampeding them over small cliffs or 'jumps'. Buffalo 'runners' located the herds; the other band members, including women and older children, waved and shouted to drive the animals down pre-established lanes to the 'jump'. Below, hunters equipped with spears and wooden-handled stone hammers would finish off the animals not killed outright by the fall. Buffalo provided the plains peoples not only with meat but with hides for tipis, robes, and shields, bones for needles, awls, and scrapers, and horns for spoons and containers.

Although the material life of the Chipewyan was less abundant than that of the Ojibwa or the Assiniboine, all five groups enjoyed a relatively high standard of living. They were better nourished than European peasants in the same historical period, and their food supplies were more secure. In times of plenty, they preserved meat for the times of scarcity that they knew were to come. The Cree, Ojibwa, and Chipewyan dried moose, caribou, and fish over their fires; the Assiniboine and Blackfoot sun-dried strips of buffalo meat into jerky, and mixed pulverized jerky with rendered buffalo fat and berries to form the high-protein mixture called pemmican. Archaeological evidence suggests that groups of Aboriginal peoples traded among themselves long before Europeans arrived in North America. Hunter-gatherer groups like the Assiniboine and the Cree journeyed south to exchange preserved meat and hides for the corn, beans, and squash grown by agriculturalists like the Mandan, Arikara, and Hidatsa. The economies of the plains peoples were not secure, but they were sustainable. As J.G. Nelson concludes, there is no evidence that Native people were responsible for the extinction of any animal species before the arrival of the newcomers from Europe.[8]

Europeans travelled to the western interior by sea from the north. The first mariners to explore the icy Arctic waters were seeking a shorter route to China, the elusive Northwest Passage. Henry Hudson imagined the huge inland sea that he investigated in 1610 to be the Pacific Ocean; in fact it was a bay, which took his life as well as his name. The English captains who retraced Hudson's voyage— Thomas Button, Luke Foxe, Thomas James— found at the end of two months' sailing neither an Arctic passage to Asia nor anything else that offered them profit, only a 'strange and dangerous' land frozen 'ten feet deepe'.

Sixty years passed before Hudson Bay gave its name, with a possessive added, to an English fur venture called the Hudson's Bay Company. It was fur that motivated renewed European interest in northern North America, specifically the fur of *castor canadensis*, the prolific 30-kilogram rodent whose short, barbed hairs made the best felt for the large hats worn by fashionable European gentlemen. Two entrepreneurs from the colony of New France, far to the southeast in the St Lawrence Valley, Pierre Esprit Radisson and Médard Chouart, Sieur des Groseilliers, recognized the potential for profit in shipping thick northern beaver pelts directly to Europe by sea. Rebuffed in France, they found in London the capital they needed to acquire ships and goods for an expedition into the Bay. After a winter trading with the Cree, Groseilliers brought back a cargo of furs rich enough to inspire demands by ministers, courtiers, and businessmen for a royal monopoly. On 2 May 1670 (a date of which the contemporary retailing firm repeatedly reminds Canadians) King Charles II chartered the 'Governor and Company of Adventurers of England tradeing into Hudson's Bay'. The 'Governor' was the King's cousin, Prince Rupert; thus 'Rupert's Land' became the English name of the 7.7 million square kilometres draining into Hudson Bay over which the 'Adventurers' became 'true and absolute Lordes and Proprietors'.

The Hudson's Bay Company's commercial strategy was simple: to establish 'factories' at the mouths of rivers running into Hudson and James Bay, and to wait for Indians to bring furs down river to trade. Necessity dictated this approach: company employees lacked the skills to travel let alone to support themselves in the interior. Native people, on the other hand, were expert hunters; in addition, many were accustomed to trading with other Native groups, and they wanted the Europeans' guns, knives, hatchets, and kettles. The resulting mutual dependency made Indians and traders 'partners in furs'. The prices paid for trade goods were expressed in terms of 'Made Beaver', the value of a prime beaver skin; other furs like muskrat and marten were credited as part of a Made Beaver. The Native traders demanded good value for their furs. They wanted light and durable kettles and preferred sturdy guns with short barrels that would stand up under winter hunting conditions. Factors—the commanders of the Hudson's Bay Company posts—warned their superiors in England to send appropriate high-quality merchandise; 'if your honours do not conceive the difference, the natives do,' wrote Richard Norton from Churchill in 1739. For products like powder, shot, and tobacco, Indians insisted that the Europeans 'give us good measure'. And once a standard price system for trade goods was in place, they refused to tolerate dramatic price increases, however much the Europeans complained that their costs had risen.[9]

The Cree and Assiniboine who travelled to the Hudson's Bay Company factories each summer to trade arrived in canoes loaded with eighty to a hundred Made Beaver. They had not trapped all these furs themselves; in fact, they were middlemen in the trade, reselling European goods at much higher prices to the Blackfoot, Mandan, and Gros Ventre to the south and west. In 1682 the factor at York Fort reported that the Cree and Assiniboine had become 'the only brokers between all strange Indians and us'. When the company opened a post at the mouth of the Churchill River in 1717, the Chipewyan took on the same role as

intermediaries with the people northwest of Hudson Bay. A Chipewyan trader who bought a hatchet for one Made Beaver could get nine or ten skins for it from the 'Far Indians', reported Churchill factor Moses Norton in 1766.[10]

Other Europeans challenged the Hudson's Bay Company's monopoly of the fur trade. French traders based on the St Lawrence and their Native partners fought to prevent the English company from drawing north the furs that had once gone east and south through their own trade networks. From 1683 until 1713, the French competed commercially and militarily for control of the European side of the western interior trade. York Factory, on the Nelson River, changed hands—and names—seven times, providing colourful gore for the textbooks of later centuries. Naval victories in the Bay ensconced Pierre LeMoyne, Sieur d'Iberville, among the 'great men' of Canadian high-school history; he is one of few heroes to be celebrated in both English and French. But if the French won the shooting battles, they lost the business war. The high cost of crossing the Shield meant that their trade from the Bay never earned a profit, while less expensive ocean transport directly from Hudson Bay allowed the HBC modest returns on its capital. In 1713, the French ceded the Bay route to the English in the Treaty of Utrecht.

They did not, however, cede the fur trade of the western interior. The French traders continued to operate from their base in Montreal, using an east–west lake and river route. Between 1727 and 1743, Pierre Gaultier de Varennes, Sieur de La Vérendrye, and his sons Jean-Baptiste, François, and Louis-Joseph held a government-granted monopoly on the western trade. In return for exclusivity, the

'Bombardement et Prise de Fort Nelson' (York Factory), 1697, from Bacqueville de la Potherie, *Histoire de l'Amérique septentrionale* (Paris, 1753), vol. I. This much-reproduced image, drawn long after the event, purports to depict Iberville's second successful assault on the fort in September 1697. A close reading of written descriptions of the battle, however, suggests that the assault depicted here is that of September 1694. In 1697 Iberville did not land guns to shell the fort, and the issue was resolved by a naval battle between Iberville's *Pélican* and the English vessel *Hampshire*. Nevertheless, several historians have used this picture to accompany written descriptions of the 1697 battle, apparently oblivious to contradictions between the written sources and the image. NAC C-21939.

Vérendryes were to assert the French imperial presence and use their fur profits to finance the continuing search for a passage to the Pacific. Futile as this quest seems to our twentieth-century sense of geography, until the mid-eighteenth century no chronometer was able to measure longitude accurately: thus Europeans persisted in the hope that the shores of the 'Western Sea' lay just beyond the next set of hills.

When they opened trade with the Cree and Assiniboine on Lake of the Woods, the Vérendryes quickly discovered that Native groups sustained imperial rivalries as fierce as those of the Europeans. Trading guns to the Cree and Assiniboine earned the animosity of their enemies the Sioux; the hostilities that ensued cost Jean-Baptiste La Vérendrye and eighteen others their lives, and the French lost the opportunity to expand their trade southwest along the Missouri River. Instead the Vérendryes turned northwest, across lakes Winnipeg, Manitoba, and Winnipegosis to the Saskatchewan River. They constructed a system of small *postes du nord* at important junctions along the route, and were accordingly venerated two centuries later as 'the first Europeans to open and chart Manitoba'. An enthusiastic popular history of that province celebrates Pierre La Vérendrye as 'the first European to see the future site of Winnipeg'.[11]

The Vérendryes found no 'Western Sea' for France, but they did build a successful fur business. Their posts intersected the river routes along which the Cree and Assiniboine brought furs north to trade with the English at York Factory or Fort Prince of Wales, and after 1730 the HBC's volumes and profits began to decline. 'The French . . . not only Beats the Bush but runs away with the Hair also,' complained the factor at York, James Isham, in 1743. But the real beneficiaries of French–English competition were the Native peoples: now fewer skins bought more guns, awls, and blankets. A gun that had cost fourteen Made Beaver in 1740 could be had for eleven in 1750. When two groups of Europeans contended for their pelts, argues E.E. Rich, 'the Indians were in control'.[12]

The conquest of New France by the English in 1760 granted the HBC only a brief respite from competition. By the end of the decade, the century-old company faced a threat more serious than the French. A throng of new entrepreneurs based in Montreal—Scots, Englishmen, New Englanders—were following the Vérendryes' route to the western interior and pushing still farther west along the Saskatchewan River. Because these 'pedlars from Quebec' could not make the 6,000-kilometre round trip in a single year, a two-stage trading and transportation system rapidly evolved. A Montreal merchant, a 'bourgeois', provided trade goods on credit to an *hivernant,* the 'wintering partner' who actually conducted the trade. The conquest had eliminated or marginalized French entrepreneurs, but

The La Vérendrye Monument, St Boniface, Manitoba. Erected two centuries after La Vérendrye's voyages, the monument states the historic claim of French-speaking Catholics to a place in a Manitoba increasingly dominated by English-speaking Protestants. The poses of the Catholic missionary and the French trader suggest the French lyrics to 'O Canada': 'Car ton bras sait porter l'épée/Il sait porter la croix!' The Native people who were La Vérendrye's trading partners are represented, but the warrior is portrayed as contentedly subservient to Père Jean-Pierre Aulneau's cross and Pierre de La Vérendrye's musket. With his buckskin and braids, the warrior seems patterned on 'Grey Owl', Canada's most celebrated 'Indian' of the 1930s, who was revealed on his death in 1938 to be Englishman named Archie Belaney, pretending to be a part-Apache. WCPI A0076-02359.

French-Canadian voyageurs continued to do the back-breaking physical work of transporting goods and furs. These *engagés,* who signed on for the season, were similarly divided into two groups: the *mangeurs du lard*, the 'pork eaters' who never saw the West, and the *hommes du nord* who spent the winter in the interior. In spring, crews of ten *mangeurs du lard* paddled 11-metre *canots de maître* west from Montreal, all with 4-tonne loads and some with 'bourgeois' as passengers. At every portage, the voyageurs made four trips, carrying the cargo in 40-kilogram packs. In July the canoes from Canada would meet the winterers from the interior at Grand Portage, on the western end of Lake Superior. The winterers made the journey east in 7-metre *canots du nord*, hauling their loads of a tonne and a half of furs across equally difficult portages. At Grand Portage, the two birchbark flotillas exchanged cargos. Then the 'hyperborian nabobs'—as the American romantic writer Washington Irving styled the fur merchants—would divide the profits of their partnership and plan a new season's strategy. The voyageurs—Irving called them 'Sinbads of the wilderness'—found what diversion they could in dancing, drinking, and gambling, amusements lovingly described by historians determined to romanticize working lives of brutal toil.

The pedlars at first competed among themselves more ferociously than they did with the Hudson's Bay Company. But the obvious advantages of working together soon led to a series of multiple partnerships. The most successful of these called itself the North West Company. Coalitions with that name existed from 1779 to 1821; after 1805, when the struggle with the Hudson's Bay Company intensified, the North West Company imposed an effective monopoly on the Montreal-based fur trade. Despite its name and its large organization—by 1795 the

North West Company had 1,200 voyageurs in its employ—it was never a chartered company and always operated as a partnership of individual merchants. Simon McTavish, James McGill, and William McGillivray were prominent among the North West Company bourgeois; the names of important wintering partners—Alexander Mackenzie, David Thompson, Simon Fraser—cover the contemporary map of Western Canada.

Winterer Peter Pond named no mighty river, but he led the Nor'Westers across the 19-kilometre Methye Portage into the richest fur territory on the continent, the Athabasca. In the winter of 1778–79, Pond and his sixteen voyageurs traded for twice as many furs as they could transport; they cached half of them for the next year. Pond's commercial coup was possible because, like all successful fur traders, he relied on Native people: 'here every information must be procured from the savages,' a winterer reported to Montreal.[13] Pond used Native maps and oral information to make his way northwest and create maps that other Europeans could follow; he also solved the problem of provisioning fur brigades in the distant northwestern interior by purchasing 'dry'd buffalo's meat . . . pounded to a powder and mixed up with buffaloes greese'—pemmican—from the Plains Cree. By incorporating the Athabasca into their trading network, the Nor'Westers leapfrogged over the Hudson's Bay Company to barter directly with the Chipewyan and with the Indians of the Peace and Mackenzie rivers. The North West Company's Fort Chipewyan, established on Lake Athabasca in 1788, awed a Hudson's Bay competitor: 'this is the compleatest Inland House I have seen in the country; this is the

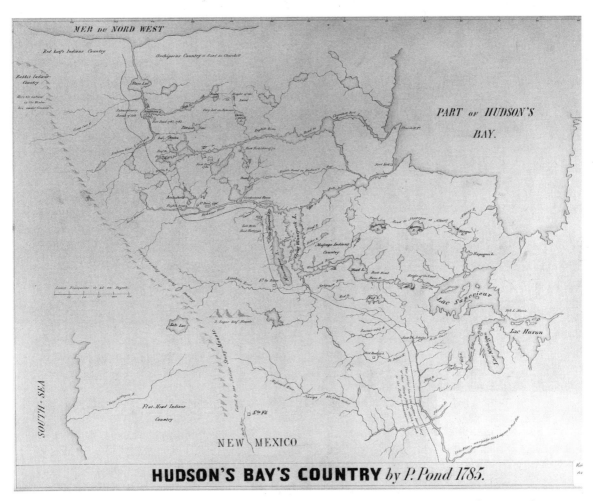

Peter Pond's map of the western interior of North America, *c.* 1785. Pond (1739–1807) was the first map-maker to
define the Prairies as bounded on the east by the Great Lakes and the Shield and and on the west by the Rocky
Mountains. Like later European map-makers, he made extensive use of Native maps and geographical descriptions.
Library of Congress, Geography and Map Division, Kohl Collection #137.

Grand Magazine of the Athapiscow Country,'
reported Peter Turnor to his superiors.[14]

The rival companies could not have been
more different in their structure or in their
commercial behaviour. The flamboyant, aggressive Nor'Westers never paused in their pur-
suit of profit even when Alexander Mackenzie
reached the Pacific, the long-sought 'Western

Sea', in 1793. The Hudson's Bay 'Company of
Adventurers', in contrast, was anything but
adventurous. It had earned modest returns for
over a century with a cautious, conservative
trade strategy. Its London directors had never
seen the western interior, nor did they care to;
they ignored critics who charged that the company 'slept at the edge of a frozen sea'.

Prince of Wales Fort (Churchill, Manitoba), *c.* 1777. This sketch accompanied the narrative of HBC factor Samuel Hearne (1745–92), *A Journey from Prince of Wales's Fort in Hudson's Bay to the Northern Ocean*, published three years after his death. Attributed to Hearne, it was probably redone by a professional illustrator. The image is crafted to communicate a sense of gentility and to convey the solidity and permanence of the company's presence. The over-sized Union Jack suggests that the HBC is representing British imperial interests in the western interior of North America. NAC C-41292.

In 1754, spurred by the Vérendryes' success, the company had ordered Anthony Henday to probe inland from York Factory. Travelling with a party of Cree, Henday went as far as the Red Deer River, where he visited Blackfoot villages, and returned with geographical information and prime furs. But twenty years passed before declining fur volumes forced the company to build its first post in the interior, Cumberland House. 'The greatest obstical' to a more aggressive expansion, wrote Samuel Hearne from Fort Prince of Wales at Churchill, was transportation. To build canoes the HBC needed birch trees, but none were available near the Bay, and company employees, hired from the Scottish lowlands or the Orkney Islands, were 'intirly Unhandy in Cannoes' in any case. Gradually, however, the HBC did respond to the Nor' Westers, using 10-metre flat-bottomed wooden York boats, portaged on log rollers, as well as canoes. By 1795 a sequence of Hudson's Bay Company posts stretched along the edge of the grasslands and the park belt to Edmonton House, then to Acton House in the Rocky Mountain foothills in 1799, and finally into the Athabasca country in 1802.

A distribution pattern similar to that of twentieth-century service stations emerged as the two companies competed fiercely to construct posts at strategic locations. Half of the Hudson's Bay Company posts sat within 15 kilometres of a North West Company competitor.[15] At first their staffs maintained the 'distant civility' that the older company ordered of its employees. The Nor'Westers had little reason to be uncivil: in 1800 they took in four times as much as the HBC—£144,000 to £38,000. For four years thereafter, the older company was relegated to third place in the trade, as Alexander Mackenzie's 'XY' Company challenged the Nor'Westers for supremacy in the Montreal-based trade. In this period of intense competition, writes E.E. Rich, 'the Indians were not only spoiled and debauched, they were bullied and abused as well.'[16] European traders had always offered gifts of liquor before proceeding to actual exchange, but between 1800 and 1803 the amount of rum brought west from Montreal doubled to 90,000 litres. The Hudson's Bay Company also provided generous amounts, for 'without that many a skin would go to our neighbours that now comes to us.' 'What a contrast,' wrote Peter Fidler of the Hudson's Bay Company: 'the greatest Chief of the Chipewyans used to get only 10½ pints of mixed [diluted] rum . . . ; now every [Chief] gets an 8 Gallen keg also of rum for nothing.' Their competitors alleged that Nor'Westers kidnapped Indian women and beat Indian men to force them to trade. 'It is a great pity that such a body of Natives should be destroyed by a parcel of wild fellows,' intoned another Hudson's Bay employee.[17]

This oft-repeated accusation that competition among Europeans 'debauched' their Native trading partners was in part a strategy used by both companies' traders to condemn their rivals and excuse falling revenues to their

'The Rival Companies Soliciting Trade a Hundred Years Ago', *Harper's Monthly*, June 1879. This image idealizes the competition for the interior trade between the Hudson's Bay and North West companies; violence and murder sometimes characterized the bitter rivalry. It does suggest, however, the extent to which the fur trade was a family-based affair, and illustrates the importance of gift-giving as a preliminary to trade. Glenbow NA-1406-39.

bosses. More deadly by far than over-proof rum was European disease. Expansion of the fur trade brought epidemic smallpox to the Peigan and the Chipewyan, cutting populations in half; in 1783 trader William Walker reported Chipewyan 'lying dead . . . like rotten sheep, . . . the wild beasts devouring them'.[18] Intensive competition also had an environmental impact. The North West Company hired Iroquois from Lower Canada, who trapped entire areas along the Saskatchewan River bare. 'Like the Locusts of Egypt', these

Iroquois interlopers brought 'Devastation & Ruin along with them' objected a Hudson's Bay trader.[19] But neither liquor, disease, nor environmental destruction made Native people pawns to be pushed around by European chess masters: they retained considerable autonomy. Sometimes they expressed their agency through violence, as when Chipewyan killed ten traders from Canada on Lake Athabasca in 1804; and three Nor'Westers starved to death in 1811 because Indians refused to hunt for them. As they had throughout the history of the trade, the Native people played off the European traders against one another. Because they could now satisfy their needs at the cost of fewer pelts, they hunted less aggressively, and as a result the volumes of the European trade declined after 1805.[20] The expansion of the European fur trade also provided new opportunities for Native people. 'Home Guard' Cree had begun to sell game and fish to Hudson's Bay Company posts from their first foundation; when the North West Company needed pemmican to feed its voyageurs, the Cree and Assiniboine, their role as trapper-trader middlemen in decline, swiftly adapted to a new role as provisioners. With astonishing speed, bands of these two tribes completed the transition from a woodland- to a grassland-oriented economy centred on the mounted buffalo hunt.[21]

The plains horse–gun culture that they adopted represents little more than a century among the millennia of Indian history, but it provides dramatic evidence of how Native people were able to adapt to the changes brought by the arrival of Europeans and incorporate into their own cultures those aspects of European technology that they chose. Horses,

introduced to the Americas in the Spanish colonies, moved north through inter-tribal trading and raiding. The Blackfoot acquired them by the 1730s, the Assiniboine and the Plains Cree by the 1770s; and by the 1790s the Ojibwa bands who had moved onto the plains had them as well. The economic advantages were obvious: a horse could carry or pull on a travois four times as much as a dog, and a rider could cover ten times more ground in a day than a person on foot. On horseback, hunters could search for buffalo over longer distances, and instead of stalking individual animals, could fire on the entire herd or stampede it to a jump or a pound. Mounted Blackfoot, Plains Cree, Assiniboine, and Ojibwa continued to hunt with bows or lances, but in battle they now used guns, which transformed war on the plains. 'A musket ball was harder to dodge than an arrow or a spear', writes Olive Dickason, and 'when it hit, it rendered traditional armour obsolete. . . . In the hands of a mounted warrior . . . even the smooth-bore musket . . . could be overpowering.'[22] Better armed because of their closer trade relationships with Europeans, the Cree and Assiniboine ended their peace with the Blackfoot and made them their bitter enemies as they moved farther south and west on the plains. Horses brought their owners affluence, prestige, and power, and helped the Plains tribes to maintain their independence.[23]

Determined to end the competition that had allowed the Native traders to charge more for their furs, the XY and North West Companies amalgamated in 1805 and launched a campaign to drive the Hudson's Bay Company out of business. Their first tactic, a takeover through the purchase of the smaller company's shares, failed. Three British brothers-in-law—John Halkett, Andrew Wedderburn Colvile, and Thomas Douglas, fifth Earl Selkirk—outbid the Nor'Westers' agents for HBC stock. The new majority stockholders belligerently took on the North West Company and, overturning HBC tradition, created a more flexible administrative system with more local autonomy for factors and chief traders as well as a new profit-sharing scheme giving Hudson's Bay employees the same incentives that drove the North West Company's wintering partners.

The triumvirate's most stunning initiative, however, was their decision to establish a European agricultural colony in the western interior. The corporate reasons were complex: to confirm the company's title to Rupert's Land, to provide land for HBC servants married to Native women who wanted to retire in North America, and to grow provisions to feed HBC traders for a new assault on the Athabasca. For Lord Selkirk, however, the creation of the colony represented more than a business decision. It was an act of personal philanthropy, his third attempt to transplant to new homes in British North America Scottish crofters displaced from their farms by large-scale sheep-raising. In May 1811 the company granted him Assiniboia, a 300,000-square-kilometre block centred on the forks of the Red and Assiniboine Rivers. This decision, Hudson's Bay Company historian Douglas MacKay wrote melodramatically a century later, 'brought upon the fur trade ten years of violence, recrimination, and incidents of bloodshed more savage than the northwest had known since white men came'.[24]

Despite Nor'Wester propaganda that emigrants would meet gruesome deaths on the scalping knives of 'warlike savage nations', some 300 colonists signed on over the next three years, making a two-month voyage on company ships to Hudson Bay and then an arduous six-week trek inland to the Red River. This first serious attempt to transplant European-style agriculture to the western interior of North America at first failed pathetically: the initial crops of winter wheat, planted with hand tools because the colonists had neither oxen nor plows, froze in the soil. The settlers relied on the buffalo hunt to survive, just as the plains tribes and fur traders did. Lest the colonists starve, in January 1814 Selkirk's governor, a former Upper Canadian militia officer and sheriff named Miles MacDonell, unilaterally embargoed the export of provisions from the Selkirk grant. Given that much of the 30 tonnes of pemmican required each year to fuel the Nor'Westers' fur brigades originated within Assiniboia, MacDonell had effectively declared war on the North West Company.

The Nor'Westers' allies in this 'pemmican war' were the Métis, the mixed-blood community of Red River. After two centuries of the fur trade, thousands of children had been born of Native mothers and European fathers. French traders, and the Nor'Westers who came after them, entered marriages *à la façon du pays*—'by the custom of the country'—with Native women. Much more than mere sexual liaisons, these unions in many practical ways made it possible for the fur trade to function in the western interior. By the end of the eighteenth century, Indians and Europeans recognized the Métis, or *bois brûlés*, as a distinct social and racial category.[25] Concentrated in the Red River area, some Métis men worked permanently or casually for the North West Company; others, with their families, hunted buffalo for subsistence and sale to the Nor'Westers. By embargoing the export of pemmican, therefore, the impetuous MacDonell had also declared war on this 'New Nation'. The North West Company styled one of its Métis clerks, Cuthbert Grant, 'Captain-General of the Métis'; with Nor'Wester support, Grant equipped a Métis army to harass the Hudson's Bay Company and its Selkirk settlement.

The pemmican war was only the first campaign in a general war between the two fur companies. It ended with MacDonell a prisoner in the North West Company's Fort Gibraltar and the colonists dispersed, their crops trampled and their log shelters torched by Métis horsemen. But the HBC's Colin Robertson persuaded a group of settlers to return, and with company assistance they rebuilt the colony. Selkirk's second governor, Robert Semple, arrived in November 1815 with a fourth contingent of Scottish emigrants. A London merchant and travel writer selected for no reason that any historian has been able to discover, Semple guided the colony to a second disaster: he destroyed Fort Gibraltar and denied river passage to the North West Company's boatloads of pemmican. To retaliate, Cuthbert Grant and his Métis riflemen captured the HBC's pemmican supplies at Brandon House and rode down the Assiniboine toward the colony. Determined to 'give the N.W. scoundrels a

---

Facing above. Peter Rindisbacher, 'Indian Hunters. Pursuing the Buffalo in the Early Spring', 1824 or earlier. Historians praise Rindisbacher (1806–34) as a realist, free of the romantic flourishes of later nineteenth-century painters. The hunters depicted here were Assiniboine, and the image is used to prove the persistence of the bow as a hunting weapon among Native peoples. Like all artists, however, Rindisbacher had to reconcile realism with the necessity of making a living. In 1833 he redid the painting for a US patron, adding a feather head-dress to the hunter in the foreground and changing the tribal identification to 'Blackfeet'. NAC C-114467.

Facing middle. Frances Hopkins, 'Canoe Manned by Voyageurs Passing a Waterfall', *c*. 1860. Eight voyageurs paddle a loaded *canot de maître* with an HBC employee and his English wife, the artist Frances Hopkins (1838–1918). The canoe and the costumes are accurate as to detail, but Hopkins romanticizes the voyageurs' toil and represents the journey as a pleasure trip: one paddler even reaches over the side to pluck a water lily for her! Written sources suggest that no crew transporting a company officer dared to let its speed fall below forty strokes a minute: given that Hopkins's husband was Sir George Simpson's private secretary, this leisurely pace seems most unlikely. NAC C-2771.

Facing below. George Back, 'Fort Chepewyan [*sic*]—An Est. of the N.W. Coy [North West Company] on the Athabasca Lake, North America'. Captain (later Sir) George Back (1796–1878) sketched this scene during his visit to Fort Chipewyan in 1820, but by the time he painted it in 1832, the amalgamation of the fur companies had made it a Hudson's Bay Company post. NAC C-15251.

Overleaf above. Peter Rindisbacher, 'A Hunter-family of Cree Indians at York Fort, drawn from nature, 1821'. 'Home Guard' Cree like the family depicted here had been provisioning Hudson's Bay Company posts for a century and a half when Rindisbacher made the sketch for this watercolour. NAC C-1917.

Overleaf below. William Armstrong, 'On Kaministiquia River', west of Lake Superior, *c*. 1860. Described in Dennis Reid's *Concise History of Canadian Painting* as 'an earnest craftsman with an essentially documentary aim', Armstrong (1822–1914), an Irish immigrant, travelled west on the Great Lakes to search out scenes like this. His 'modest works of art' were very popular with patrons who wanted realistic depictions of Canada's westward growth. NAC C-40292.

C.W. Jefferys, 'The Massacre at Seven Oaks, 19 June 1816'. When Jefferys (1869–1951) created this image for *The Picture Gallery of Canadian History* (1945), he drew on a long-established Anglo-Canadian tradition that bore little resemblance to what we can know of the incident. The written evidence is unambiguous: the Semple party fired first, and the fighting took place with the Métis dismounted. Jefferys depicts the Métis as the aggressors, and shows them riding down Semple and the colonists. To demonstrate that the 'savage' Native ancestry of the Métis had overwhelmed their veneer of European 'civilization', he represents six of the eight riders in the picture as Indians—one with a full feather bonnet. NAC c-073663.

drubbing', Semple and a group of colonists confronted Grant's force at an oak bluff near the Red River on 19 June 1816. In minutes, the governor and twenty of his followers were dead. A subsequent investigation into the incident concluded unambiguously that the Selkirk party had fired the first shot, initiating the conflict. A heroic ballad in the Métis oral tradition commemorates their defeat of the

'men from across the sea/who'd come to pillage our country'. But when Anglo-Canadians became the majority in the prairie region in the 1890s, their historians reconstructed Semple's stupidity as a sort of western Canadian Alamo, at which their martyr-ancestors fought gallantly so that 'civilization' might eventually triumph over 'savagery'. As the 'Seven Oaks *Massacre*', the incident lives on in textbooks and popular histories, and thus in the collective memory of the Anglo-Canadian Prairies.[26]

The struggle between the fur companies continued for another four years after Seven Oaks. Even before he learned of Semple's catastrophe, Lord Selkirk had arranged his own appointment as a magistrate in Upper Canada and hired ninety Swiss mercenaries of the de Meuron Regiment, demobilized in Canada after the War of 1812–14. With this private army he captured Fort William, the North West Company's post at Grand Portage, and 'arrested' the Nor'Westers he found there, charging them with 42 counts of murder, 18 of arson, 16 of robbery, 9 of 'stealing boats on a navigable river', and 7 of 'malicious shooting'. Selkirk then moved on to the Red River colony, where the de Meuron soldiers reinforced and reassured the colonists. Thereafter, although the Selkirk settlement had to survive floods, fires, and locusts, the European agricultural presence in the western interior was permanent. The colony secured, the Hudson's Bay Company renewed its commercial war with the Nor'Westers, pushing their trade into the Athabasca territory. There they matched the Nor'Westers outrage for outrage. The HBC stuck its hardest blow in 1819, when William Williams, the new governor of Rupert's Land, ambushed seven Nor'Wester winterers at cannon-point on the Saskatchewan River.

After a decade of strife that had almost bankrupted both businesses, the winterers of the North West Company, the toughest and most ruthless combatants, were the first to blink. A new partnership agreement with the bourgeois partners was to be negotiated in 1821, and the winterers demanded a larger share of the profits; with justification, they felt that the Montreal partners risked only their capital, while the wintering partners risked their lives. The winterers threatened mass defection to the Hudson's Bay Company if their demands were not met. This regional tension within the North West Company was only the first of many disputes between producers in the west and investors in the east. Geopolitical considerations demanded that the British government lend its authority to support a merger. The United States of America, born in revolution only three decades earlier, had proved its aggressiveness in the War of 1812–14. Having extended its empire across the continent, the new country now challenged Britain, Russia, and Spain for the Pacific coast: only with unity among the various participants in the British North American fur trade could Britain maintain its claims to the western interior. Lord Selkirk's death in 1820 removed the most bitter opponent of compromise. A year later, the exhausted adversaries chose collusion over continued conflict. The intra-European struggle for control of the fur trade had ended.

CHAPTER THREE

Fur Trade to Settlement: 1821–1870

The new Hudson's Bay Company that emerged from the resolution of the ten-year war resembled both and neither of its fur-trade parents. From the older company came a name, the geographical advantage of the Bay transportation route, and the ancient, now meaningful, monopoly, broadened by a 'License of Exclusive Trade' to take in the Pacific slope as well as Rupert's Land. From the Nor'Westers came a compensation system that extracted maximum effort from senior employees: each Chief Factor, commanding a district, and Chief Trader, commanding a post, would be paid a share of the annual profit. Amalgamation continued the gradual transformation of the Hudson's Bay Company from a merchant enterprise into a modern capitalist corporation, which had begun with Lord Selkirk's takeover. The merged company's choice of governor for its operations in Rupert's Land reflected an increasing attention to efficiency and the bottom line, and a diminishing concern for the consequences for company employees, their mixed-blood families, and the Native people with whom they traded.

George (after 1841 Sir George) Simpson's contemporaries commented on his administrative skills, his attention to detail, and his increasingly autocratic style of management; but 'no one,' observes Keith Wilson wryly, 'ever called "the Little Emperor" a prince among men.' During his thirty-nine years as governor, Simpson eliminated both the paternalism of the old HBC and the partners' democracy of the Nor'Westers. The London Committee that had run the company since 1670 gave the North American operation more autonomy, but Simpson kept the exercise of that autonomy for himself and immediate subordinates such as John Rowand, Chief Factor of the Saskatchewan district. Although the agreement of 1821 required annual councils of Chief Factors and Traders, modelled on the old Nor'Wester gatherings at Grand Portage, this system soon collapsed. Instead, to hold his fur empire together, Simpson toured in a light canoe with a hand-picked crew capable of paddling 150 kilometres in a 16-hour work day. En route, he dictated letters to his secretary or jotted notes in the 'Character Book' that he maintained to keep track of his subordinates. Complaints about Simpson's manage-

'Making a Portage', *Harper's Monthly*, June 1879. HBC tripmen portage York Boats around rapids. The amalgamated company used its monopoly to 'rationalize' its transportation system, discharging employees and cutting costs. Glenbow NA-1406-48.

ment style were muted because his policies made the company's owners and executives lots of money. Between 1825 and his death in 1860, HBC stockholders never earned less than a 10 per cent annual dividend, while Chief Factors earned an average of £720, and Chief Traders £360, each year.[1]

It was the company's trading hegemony over much of the western interior that made this unparalleled prosperity possible. Simpson immediately closed duplicate posts and swiftly reorganized the transportation system. York Factory became the hub of an integrated sys-

tem, with a regular north–south river- and lake-spoke to carry trade goods to Fort Garry in the Red River settlement. Norway House on Lake Winnipeg developed as a mid-way point for shipping goods on to the Athabasca. Without competition, speed mattered less than increasing carrying capacity and reducing costs. York boats supplanted freight canoes on major rivers, and two-wheeled wooden 'Red River carts' creaked 450-kilogram loads northwest from Fort Garry to Fort Carlton on the North Saskatchewan and then to Fort Edmonton. By 1840, company hauling costs had been cut by two-fifths.

With restructured transportation routes going to fewer posts, Simpson radically downsized (to use the modern corporate jargon) the company's work force: 1,300 workers, six in every ten, were dismissed in the first five years after union. Employees with large mixed-blood families were the first to be let go, to save on company provisions. When expansion of operations in the North and in British Columbia after 1830 required more workers, new permanent employees were hired at £17 a year, as compared to £25 to £40 at the height of the fur war. The company took on as few permanent workers as possible, however, and instead used seasonal employees, usually mixed-bloods, who received none of the paternalist benefits that company 'servants' had received from the old Hudson's Bay Company.[2]

Increased corporate profits also came from squeezing the Native people who had been the company's partners in furs. In 1822, Simpson told his factors and traders that henceforward 'Indians . . . must be ruled with a rod of Iron to bring and keep them in a proper state of subordination.' Traders were to make Native people 'feel their dependence on us' by refusing the customary advances of supplies: Simpson ordered 'no credit, not so much as a load of ammunition . . . until they renew their . . . habits of industry.' To enforce this decree, the company established a more thorough accounting system, and assigned Aboriginal families to trade at specific posts, to prevent them from evading debts by moving from post to post. Simpson also ordered an end to the 'ruinous practice' of 'giving presents and treats' in pre-trade ceremonies.[3] Virtually all the Native peoples of the western interior now participated in the market economy of the fur trade, but not all participated to the same degree or in the same capacities. Thus the Hudson's Bay Company's new ruthlessness affected the various Native peoples in different ways. The Plains Cree, the Assiniboine, and the Blackfoot retained considerable autonomy because they hunted with traditional weapons rather than guns, and because the company depended on pemmican. 'The Plains tribes,' Simpson grumbled in 1823, 'continue as insolent and independent if not more so than ever.' After 1820, growing demand in the United States for buffalo robes actually increased the independence of the Blackfoot, who sold robes to American traders at Fort Union and Fort McKenzie on the Missouri River. Chief Factor John Rowand—'Iron Shirt' to the Blackfoot—found himself passing out presents and buying buffalo robes that the company could not resell, in order to keep the Blackfoot trading at Fort Edmonton.[4]

The Woodland peoples, however, had become more dependent on trade with Europeans for guns, ammunition, and cloth. An English visitor to the Athabasca country in 1830 observed that the Native peoples had 'lost their original mode of hunting; the use of the bow and arrow is gone, the gun [makes them] . . . dependent upon the company for their powder and shot. To make an Indian really a hunter with the bow and arrow, a deer-stalker, takes a whole life; you cannot re-teach the present generation; it takes a whole life to learn.' Nor were there any American traders nearby to challenge the HBC's monopoly. The Woodland Cree and Ojibwa, and the Chipewyan, thus had no alternative but to accept the company's new prices and new rules. Among the latter were regulations intended to limit trapping in areas where fur-bearing populations had declined severely during the years of intense competition. Simpson ordered company traders to reject pelts from immature beavers, and to prohibit the use of steel traps; at some posts he imposed annual maximum quotas for pelts. This experiment in a sustained-yield fur trade did not represent a general corporate policy of conservation, however. To the south and west, where the Hudson's Bay Company competed with American traders, Simpson ordered a policy of 'trapping clean'. Between 1824 and 1830 the company hired 'the very scum of the earth'—Simpson's own description—to exterminate every fur-bearing animal in the Snake River Valley, in order to deny the valley to American mountain men. 'An exhausted country,' wrote Simpson, was 'the best protection we can have from opposition.'[5]

In areas without American competition, Simpson gradually eliminated liquor from the company's fur trade, both as part of pre-trade ceremonies and in its less common role as a trade good. His professed explanation was humanitarian: 'to wean the Indians from their insatiable thirst for Spirituous Liquors.' But the

Peter Rindisbacher, 'Scene in an Indian Tent', *c.* 1824. Here Rindisbacher depicts himself inside an Ojibwa tent. Ethnohistorians use this image as evidence of cultural exchange among Native peoples; Rindisbacher's clay pipe is of Plains origin, while the others smoke Woodland carved stone pipes. NAC c-114484.

corporate motivation was more complex. Discontinuing 'treats' of alcohol saved the company the thousands of pounds it had spent each year on buying and shipping kegs of rum. Abolition of alcohol also gave the Hudson's Bay Company the moral high ground when critics in Britain challenged its monopoly: a return to competition, Simpson warned, would 'debauch' the Indians of Rupert's Land with liquor. This discourse made it easy for the company to persuade Parliament to renew its License for Exclusive Trade in 1839.

The company's response when smallpox swept the northern plains in 1837–8 added further lustre to its image. The virus had travelled west on the American Fur Company steamboat *St Peter* with the annual load of trade goods to Fort Union, where Assiniboine robe-traders were infected with it. A longboat of supplies then carried the smallpox west along the Missouri to Fort McKenzie and the Blackfoot, Peigan, and Blood peoples. Native people scoffed at the idea of quarantine; as one Cree told David Thompson, 'a wounded man could not give his wound to another.' Thus they rode north with the pox to their villages: 6,000 of 9,000 Blackfoot, Blood, and Peigan, and 2,000 of 3,000 Assiniboine, died in the epidemic. Because smallpox was not a stranger to Rupert's Land, however, for humanitarian and business reasons the company had provided its traders with Jenner cowpox vaccine. At most posts the vials sat unopened, but at Fort Pelly, on the Assiniboine River, Chief Factor William Todd had been a company physician before he became a trader. On hearing the first reports of smallpox at Fort Union, Todd vaccinated the Plains Cree who traded there; he also trained one of his clerks, who then journeyed to other posts to do the same. Todd's rapid response saved most of the Plains Cree from infection and prevented the contagion from spreading to the Woodland peoples.[6]

The 1821 merger changed the Hudson's Bay Company's attitude towards the Selkirk settlement. Since the new company's requirements for labour and provisions had decreased, there was no longer any compelling reason for its existence. Quite the reverse: the Red River colonists represented a potential fifth column of competitors who might smuggle skins south across the nearby forty-ninth parallel, negotiated in 1818 to separate British territory from the United States. George Simpson suggested abandoning the colony, but Lord Selkirk's brother-in-law, John Halkett, rejected the proposal. They reached a compromise that no new immigrants should be admitted to the tiny communities of Scots, de Meuron soldiers, and French Canadians clustered around the Forks of the Red and the Assiniboine. The last contingent from Europe, fifty-seven families recruited in Switzerland, arrived in York boats from the Bay in November 1821. 'Only' one man and 'only' six children died on the long trip to the Forks, noted John West, the Anglican missionary who had accompanied the Swiss inland. As a group, the Swiss were an ephemeral presence at Red River; like many European immigrants to British North America, they moved south to the United States. One of them, however, left an enduring legacy.

'Rindisbacher, Pierre, 15, draughtsman, character good'—so an 1822 report to the governor of the colony described him—created hundreds of images of life in the western interior during his five-year sojourn. Peter Rindisbacher (1806–34) earns no more than a line, sometimes not even that, in histories of Canadian art. But his sketches and watercolours are invaluable as a visual record, in large part because his youth and limited formal training meant that his work was relatively free of formalistic clichés. Although he depicted Native people in classical poses borrowed from antique art, he lacked the romanticism of later painters, like George Catlin, who were determined to chronicle a 'vanishing race'. Rindisbacher's draughtsman's eye and meticulous attention to ethnohistorical detail made him 'an ideal painter for the anthropologist because he did not deviate from accuracy for the sake of making pleasing pictures'. The demands of patrons did constrain and shape Rindisbacher's work, however, as they do that of all artists. Several Hudson's Bay Company officers and three governors of Red River commissioned the 'boy artist' to depict specific subjects. But the usual fee of about £6 for a custom watercolour was not enough to keep young Rindisbacher in the Red River colony; with his family, he left for the United States in 1826.[7]

The Red River population grew as a result of natural increase and Hudson's Bay Company employment policies as the settlement became a magnet for those abandoned by the fur trade. Soon three-quarters of the inhabitants were of mixed race, the issue of fur-trade marriages *à la façon du pays*. Protestant missionaries and the small number of genteel British women who accompanied their husbands to the settlement, like George Simpson's bride Frances, regarded both the marriages and their offspring as evidence of the colony's barbarity. Studies by the historians Sylvia Van Kirk and Jennifer S.H. Brown describe such relationships as enduring and often caring, but suggest that as European newcomers not connected with the fur trade became more numerous in Red River, racism and the Victorian double standard made life more difficult for mixed-race families. The titles of their books, both direct quotations from primary documents, illustrate the two sides of such marriages: Van Kirk's *Many Tender Ties* captures the caring and stability, while Brown's *Strangers in Blood* reminds us that, however much the children of fur-trade marriages might have been

, 2. A Swiss colonist with wife and children from the Canton of Berne.   3. A German colonist from the disbanded De Meuron Regt.   4. A Scottish Highland colonist.   5. An immigrant colonist from French Canada.

TYPES OF LORD SELKIRK'S SETTLERS IN 1822.

Peter Rindisbacher, 'Colonists on the Red River in North America', 1822–25? *A Manitoba Free Press* artist gave this line drawing a new title and added the shading when the newspaper reproduced it during the 1920s to commemorate the Selkirk settlers as the founders of Manitoba. Subsequently, some historians have used this line drawing to depict ethnic heterogeneity in Red River, emphasizing that the figures represent Swiss, German, Scottish, and French-Canadian 'types'. Alvin Josephy argues persuasively, however, that 'the artist was probably depicting his family in the company of some friends', and that the central figures are Peter and his father.

cared for and loved, in European eyes they were illegitimate.

The longer presence and larger numbers of French-Canadian *engagés* in the western interior meant that francophone Métis outnumbered the English-speaking progeny of Scots or Orkney HBC servants. Neither group fitted smoothly into either the European or the Native culture, although each had contacts with both. Residence in different parishes and high levels of marriage within their own communities created fairly distinct cultural com-

Paul Kane, 'Half Breeds Travelling'. Kane (1810–71) sketched this scene when he accompanied the Red River Métis on the hunt in 1846, but the panoramic oil reproduced here, like all his paintings, was done several years later in his Toronto studio. ROM 912.1.24.

munities. Historian Jacqueline Peterson writes of 'the sudden florescence of a distinctive métis population and culture' that 'radiat[ed] outward from the junction of the Assiniboine and Red Rivers' between the 1820s and the 1850s. The French-speaking Métis made up the largest group in the Red River settlement, numbering 2,400 in 1831 and 4,000 a decade later; other Métis settlements developed farther west, at Batoche on the Saskatchewan River and near Fort Edmonton. In addition to the French language, the Métis shared with French Canada their Roman Catholic faith: Father J.N. Provencher, a priest from Lower Canada, had founded a mission at the Forks in 1818, and missionary-priests served the Métis settlements. Before the 1821 merger, Cuthbert Grant and others had found careers as clerks with the North West Company, but after it more restrictive attitudes to race made such opportunities rare. Métis men worked seasonally for the Hudson's Bay Company at manual jobs as provisioners, 'tripmen' on York boats, or teamsters; and with their families they farmed narrow lots fronting the rivers south and west of the Forks.

The English-speaking Protestants of mixed ancestry remain a subject of debate among historians, who disagree on their relationship with the Métis, and even about what to call them. 'Country-born', the Hudson's Bay Company's preferred euphemism, has become the accepted term in academic circles, replacing the now embarrassing 'English half-breed'. Traditional historians like George Stanley identified the francophone Métis as 'improvident and happy-go-lucky', unsuccessful farmers who were 'inclined to the roving life' of the hunt, while the 'English half-breeds' were described as 'steady, economical, industrious and prosperous' farmers who eschewed the 'wild' life on the prairie. Recent exhaustive research by Gerhard Ens finds few socio-economic distinctions between the two groups, apart from the obvious differences of language and religion. Ens concludes that both the Métis and 'country-born' communities were composed of peasant families who combined buffalo hunting, and whatever seasonal labour they could find with the Hudson's Bay Company, with subsistence farming.[8]

Hay cut from the tall grass prairie mattered more to these families than cultivated crops of grain and potatoes, because hay fed their oxen and the horses used in the June and October buffalo hunts. Whole families took part, men as hunters, women and children as processors. The larger June hunt left only the very oldest and youngest Métis and country-born residents behind to share the settlement with the Scottish Selkirk families and the Hudson's Bay employees. Because of the complexity of co-ordinating as many as 1,500 people, the hunt required a quasi-military discipline, with an elected captain and officers to organize and regulate it, and 'courts martial' for offenders who refused to follow the rules of the hunt. Another reason for

military discipline was that the search for buffalo took the hunters far to the southwest, into the territory of the Sioux. In July 1851, on the Grand Coteau of the Missouri River, an advance party of seventy Métis circled their Red River carts to defeat a vastly superior force of Dakota Sioux without the loss of one life. Métis and country-born living near the Forks soon dominated the business of supplying pemmican to the Hudson's Bay Company in the eastern prairies, especially after the smallpox epidemic of 1837–8 decimated the Assiniboine. By the early 1840s these hunters were producing more pemmican than the company could absorb, and thereafter they diversified into the trade in buffalo robes and hides.

Lord Selkirk's heirs formally returned Assiniboia to the Hudson's Bay Company in 1834, making it legally as well as practically responsible for maintaining rudimentary institutions of civil government. A governor, usually the Chief Factor of the company, was advised by a Council of Assiniboia, appointed at the company's pleasure, and by a recorder, the legal officer who administered the English common law. These officials governed only in theory, however; given that seven or eight of every ten males in the colony were buffalo hunters with rifles, 'such government as there was depended on the consent of the governed,' as W.L. Morton puts it. The Métis never accepted HBC rule docilely. In particular, the more ambitious young men challenged the company's trading monopoly by selling furs and buffalo robes to American traders. During the 1840s, the demand for buffalo robes in the US expanded and Red River hunters eagerly supplied them, freighting robes 750 kilometres for sale in St Paul in the Minnesota

Territory. The Hudson's Bay Company could not turn a blind eye to the trains of Red River carts heading south. In 1849, Chief Factor John Ballenden charged a Métis named Pierre Guillaume Sayer with illegal trading. Despite a spirited defense by the country-born James Sinclair, a jury reluctantly found Sayer technically guilty but recommended that he be set free. The 300 armed Métis surrounding the Assiniboia courthouse persuaded recorder Adam Thom that a sentence of no sentence would be prudent. As Sayer left the courthouse, unpunished, celebratory gunshots and shouts of 'Le commerce est libre!' announced the effective end of the Hudson's Bay Company's trading monopoly.[9]

The Sayer case signalled the challenges that the Hudson's Bay Company faced, but did not end its paramount commercial power in the western interior. One of the company's most effective allies as it struggled to maintain that paramountcy was painter Paul Kane (1810–71). Kane toured the west between 1846 and 1848 as Sir George Simpson's official guest. More than any other image-maker, Kane defined (and continues to define) the pre-Confederation Canadian West and its peoples. Formally trained in Europe and explicitly imitative of George Catlin, Kane returned to his Toronto studio to reshape the realistic field sketches made on his journey into preconceived portraits of 'noble savages' interpreted according to the conventions of nineteenth-century romantic art.

Kane's account of his tour, *Wanderings of an Artist among the Indians of North America* (1858), is mistitled, for he was hardly a 'wanderer'; Simpson had commanded that he receive the 'kind attentions and hospitalities . . . of the Company's posts' and ordered that Kane be car-

Paul Kane, 'Kee-akee-Ka-Saa-Ka-Wow, The Man that Gives the War Whoop', 1848, and 'Kee-A-Kee-Ka-Sa-Coo-Way', *c.* 1852–53. Kane's sketch of a Plains Cree at Fort Pitt contrasts sharply with the romanticized portrait later created in oil in his studio. Not only did he add the Plains Indian props, but he narrowed the features of his subject's face to better fit the 'noble savage' stereotype. Sketch, NAC C-114386; oil on canvas, ROM 912.1.42.

 Boundary Commission photographers, 1872. Nineteenth-century photographers struggled with awkward equipment, including the chemicals required to develop their wet-plate negatives, and portable darkrooms. This photo also suggests the nineteenth century's pride in the new technologies that facilitated westward expansion. PAM N11938.

ried 'from post to post in the Company's craft—free of charge'. Not surprisingly, a grateful Kane echoed the official HBC version of life in the western interior in his book:

> The half-breeds are much inclined to grumbling . . . [but] as far as the Company is concerned, I cannot conceive a more just and strict course than that which they pursue in the conduct of the whole of their immense traffic. . . . No drunkenness or debauchery is seen around their posts, . . . so strict is their prohibition of liquor. . . . The firm conviction

which I have formed from a comparison between the Indians in the Hudson's Bay Company territories and those in the United States, [is] that opening up the trade with the Indians to all who wish indiscriminately to engage in it, must lead to their annihilation. . . . Those [Native peoples] in contact with the Hudson's Bay Company maintain their numbers, retain native characteristics unimpaired, and in some degree share in the advantages which civilization places within their reach.[10]

Kane's book appeared, to excellent reviews, in the midst of unprecedented outside attention to the western interior and to the company that governed half a continent. His words and images defended the HBC at a time when it was besieged by critics who wished to incorporate the fur traders' domain into the world-wide British Empire of settlement. Gold on the Fraser River had created the colony of British Columbia on the Pacific; soon, editorialized the London *Daily Telegraph*, 'the time must come when the two tides of civilization flowing inwards from either shore will meet and coalesce.' In 1857 a Select Committee of the British House of Commons inquired into the future of Britain's North American West. Concern about the expanding United States recurred in the questions that members of Parliament put to company officers: if Minnesota could grow from a wilderness to a state with a white population of almost 200,000, why had Rupert's Land not done the same? Sir George Simpson's adamant answer that 'no part of the territories of the Company is well adapted for settlement' was interpreted as evidence of self-interested conspiracy to conceal the rich agricultural potential of the prairies.[11]

The Hind expedition in camp on the Red River, June 1858. The three Europeans crowd the foreground, while six Métis canoemen-guides are out of focus in the background. Hime featured Native people only when they fitted the same 'noble savage' stereotype that preoccupied Paul Kane. H.L. Hime photo. NAC C-4572.

At least equally self-interested were the growing demands for Canada to expand west into the Hudson's Bay Company's territories. Centred in Canada West (the future province of Ontario), the expansionists had the political support of the Reform Party and the editorial blessing of George Brown's Toronto *Globe*. English-Canadian expansionists cheered the British parliament's decision not to renew the HBC's Licence of Exclusive Trade, and the parliamentary committee's recommendation that Rupert's Land be developed 'to add to the strength of the great colony of Canada'.

Canadian expansionists vowed to be worthy trustees of this patrimony: 'the region between Canada and the Rocky Mountains, with a railway and a telegraph linking the Atlantic and the Pacific,' wrote Alexander Morris, would become 'the Great Britannic Empire of the North.'[12]

Beyond their common conviction that vast resources awaited European exploitation, neither the parliamentary committee nor the Canadian expansionists had any detailed information about the western interior. In 1857, two scientific expeditions set out to find the evidence to prove what the expansionists

H.L. Hime, 'Ojibway Squaw and Papoose', 1858. Ethnohistorians compare this photo with Rindisbacher's images to document Ojibwa adoption of European-style cloth garments. The child's blurred face is evidence of the long exposures necessary in early photography; children and animals made poor subjects because they wouldn't keep still long enough. PAM Hime Collection 31, N12579.

park belt. They identified transportation routes, catalogued mineral and timber resources, and, most important, assessed the capacity for agriculture. Palliser and Hind discovered what the expansionists needed: a 'Fertile Belt' that arced northwest across 'the vast plains of Rupert's Land' from the Red River to the Rocky Mountains. 'No other part of North America [has] this singularly favourable disposition of soil and climate,' reported Hind, with virtually no meteorological data to support his 'scientific' conclusion. 'Only the difficulty of access' to the Saskatchewan country, wrote Palliser's geologist, Dr James Hector, 'prevents its immediate occupation.' The two expeditions concurred that this 'Fertile Belt' wrapped around a 44,000-square-kilometre 'arid district' along the 49th parallel, the northern tip of a 'Great American Desert' that they believed covered the interior of the United States. But the arid 'Palliser's triangle' was an insignificant caveat to the unlimited promise of the 'Fertile Belt'. Palliser and Hind had contradicted the perception, crafted by the fur traders, of the western interior as a wilderness wasteland. In its place they constructed a competing image of the northwest as a garden in waiting, as fertile soil in which, in Hind's words, 'to plant British institutions and civilization . . . a spirit of loyalty, of order, and of obedience to the law'.[13]

already believed. The British government financed a party led by Captain John Palliser, while Canada chose a University of Toronto professor of chemistry and geology, Henry Youle Hind, a committed advocate of western expansion, to lead its excursion. The work of Palliser, Hind, and their colleagues was 'inventory science', consisting of systematic surveys of the material potential of the prairies and

A new image needed new images. Photography was less than twenty years old, but its bond with scientific exploration had already been established by American expeditions west of the 100th meridian. Accordingly, H.Y. Hind insisted that the Toronto 'photographist' Humphrey Lloyd Hime be assigned to his team in 1858. Hime thus 'took' (like sci-

H.L. Hime, 'The Prairie looking west', 1858. Historian Andrea Kunard argues persuasively that Hime planted the human skull and the (human?) bone in this photograph. In his diary for 28 June 1858, Hime imagined a lurid origin for his prop: 'found a skull close to a grave on the prairie—it was all pulled about by wolves—kept the skull which was apparently that of a squaw: perhaps the victim of a savage husband.' NAC C-017443.

entific specimens, photographs were said to be 'taken') the first of the many thousands of photographs that would represent the landscapes and peoples of the western interior to the world. Hime was a photographic innovator, according to historian Lilly Koltun, with a 'stark style and innovative compositional designs [that] set him apart from the usually pictorial or illustrative photographer'. But photographic technology imposed limits. Hime used the cumbersome wet-plate process, common until the 1880s. In addition to the heavy camera, lenses, and tripod, wet-plate photography in the field required cases of glass plates, bottles of chemicals, a barrel of water, and a 'dark tent'. For each photograph, Hime had to coat a clean glass plate with collodion (gun-cotton dissolved in ether and alcohol) dip the plate in a silver nitrate solution, expose the moist plate without delay, and then immediately fix the negative in a potassium cyanide solution. Under these trying conditions, Hime created images that historian Ralph Greenhill describes as 'among the finest early photographs taken in Canada, . . . an astonishing achievement'. A portfolio of Hime's photographs was published in 1860, and engravings based on them illustrated the reports of the Hind expedition. Nineteenth-century readers of Hime's photographs accepted them as objective renderings of reality. Like Paul Kane's paintings, however, Hime's photographs were carefully composed according to stylistic conventions, and created with a specific objective explicitly stated: to be 'useful and interesting to parties wishing to visit the country for purposes of settlement'.[14]

Photography was just one of the new technologies that were changing the European-centred world in the mid-nineteenth century.

Expansionists were able to imagine a transcontinental Canada only because steam-powered ships and railways were shrinking time and space. A transcontinental railway was still a dream for the future, but in 1859 the paddle-wheeler *Anson Northup* inaugurated service between Red River and St Paul: Sir George Simpson made his last trip to Red River not in a canoe but via Minnesota in a steamboat. And the industrial revolution transformed the western interior long before it actually arrived there. When less expensive mass-produced silk hats replaced beaver in the 1850s, cash prices began to replace the Made Beaver as the standard of exchange. Similar changes occurred in Indian and Métis societies, where in the past resources

Facing above. Alfred Jacob Miller, 'A Buffalo Rift', 1837. This image of a buffalo 'jump' is often misdated to 1867, the year the Canadian government commissioned a copy of the original, rather than 1837, the year Miller (1810–74) painted it. In his journal, the artist expressed alarm over 'the wholesale destruction of these valuable animals, [and] the vast hecatombs of victims'. He noted with grim satisfaction that 'sometimes . . . the Indians get entangled and are hurled down with the Buffalo; almost a just retribution for the deplorable waste of animal life' (Miller, *Braves and Buffalo: Plains Indian Life in 1837* (Toronto: University of Toronto Press, 1973). NAC C-403.

Facing below. Peter Rindisbacher, 'Governor of Red River in a Canoe', 1823–24. Historians sometimes claim that this watercolour represents HBC governor Sir George Simpson and his crew of 'hand-picked canoemen', but in fact it was commissioned by its actual subject, Red River governor Andrew Bulger. The younger man wearing a cap and sitting next to Bulger may represent Rindisbacher himself. According to Alvin Josephy, the painting is in 'Rindisbacher's usual style, in which he first made careful pencil and pen-and-ink outlines and then filled in the pictures with watercolors'; he created several versions of this painting, with the canoe facing in different directions. PAM CT5, CN14.

Overleaf above. Peter Rindisbacher, 'Winter fishing on the Assynoibain [sic] and Red River, drawn from nature in December 1821', c. 1822. The HBC's Fort Douglas appears in the background of this busy winter scene. Ethnohistorian Laura Peers who has compared Rindisbacher's paintings with written sources, argues that his work reliably depicts Ojibwa winter clothing and weapons, and that the extensive interaction he portrays between Native people and settlers is accurate as well (*The Ojibwa of Western Canada, 1780–1870*. Winnipeg: University of Manitoba Press, 1994). NAC C-1932.

Overleaf below. Peter Rindisbacher, 'Arrival at the Mouth of the Red River in North America . . . and welcome from the Sautaux Indians . . . after a river and sea voyage of 4836 English Miles', 1821. This seldom-reproduced painting represents the Swiss settlers pausing as they reach the last leg of their long journey inland from Hudson Bay to the Selkirk colony. One York boat has landed at the Saulteaux camp, and two others steer with oars toward the shore. Note the ducks (or geese—Rindisbacher was just learning how to depict the fauna of his new home) in the foreground. The abundance of wild game excited the young artist, as it did other European newcomers. NAC C-1926.

had been shared, common property to which all had access. Just as the 'money way' superseded the 'skin way' of fur trading, so the ideology of private property and individual land ownership, essential to capitalist development, began gradually to displace the idea that resources might be held in common.[15]

These new values came as baggage with the trickle of Canadians, virtually all English-speaking Protestants from Ontario, drawn west by Hind's report. By 1867, when Ontario and Quebec confederated with Nova Scotia and New Brunswick, some 800 of them lived in or near Red River—an advance guard, they believed, for the tens of thousands who would follow when the new Dominion of Canada annexed the Hudson's Bay Company territories. Canada could scarcely have had worse ambassadors than this 'Canadian party' and *The Nor'Wester*, an annexationist newspaper founded in Red River by two former Toronto

Globe journalists. They made no secret of their contempt for the French-speaking Catholic Métis, and they were eager for union with Canada, when, as a *Nor'Wester* editorial put it, 'the indolent and the careless, like the native tribes of the country, will fall back before the march of a superior intelligence.' After long negotiations, and with the encouragement of the British government, Canada and the Hudson's Bay Company agreed to terms in 1869. The company would surrender its rights and privileges for £300,000 (about $1.5 million—one-quarter of what the United States had paid Russia for Alaska two years earlier), one-twentieth of the land in the 'Fertile Belt' as defined by Hind and Palliser, and the right to continue trading without 'hindrance or exceptional taxation'.[16]

Neither Britain, Canada, nor the company made any effort to consult or even to inform the inhabitants of the western interior about

---

Facing above. Paul Kane, 'Winter Travelling', *c.* 1852. Kane painted this oil to please a specific HBC patron. It portrays a factor's daughter, her husband, and the guests who had attended their wedding leaving Fort Edmonton for Fort Pitt in 1848. The authors of the 1927 high-school text *The Story of the Canadian People* captioned it 'Fur Traders on their way to Northern Posts', eliminating the inconvenient concepts of women and weddings from the heroic male story of the conquest of the Northwest. ROM 912.1.48.

Facing below. Paul Kane, 'The Death of Omoxesisixany or Big Snake', 1848. Native peoples did make war on each other, but in ways unsuitable for heroic paintings. If reality did not lend itself to the composition he wanted, Kane simply fabricated the scene. The Blackfoot chief Omoxesisixany ('Big Snake'), shown dying with a Cree lance in his chest, in fact lived until 1858. Russell Harper concludes that Kane 'painted this imaginary view of the incident after reaching Toronto', and that 'the composition suggests that the canvas was based on a European prototype.' Glenbow Collection, Calgary, Alberta, Canada. 61.109.

Overleaf above. Paul Kane, 'Métis Running Buffalo', *c.* 1850. Kane's original title was 'Half Breeds Running Buffalo', but the painting has been informally renamed since the 1960s. Kane had little skill in depicting people or animals in action. ROM, Ethnology Department, 912.1.26.

Overleaf below. Paul Kane, 'Rocky Mountain House with Assiniboin [*sic*] lodges in the foreground', *c.* 1848. Because Sir George Simpson was his patron, and because the company helped him to travel through the western interior, Kane painted several HBC posts, but none with much conviction. Portraying 'vanishing' Native people was his real objective, as the absence of whites in this painting suggest. NAC C-114374.

the negotiations. The new Canadian federal government behaved as if annexation were a *fait accompli*: in the summer of 1869, well before the transfer eventually negotiated for 1 December, Canada sent road builders and surveyors into the Red River district. By the Act for the Temporary Government of Rupert's Land, the Canadian Parliament attempted to make all of the western interior, Red River included, into a colony such as Canada itself had been a century earlier, with an appointed lieutenant-governor, executive, and council, and without an elected assembly. Prime Minister John A. Macdonald's choice of governor for his new colony—William McDougall, an arrogant Ontario annexationist with a reputation for anti-Catholicism—turned a serious situation into a dangerous one. It is difficult to understand how politicians astute enough to create the Canadian confederation could bungle western expansion so completely; their disregard for the human rights of the residents of Rupert's Land was callous, but their nonchalance regarding the military capacity of the Métis was irresponsible. Historian Doug Owram offers the best explanation: that the images created by Paul Kane and H.L. Hime combined with the racist discourse of the annexationists in the Red River colony to persuade Canadians that the Métis were 'a quaint, colourful, and somewhat romantic people' unable to offer serious opposition to Canada's western destiny. 'Easily dealt with and easily controlled,' sneered one Red River expansionist to the Toronto *Globe* in February 1869.[17]

Métis protests soon belied this boast. Apart from the Canadian party, no one in Rupert's Land welcomed annexation on the terms dictated by Ottawa, but it was the French-speaking Catholic Métis who led the resistance to the transfer. Louis Riel emerged rapidly as the leader of the Métis. Born in Red River in 1844, the son of a leader in the Métis challenge to the Hudson's Bay Company's trading monopoly, Riel had left in 1858 for a Catholic education in Montreal. Back in the settlement for less than a year when rumours of impending annexation exploded, the young seminarian seemed an unlikely commander for an army of buffalo hunters. Riel won their loyalty because he spanned the gap between the traditional oral society of the western interior and the literary, textual society that was supplanting it. Riel could read and write, and the Métis recognized these skills as important even if they did not share them. He also had the support of several Roman Catholic priests in Red River who, like the Métis, feared that annexation would bring a flood of immigrants from Protestant Ontario. The strategy of the National Committee of the Métis of Red River, with Riel as its secretary, was not to reject union with Canada, but to delay until they could negotiate terms that would take their concerns into account, so that they could join Canada as citizens rather than as colonial subjects. To this end, armed Métis first stopped the work of the Canadian surveyors. When the governor-designate, William McDougall, entered Rupert's Land on the trail from St Paul, a month before the legal date of the transfer, mounted riflemen forced him to retreat back across the 49th parallel. The National Committee's soldiers seized the HBC's Upper Fort Garry and the stores it contained, and established themselves in effective control of Red River.[18]

In the early morning of 1 December 1869, the would-be governor slipped briefly across

Louis Riel and the Council of the Provisional Government, Fort Garry, 1869 or 1870. Riel (middle) sits surrounded by his council. The captions to various archival copies of this photo disagree about the identity of several of the councillors. The photo is attributed to James Penrose, one of Manitoba's first photographers. However, Penrose did not arrive in Manitoba until May 1871, so the attribution seems dubious. PAM N5396.

the border from his unhappy exile in the Dakota Territory. In the dark, in the midst of a snowstorm, he proclaimed himself ruler of Rupert's Land and called on all loyal subjects of Queen Victoria to suppress the Métis insurrection. McDougall's proclamation was both foolish and illegal—Prime Minister Macdonald had informed the British government that Canada would not accept the transfer until the situation had been resolved—but in Red River a group of Canadians led by Dr John Christian Schultz heeded McDougall and took up arms

to resist the resistance. Their action rallied a rough (though never complete) consensus within Red River behind Riel's strategy of negotiation. Métis soldiers quickly captured Schultz and his followers and locked them up in Fort Garry.

A Provisional Government, with Louis Riel as its elected president, convened delegates from parishes within the settlement who drafted a 'Bill of Rights' as a basis for bargaining with Canada. Three delegates took these terms to Ottawa, where on 12 May 1870 they formed

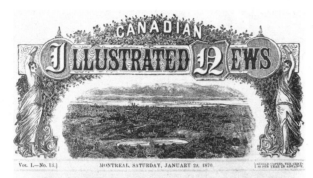

'The Situation', cover of the *Canadian Illustrated News*, 29 Jan. 1870. On a cold winter night, 'Miss Red River' must choose between the 'U.S. Hotel' and 'Hotel Canada'. A leering, whittling, smoking Uncle Sam lounges in front of the former, while the respectable Mrs Britannia keeps the latter. Victorian readers accustomed to such artistic conventions would have had no doubt about the fate that awaited 'Miss Red River' inside the 'U.S. Hotel'. NAC 48653.

the basis of the Manitoba Act. Red River and its environs would enter the confederation not as a colony but as a self-governing province, with representatives in the federal Parliament, and an elected legislature and responsible government. The new 'postage stamp' province of Manitoba scarcely extended beyond the settlement, however, and it lacked the most significant power of the four other provinces: control of its natural resources, above all its public lands, belonged to the federal rather than the provincial government. To settle the land question, the federal government recognized existing titles and reserved 1.4 million acres (567,000 hectares) for land grants for future Métis generations. The Manitoba Act also guaranteed a continuation of English-Protestant and French-Catholic duality in Manitoba's government, courts, and public schools. French–English duality had not been among the Red River community's original list of demands; historians have identified Riel and Roman Catholic Bishop Alexandre Taché as the authors of this provision. Whatever its source, it reflected the reality in Manitoba, which had a French-Catholic majority when it officially joined Canada on 15 July 1870.[19]

Canada had worried that the United States would exploit the Métis resistance to add Rupert's Land to its manifest destiny, just as it had prised Texas and California from Mexico. Fear of US intervention encouraged Canada to negotiate, but Riel never considered joining the United States. He adroitly outmanoeuvred the minority in Red River who sought annexation to the US, and insisted that the Union Jack fly over Fort Garry. Far from being a 'traitor' to Canada in 1869–70, as English-speaking Canadian children were once taught, Louis Riel helped to ensure that the western plains would become part of the new Dominion rather than the American republic.[20]

For a settlement in insurrection, Red River remained remarkably tranquil under Riel's Provisional Government. Only one serious

'The Execution of Scott'. The captain of the Métis firing squad finishes off Thomas Scott with a pistol shot to the head, while other armed Métis laugh in the background and a well-dressed Louis Riel looks on. In fact, Riel was not present at the execution. Ontarians imagined the 'murder' of Scott in such terms or worse; some stories had him buried alive, clawing helplessly at the coffin lid with bleeding fingers. NAC C-118610.

incident broke the calm in the colony: the execution of Thomas Scott, a Protestant Irish immigrant who had been arrested with Schultz's force. Scott was an unmanageable prisoner who regularly shouted out his contempt for French-speaking Catholics; taunted beyond endurance, his Métis jailers demanded that he be charged for 'insubordination and striking the guards'. Riel justified Scott's sham trial and subsequent execution on the grounds that 'we must make Canada respect us', but Scott's death had consequences beyond anything that

could have been predicted. In Protestant Ontario, the young hot-head became a martyr 'cruelly murdered by the enemies of our Queen, country, and religion'. Canadian expansionists manipulated longstanding anti-French bigotry. Mass meetings, at which John Christian Schultz was the featured speaker, demanded that the Macdonald government avenge Scott's death and punish his French-Catholic Métis 'murderer', Louis Riel. Macdonald took care to ensure that Riel was not captured. But to pander to Ontario's ethnocentric outrage at Scott's death, the prime minister excluded Riel from the general amnesty granted to others who had been active in the Red River Resistance.

The Prairie West thus became contested terrain in French–English ethnic conflict in Canada from the moment it entered the confederation. The Canadian soldiers sent by Macdonald to Manitoba carried that conflict west in their packs. Ostensibly the 800 militia and 400 British regulars were to help the new lieutenant-governor, Adams Archibald, maintain law and order and establish a provincial government; in fact, the militiamen themselves believed their mission was to punish the Métis and capture Riel. 'Had we caught him', wrote Colonel Garnet Wolseley, British commander of the expedition, 'he would have had no mercy.' To the frustration of the militiamen—and the relief of both the Canadian and British governments—Riel prudently departed before the troops arrived on 24 August 1870. Governor Archibald's oath of office on 2 September made the Prairie West legally part of Canada; the more difficult task of the Canadian government would be to make the Prairie West Canadian.

CHAPTER FOUR

※

Making the Prairie West Canadian: 1870–1900

Canada stretched its nominal sovereignty west to the Pacific in an astonishingly short time. When British Columbia entered the confederation in July 1871, the new Dominion had accomplished in four years what had taken the United States fifty. But British Columbia's provincehood differed sharply from Manitoba's. Because it had been a British colony with representative institutions and a larger white settler population, BC had to be bribed to join Canada with lavish terms of union that made it what many called 'the spoilt child of Confederation'. In Manitoba, by contrast, the Métis resistance had won the grudging concession of provincehood, but the new government in Winnipeg lacked the most important provincial prerogative: control of natural resources. Lands, forests, and minerals within Manitoba, as in the North-West Territories surrounding the new province, were to be developed 'for the purposes of the Dominion', regardless of how the residents of province and territories might feel about those purposes.

The Conservative government of Sir John A. Macdonald refused the North-West Territories even representative institutions: they

were governed by an appointed governor and appointed councillors who lived in Winnipeg. Self-government, Secretary of State Joseph Howe explained, would not be 'compatible with the preservation of British interests on the Continent, and the integrity of the Empire'.[1] In 1875 the North-West Territories Act, passed by the Liberal government of Alexander Mackenzie (1874–78), created a capital within the Territories (Battleford until 1882, and Regina thereafter) and permitted the gradual introduction of elected members to the territorial council. Macdonald criticized even these minor concessions as capitulation to 'the popular element'. But the representative government that Mackenzie permitted in the Territories was far less than the 'responsible' government that Canadians themselves had struggled for in the 1840s. Decisions of any significance were made in Ottawa, where the North-West Territories went unrepresented until 1882. The real government of the North-West Territories was the Dominion Department of the Interior, responsible for Crown lands, natural resources, and Indian affairs. The department's first minister, Senator Alexander Campbell, described him-

Sappers of the Royal Engineers building a boundary mound, August or September 1873. The Boundary Commission erected a mound every three miles and planted an eight-foot hollow iron pillar every mile. Marking the forty-ninth parallel and photographing the act of marking demonstrated that Canada and the British Empire now possessed the land north of the line. Glenbow NA-218-1.

self as the 'Secretary for the Colonies'. This was entirely appropriate: the developing Prairie West had been designed to be a colony of the Canadian government.

By refusing to delegate authority or to foster the development of local autonomy, Canadian governments specifically rejected the American model of a systematic evolution towards full self-government for territories. In the formula for statehood, a population of 5,000 adult males brought an elected territorial legislature, and with a population of 60,000 adult males a territory could petition for statehood. Thus after enduring a period as 'colonies' of Washington, male citizens of the western territories of the United States could look forward to equality with the 'mother country': by 1870, eighteen territories had become states on an equal footing with the others. Canada drew up no such pattern for provincehood, even for limited provincehood like that of Manitoba. The federal government wanted no inconvenient local interference with its project of making the Prairie West Canadian.

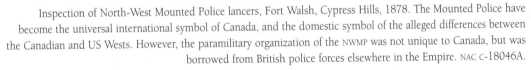

Inspection of North-West Mounted Police lancers, Fort Walsh, Cypress Hills, 1878. The Mounted Police have become the universal international symbol of Canada, and the domestic symbol of the alleged differences between the Canadian and US Wests. However, the paramilitary organization of the NWMP was not unique to Canada, but was borrowed from British police forces elsewhere in the Empire. NAC C-18046A.

Canadian governments, Conservative or Liberal, were in fact determined to make the Prairie West as explicitly *un*-American as they possibly could. Macdonald believed that the United States would do anything, 'short of war, to get possession of the western territory', and accordingly took 'immediate and vigorous steps to counteract them'. Canada took these steps not on its own, but as the North American unit of a world-wide British Empire. The first essential was to give physical reality to a boundary that so far had been drawn only by

the pens of cartographers. Between September 1872 and August 1874, fifty British Royal Engineers and a group of Canadian surveyors marked 1,600 kilometres of the forty-ninth parallel from the eastern edge of the plains to the mountains. Once surveyed, the line of stone cairns and iron stakes erected by the boundary commission had to be watched. A large western army like the one deployed by the United States would have been prohibitively expensive: in 1870, the American government spent more on fighting Indians than the

SITTING BULL ON DOMINION TERRITORY.

U. S. Soldier.—Send him over to our side of the line and we'll take care of him.
N. W. Mounted Police Officer.—So long as he behaves himself, the British right of asylum is as sacred for this poor Indian as for any royal refugee.

Henri Julien, 'Sitting Bull on Dominion Territory', cover of the *Canadian Illustrated News*, 22 Sept. 1877. The caption includes a brief exchange between the two white characters. The US soldier says, 'Send him over to our side of the line and we'll take care of him'; the NWMP constable replies, 'So long as he behaves himself, the British right of asylum is as sacred for this poor Indian as for any royal refugee.' Sitting Bull and his people fled to Canada after destroying Lt Col. George Armstrong Custer's 7th Cavalry at the Little Big Horn. The Canadian government refused American entreaties to send the Sioux back to the US. As Julien's cartoon suggests, this reinforced Canadians' conviction that their West was morally superior to the 'wild' US West, but Sitting Bull's demeaning posture suggests that Canada's Indian policy was founded on the same racist assumptions as that of the United States. NAC C66055.

Canadian government spent for all purposes. Instead Macdonald adopted a solution used successfully elsewhere in the British Empire: a paramilitary police force of mounted riflemen, modelled after the Royal Irish Constabulary.[2]

Parliament had already passed a bill authorizing the creation of such a force when the government learned that, on 1 June 1873, 'American Outlaws' had gunned down between twenty and thirty Assiniboine men, women, and children (accounts differ as to numbers) in a dispute over horses in the Cypress Hills, just inside the Canadian border. The Cypress Hills Massacre dramatized the perfidy of Americans and underscored the need for a Canadian response. Indignation at the American intrusion on Canadian sovereignty outweighed concern for the dead Assiniboine. Untroubled by evidence that some of the trigger-happy wolf hunters who committed the murders were actually Canadians, editorials thundered that 'if the Republic cannot teach its subjects to respect law it is time that the Dominion should.' In the summer of 1874, 275 North-West Mounted Police, dressed in the scarlet tunics of the British army, rode west from Manitoba to the foothills. They went, according to Governor-General Lord Dufferin, 'not as the Americans have done, for the purpose of . . . controlling the Indian tribes, but with the view of avenging injuries inflicted on the red man by the white.'[3]

If the North-West Mounted Police fell short of Dufferin's grand design, for the rest of the century they nonetheless maintained a remarkable peace between Euro-Canadian settlers and Native people—remarkable, that is, when contrasted with the violent conflict between the US Cavalry and the Plains tribes on the other side of the forty-ninth parallel. And Canadians from the first did contrast the US and Canadian western experiences: to Canadians, the Mounties symbolized the aspirations of their new nation-state. The NWMP hierarchy and Canadian élites carefully constructed a heroic legend in which red-coated Mounties defended grateful Indians from American desperados. The founding commissioner of the force, G.A. French, began the image- and legend-making by paying for Henri Julien, an artist-journalist for *The Canadian Illustrated News* and *L'Opinion publique*, to accompany the police on their western trek. Thus began the process of Mountie mythologizing that reached its apogee with Wallace Stegner's description of the US–Canada boundary as 'a color line: blue below, red above, blue for treachery and unkept promises, red for protection and the straight tongue'.[4]

The Mounted Police averted violent Indian–white confrontation (with the notable exception of the North-West Rebellion of 1885) for several reasons. Like the Canadian government, the Assiniboine, Blackfoot, and Plains Cree had also learned from the American example: they knew that the Canadian government could wage war and ultimately destroy them should it choose to.

Hunger was the second brutal cornerstone of Canada's successful Indian policy: by the 1870s, the Plains tribes were slowly starving. The near-extinction of the plains bison began in the 1840s, as the herds disappeared from the eastern prairies and contracted south and west beyond the Cypress Hills. The hunt to provision the fur trade had not seriously threatened the bison population, but the growth of the trade in buffalo robes put greater pressure on it as more hunters chased fewer animals. In the 1820s five million bison had migrated between the Missouri River and the Saskatchewan; by 1870 fewer than two million

remained. In that year a Philadelphia tanner sealed the fate of these survivors when he devised a process for turning buffalo hides into inexpensive leather. New breech-loading Sharps rifles could drop an animal at 500 metres; new US railroads transported the hides to tanneries in the eastern United States. American 'pot' hunters killed tens of thousands of animals annually throughout the 1870s, and Métis hunters on the Canadian plains enthusiastically enlisted in the slaughter, selling the hides at posts on the Missouri River. White or Métis, the hunters simply skinned the carcasses and left the meat to rot; the boundary surveyors held their noses to shut out the stench. The Native people had difficulty believing what was happening. 'They come again and again to us,' one Plains Cree told William Francis Butler in 1872, 'we cannot kill them all.' The end came with surprising suddenness. In 1879, the Métis' Red River carts returned empty from the hunt: the herds that had seemed inexhaustible were gone.[5]

The Blackfoot and Sioux had followed the buffalo for centuries. The Cree, Assiniboine, and Ojibwa had migrated to the plains and park belt in response to the depletion of other game in the forests. None of these peoples had anywhere else to go. They hunted pronghorn antelope, mule deer, and moose more intensively, and soon these animals too were reduced from millions to thousands. Along with the larger game went the bears and the wolves—those wolves not already killed by pelt-hunters using strychnine-laced bait. In the Qu'Appelle Valley of the North-West Territories, starving Cree competed with the hawks and coyotes to catch gophers.

The rapid loss of their economic base

Loading buffalo bones onto a boxcar, Gull Lake, NWT, *c.* 1885. Bone-pickers followed the hide-hunters, shipping the bleached remains of millions of bison east to be ground up and used in refining sugar; horns were manufactured into buttons and combs, and hooves rendered into glue. Truman and Caple photo. Glenbow NA-250-15.

accelerated Canada's subjugation of the Native peoples of the Prairie West. Canadian governments followed the long-established British tradition of recognizing Aboriginal title, and bargained for possession of the lands occupied by Native peoples before distributing them for settlement. They did so, Prime Minister Alexander Mackenzie explained, not only because this policy was 'humane, just and Christian' but because it was 'the cheapest, ultimately, if we compare the results with those of other countries'—most notably the United States, where 'deplorable war' cost the government $20 million a year.[6] Between 1871 and 1877, Canada negotiated agreements with most of tribes of the Prairie West, some 34,000 people. Named by consecutive numbers according to the order of their conclusion, Treaties 1 and 2 covered Manitoba and the adjacent territory, Treaty 3 the area east to Lake Superior, and Treaty 4 the Assiniboine and Qu'Appelle River valleys and the southern plains. Treaty 5 took in the area west of Lake Winnipeg north to the Nelson River, and Treaty 6 encompassed a wide swath of prairie and park belt west along the Saskatchewan to the Rockies. By 1877, when the tribes of the Blackfoot Confederacy signed Treaty 7, Canada had acquired formal title to all those parts of the Prairie West that the government planned to settle and develop.

Textbook accounts like *The Story of the Canadian People*, used in the schools of the Prairie provinces during the 1920s, told pupils that 'the government of Canada may well be proud of its policy in dealing with the Indians of the North-West', and that they too should take pride that 'in connection with the lands claimed by the Indians care had been taken to deal fairly with the original owners.' Historians who have examined treaty-making more recently, however, conclude that the government was reluctant to negotiate unless it needed Native lands for immediate economic purposes, and that the numbered treaties were more the result of Indian than of white agency. 'It was pressure from the Indians of Manitoba that forced the government of Canada to initiate the treaty process,' writes John L. Tobias, and 'pressure from the Plains Cree in the period 1872–77 that compelled the government of Canada to continue the process with the Indians of the Qu'Appelle and Saskatchewan districts.' The Native people recognized that their traditional economy was gone, and they wanted to negotiate an alternative future for themselves as farmers. This rational response to a difficult situation that was widespread by the mid-1870s is evident in a petition sent by a delegation of Plains Cree chiefs to Governor Adams Archibald in Winnipeg. The chiefs protested the Hudson's Bay Company's sale of their land to Canada: 'it is our property, and no one has a right to sell [it].' However, understanding that 'our country is no longer able to support us,' they told the governor they wanted 'cattle, tools, agricultural implements, and assistance in everything when we come to settle. . . .'[7]

The desperate nature of their situation meant that Native people were bargaining from a much weaker position than the Canadian commissioners. Critics question the treaties because they were signed under duress—explicit when the North-West Mounted Police attended the negotiations, and implicit when bands that would not sign faced famine. But the tribes retained enough military power that the negotiations were never simply a matter of the victors' dictating terms of absolute surrender. Discussions began with extravagant ceremonies, not unlike the 'treaty trade' that had preceded the exchange of furs. Every treaty had one constant: in return for conceding their territory, the people received a 'reserve' of land for their use. Each treaty also contained unique clauses, however, hard-won by Native negotiators. According to Treaty 3, the Ojibwa were to receive an annual grant to buy fishing nets, and Treaty 6 promised the Cree medical supplies. The increasing amounts of land allotted for reserves—from 160 acres (65 hectares) for every five persons in Treaty 1 to 640 acres (259 hectares) in later treaties—testifies to the negotiators' diplomatic skill. Similarly, annual per capita cash payments to bands increased, as did the lump-sum payments made to each group as a 'signing bonus'. The most prolonged discussions concerned government support for the transition from the hunt to agriculture: Indians demanded that they be supplied with seed, livestock, tools, and implements, as well as training in how to use them, and that they be fed during the transition.

Three important Plains Cree chiefs—Big

Crowfoot in conference with Governor General Lord Lorne, Blackfoot Crossing, NWT, 1881, painted by Sydney P. Hall (1842–1922) in 1887. In these discussions the Plains tribes attempted to renegotiate existing treaties on more favourable terms. Historian John Tobias quotes Lorne's response, which was the same reply the Canadian government always made to Indian demands for renegotiation: 'I am come here to hear what you have to say but not to make any changes in [the] treaties. . . . I consider the chiefs as officers of the Queen among the Indians and I hold them responsible for what the people say and do. . . . As the chiefs on behalf of the people put their hands to a treaty . . . I expect them to keep it.' Glenbow NA-3412-20.

Bear, Piapot, and Little Pine—refused to sign Treaty 6. 'We want none of the Queen's presents,' declared Big Bear during discussions at Fort Carlton in 1876: 'when we set a fox trap we scatter pieces of meat all round, but when the fox gets into the trap we knock him on the head; we want no bait.' He hoped to rally other Cree bands and join forces with the Blackfoot to demand an Indian Territory in the Cypress Hills in which they might retain some autonomy. But the destruction of the buffalo herds put an end to that hope. In December 1882, Big

Bear 'took treaty' rather than watch the winter starve his band to death. His skepticism regarding 'the Queen's presents' proved well-founded. Territorial Governor and Indian Commissioner Edgar Dewdney broke Canada's pledges almost immediately. He ordered Indian agents to withhold rations until the Cree agreed to be scattered on separate reserves at Qu'Appelle, Battleford, and Fort Pitt, far from the Cypress Hills they had hoped to make their home. For other bands, the promised support for a transition to agriculture failed to appear. The 'sweet

Sydney Hall's pencil sketch of the negotiations, 1881. The sketch that Hall drew on the scene depicts a much less mighty Crowfoot than the painting done six years later. Crowfoot, the Blackfoot chief who refused to take up arms in 1885, had to be rendered heroically and contrasted to 'unreasonable' chiefs like Big Bear, who 'rebelled'. Crowfoot became indispensable to the evolving Euro-Canadian myth of a benevolent Canadian Indian policy. His pathetic tribute to the NWMP is still quoted today: 'Bad men and whisky were killing us so fast that very few of us would be left today. The Mounted Police have protected us as the feathers of the bird protect it from the frosts of the winter.' However, authors who use this quotation ignore the fact that it is empirically false: the population of the Blackfoot, like that of every other tribe in western Canada, dropped sharply after the 1870s. Glenbow NA-3412-1.

things were taken out' of the treaty that he had signed, Big Bear complained, and 'lots of sour things left in.'[8]

Native people were peripheral to the plans of men like Governor Dewdney and the government that had appointed them. Whatever the rhetoric about a 'humane, just and Christian' Indian policy, the government of John A. Macdonald had not bought Rupert's Land from the Hudson's Bay Company to preserve a homeland for the Cree: Manitoba and the North-West Territories were real estate much too valuable for that. In the language of western expansionists, the land had to be 'opened' to commercial agriculture and 'filled' with white settlers—as if it had been 'closed' and 'empty' before. Exploitation of the western interior was the anchor of the National Policy, the overall development strategy underlying Confederation. Through this policy Canada, the North American unit of the world system of the British Empire, hoped to emulate the

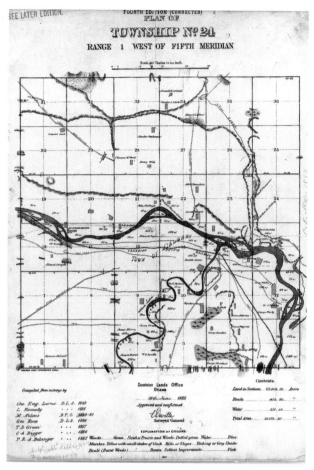

'Plan of Township No. 24 Range 1 West of Fifth Meridian', 1889 (includes town of Calgary). Canada's Dominion Lands survey and distribution system followed the US example almost exactly. NAC National Map Collection-26423.

older Canadian provinces were rejected in favour of the American plan of 36-square-mile (93.25 km²) 'townships' subdivided into 'sections' of 640 acres (259 ha). To attract immigrants to plow the prairie, the Dominion Lands Act of 1872 mimicked the American Homestead Act of 1862. The head of a family, or a single man twenty-one years or older, could claim a 160-acre 'quarter section' of western land for a $10 filing fee. If the would-be farmer 'proved up'—planted crops, built a shack, and survived on his homestead for three years—the land belonged to him (or, in many fewer cases, to her—if she were a widow, a divorcée, or a wife who could document her husband's desertion). In the past, the Native peoples had never owned land, and the Métis had cut hay for their horses on a 'commons' shared by all. But after 1872, free homesteads firmly established the ideology of private property in the Prairie West, making the land a commodity to be sold like any other.[9]

A transcontinental economy required a transcontinental railway. The Prairie West could never be Canadian as long as the only practical connection to Central Canada ran along US railways to Fargo in the Dakota Territory, and then north and west by paddle-wheel steamer—if the Red and the Saskatchewan weren't frozen—or by horse and wagon if they were. The design for railway construction again imitated the America model; like its US counterpart, the Canadian government purchased private rails to the Pacific with vast tracts of public land. After Macdonald's first attempt to charter a railway dissolved in scandal in 1873, the government traded 'a kingdom for an Iron Horse' to launch a second Canadian Pacific Railway in 1881. The CPR syndicate received 25

transcontinental economic success of the United States and eventually to supplant the US as North America's dominant nation-state.

Ironically, given the Canadian government's preoccupation with differentiating its West from the American West, basic administrative elements of its development policy were copied from the United States almost to the letter. The land survey systems used in the

The steamboat *Selkirk* unloads. Boundary Commission photo, 1872-74. From 1859 until the 1890s, sternwheel 'mudskippers' like the *Selkirk* supplanted the Red River cart trains for the summer shipment of cargo, dislocating the carting economy that supported many Métis. The steamers themselves were soon supplanted by the railway. PAM N14022.

million acres, a cash subsidy of $25 million, existing government-built lines worth $38 million, tax exemptions on its property, and a twenty-year monopoly clause in its charter guaranteeing that no competing road would be built south of its main line. This government-sanctioned monopoly was a truly distinctive characteristic of the Canadian West: in the United States, railroad barons had to collude in secret to suppress competition. The massive monetary support and the monopoly were justified as reasonable compensation for the risk of building an all-Canadian railway north of Lake Superior and across a region that would not yield commercial rail traffic until the railway itself created commerce.

The CPR chose a route west from Manitoba to the Rockies that ran south of H.Y. Hind's 'Fertile Belt', straight through the triangle that Captain John Palliser had pronounced unfit for

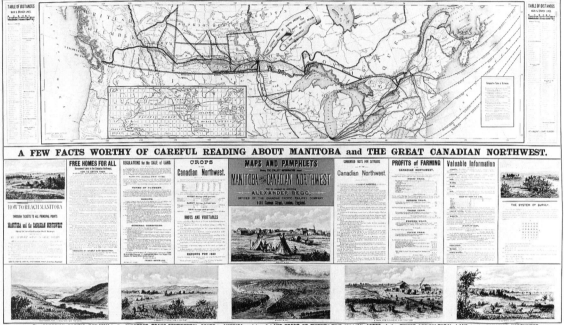

 A CPR map from 1886. This pamphlet expresses the dual themes of all Canadian propaganda aimed at attracting farm families to the Prairies, promising both 'Free Homes For All' and the 'Profits of Farming'. Emphasizing its role in the advancement of the British Empire, the CPR also advertised itself as 'the imperial highway from the Atlantic to the Pacific'. The inset on the map shows the railway linking Britain with Asia. Glenbow NA-2222-1.

cultivation. To assuage fears—their own as well as the public's—the CPR syndicate and the Department of the Interior produced a botanist named John Macoun who happily swore that Palliser had erred, and that his arid triangle didn't exist. Building closer to the forty-ninth parallel protected the CPR against potential US competitors, and laying track across the open prairie allowed the line to go forward with astounding speed. The southern route also meant that the CPR could create its own dependent towns as it moved west, rather than have to deal with the established commu-

nities on the well-worn cart trail northwest from Winnipeg to Edmonton. At the same time, the CPR syndicate was canny enough to insist that the millions of acres it was to receive be 'fairly fit for settlement', and that it have the right to choose them: very few of them were in the area through which it directed its main line. The completion of that line in November 1885, signalled with reverse ostentation by driving a last spike of plain iron, joined the trek of the Mounted Police as an iconic moment in Canada's national epic, and has been celebrated in poem, song, and a two-volume best-seller by

Farmers wait to unload their wheat at the grain elevator, Brandon, Manitoba, 1885–88. Three nearly identical versions of this image exist, one dated 1885 and two dated 1888. Showing a 'grain blockade', it suggests the frustration of commercial farmers faced with a grain marketing infrastructure that was inadequate to handle the surpluses they had to sell if the harvest was large. Glenbow NA-1406-244.

Pierre Berton. But business historian Michael Bliss pricks the nationalist balloon by pointing out that 'Canada's "national dream" of a transcontinental railway was realized by reliance on foreign capital, expertise, and labour at every stage of the work.'[10]

Even before the 'last spike' clinched the transcontinental connection, the CPR had earned a place of dishonour in an evolving litany of Prairie regional grievance. Homesteaders who had grain to ship to market complained that they faced 'grain blockades' because the company, sheltered behind its monopoly, spent little on branch lines, shipping facilities, or rolling stock, and set its rates as it pleased. When the Manitoba government chartered railways to compete with the CPR, the Dominion government used the power given to it by the British North America Act to simply disallow the charters. The Manitoba and North-West Farmers' Union, founded in 1883, bitterly protested the CPR monopoly, Ottawa's insensitivity, and the 35 per cent protective tariff on imported manufactured goods that the Macdonald government had imposed in 1879. But when a minority went so far as to

A family of Métis traders in camp. Boundary Commission photo, 1872–74. A cart like the one in the photograph carried half a tonne of freight. 'It was a marvel how well those Red River Carts stood all the jolting that they got,' wrote George Monro Grant in 1872. 'When any part broke . . . a thong of Shaganappi [buffalo hide] united the pieces. Shaganappi in this part of the world does all that leather, cloth, rope, nails, glue, straps, cord [and] tape . . . are used for elsewhere. Without it the Red River Cart, which is simply a clumsy looking, but really light, box cart with wheels six or seven feet in diameter, and not a bit of iron about the whole concern, would be an impossibility' (*Ocean to Ocean: Sandford Fleming's Expedition Through Canada in 1872* [Toronto, 1873]). Both the buffalo and the Métis hunting and carting economy would be gone a decade later. PAM N14100.

propose secession from Canada and annexation to the United States, the Farmers' Union vanished as a political force. The pattern of Prairie politics was established early: those protest movements that endured sought to change the country's policies, not to secede from the confederation.

A greater threat to Canada's conception of the Prairie West than grumbling white settlers was posed by angry Métis communities in the North-West Territories. Between 1870 and 1884, a thousand Métis families sold their claims to the lands set aside for them in the Manitoba Act and migrated west to join established Métis settlements on the South Branch of the Saskatchewan River or in the Cypress Hills. Historians hotly contest the motives behind this migration. One side, led by

Douglas Sprague, argues that these people were swindled out of their land in Manitoba by a deliberate government conspiracy to dispossess them; the other, identified with Thomas Flanagan, holds that the government fulfilled its legal obligations to the Métis: those families who sold out and moved did so in order to take advantage of the new economic opportunities available farther west. The fervour with which the two sides pursue the debate is not simply a matter of scholarly devotion: the Manitoba Métis Federation funded Sprague's research as evidence in a lawsuit against the federal government, and the federal Department of Justice financed Flanagan's riposte as the government's defence.[11]

There can be no neat historical resolution to this argument: in fact, there was no single reason for the migration. After 1870, parts of Manitoba became uneasy for Métis. The English-Canadian Protestants who moved there from Ontario manifested what Governor Archibald called 'a frightful spirit of bigotry . . . [they] talk and seem to feel as if the French half-breeds should be wiped off the face of the globe.' Between 1870 and 1872, four Métis were murdered, three others were savagely beaten, and no one was convicted for the crimes. The government dragged its feet on amnesty for important participants in the Red River Resistance, and was maddeningly slow to resolve land claims. There is plentiful evidence that federal politicians and bureaucrats shared the racist contempt that virtually every white Canadian felt towards people of Native ancestry, as well as evidence of dishonesty and inefficiency. But there is no persuasive evidence of a deliberate conspiracy to cheat the Métis of their land or to drive them out of Manitoba. The limited competence with which the Canadian government managed the western territories makes it difficult to believe that it could have been capable of such intrigue. And not all Métis felt compelled to leave. There was a class dimension to the migration: those families who combined hunting, freighting, and self-sufficient agriculture moved west, and those who had established lives as commercial farmers stayed put in Manitoba.[12]

Nor is there convincing evidence that, as some historians have contended, the Canadian government deliberately provoked the Métis into the confrontation known as the North-West Rebellion of 1885. But the Métis experience in Manitoba does help to explain how their poisoned relationship with the government made the situation explode. As in Red River in 1869, the central issue was land: government bureaucrats were attempting to impose the rectangular survey and Dominion Lands regulations on the Métis river-lot farms on the South Branch of the Saskatchewan. And as in Red River, some of the Métis turned to Louis Riel to lead them.

Since 1870, Riel's life had been a bitter succession of disappointments. Three times elected to Parliament from Manitoba, he was never able to take his seat because the Ontario government had put a price on his head for the 'murder' of Thomas Scott and the Dominion government refused to grant him amnesty. At Mass on 8 December 1875—six years to the day after the creation of the provisional government at Red River—Riel underwent the first in a series of religious experiences that convinced him he was Louis 'David' Riel, 'Prophet of the New World', chosen by God to create an independent Métis theocracy in the land that was rapid-

'Trial practice with the Gatlings at Swift Current', lithograph from *Canadian Illustrated War News*, 25 April 1885. Despite the plural, the Canadian militia had only one Gatling gun. In his biography *Gabriel Dumont* (Edmonton: Hurtig, 1975), George Woodcock mistakenly captioned this image 'Canadian Artillery at Batoche, May 1885'. The Gatling was a machine gun, not a field artillery piece, but its fire-power did play a critical role in the Canadian defeat of the Métis at Batoche. NAC C-5541.

ly becoming the Canadian Prairie West. Riel was in exile, teaching school in Montana, when Métis delegates summoned him to the Saskatchewan district in June 1884.[13]

Riel's presence ended any possibility that aggrieved white settlers and Métis might make common cause against Ottawa. And as his speeches revealed more of his deeper messianic purpose, the French-Catholic clergy and the less-committed Métis withdrew their support. Backed only by a core of militant South Branch buffalo hunters, most notable among them Gabriel Dumont, Riel repeated the steps he had taken in 1869-70, without comprehending that circumstances had changed fundamentally in fifteen years. When his Provisional Government demanded that Inspector Leif Crozier surrender the NWMP detachment at Fort Carlton and evacuate all police and bureaucrats from the territory, Crozier refused to negotiate. Instead, on 26 March 1885, 56 Mounties and 43 civilian volunteers blundered out to confront 200 Métis at Duck Lake. The deaths of three policemen, nine volunteers, and five 'rebels' lit a prairie fire that would burn for seven weeks. The new telegraph line to Central Canada quickly informed the government of this challenge to its authority, and it responded with alacrity. Militia regiments rushed west on the new railway (Parliament rewarded the CPR for its performance with a loan of an extra $5 million); looting every Métis farm they passed, the troops marched to the seat of the provisional government at Batoche. A four-day siege ended with fierce combat on 12 May. Their bullets gone, the defenders fired stones and nails at the militia in the last stages of the battle.[14]

After the fall of Batoche, only mopping up remained. Dumont and a few others escaped to the United States. Fourteen Métis were imprisoned. Riel surrendered, was convicted of treason, and—although the jury recommended mercy—was executed in Regina on 16 November 1885. His death, a week after the last spike completed the Canadian Pacific Railway, could symbolize Canada's conquest of the Prairie West. Or it could symbolize many other things. The hangman who exulted that 'the son-of-a-bitch is gone at last' could not have guessed that Riel would live on in the ethnic conflict between French-Catholic Quebec and English-Protestant Ontario, or that he would be resurrected a century later, by descendants of the white regionalists who hanged him, to serve as a symbol of Ottawa's oppression of the Prairie West.

Later that November, eleven Indians mounted the gallows with considerably less fanfare. Two dozen more, Big Bear among them, went to prison, most with stiffer sentences than the convicted Métis. Yet there had been no Indian rebellion in 1885, despite the Canadian government's pretence that the whole of the North-West Territories had been in the grip of a co-ordinated Métis-Indian insurrection. Some Cree and Dakota Sioux had joined the Métis at Duck Lake and Batoche, and at Frog Lake there had been a spontaneous attack

Gabriel Dumont, May 1885. Woodcock's biography substituted Dumont for Riel as the 'great man' who led the Métis. Unlike Riel, Dumont looked to Woodcock the way a manly hero should: uncomplicated, unconflicted, unambiguous. However, Bob Beal and Rod Macleod remove the mantle of military genius from Dumont's shoulders by pointing out that, for the Métis during the North-West Rebellion, 'group decision-making covered everything from basic strategic matters to instructions for the cooks'. Glenbow NA-1063-1.

by angry Cree warriors on whites they felt had treated them cruelly. But most Plains Cree, including Piapot's band, stayed at peace on their reserves; the Blackfoot, ancestral enemies of the Cree, volunteered to ally themselves with the government against them. The government declined the offer. Instead, territorial Governor

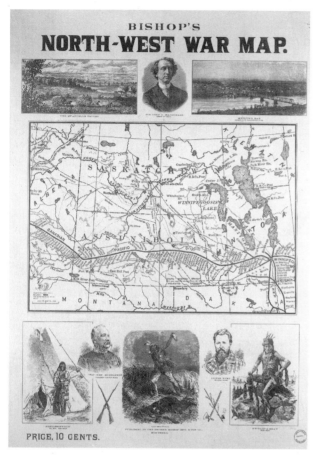

'Bishop's North-West War Map', 1885. There never was an Indian 'war' in 1885, yet three pictures in this composite published in Montreal depict Indians on the 'warpath'. Apparently the publisher believed that images of Indians would sell more maps than images of Métis. Library of Congress—Geography and Map Division, 711493 #380.

Edgar Dewdney used the militia troops and the NWMP to repress the Cree movement for treaty revision, and to begin a final assault on the remnants of Plains Indian autonomy.

The stated goal of Canadian Indian policy, codified in a revised Indian Act in 1876, was 'to lead the Indian people by degrees to mingle with the white race in the ordinary avocations of life.' Hayter Reed, deputy superintendent general of Indian Affairs, called this policy of assimilation 'detribalization': Aboriginal peoples were to be Christianized, educated, and turned into farmers. As a first step, Indian agents attempted to confine Native people on their reserves with a pass system, and the NWMP co-operated with the US Cavalry to suppress horse-raiding across the international boundary. To extirpate traditional political and religious practices, laws required that chiefs and band councils be elected, and forbade religious ceremonies like the Sun Dance, the Thirst Dance and the Give Away Dance. This last ritual was considered particularly dangerous: it involved obligatory sharing, and thus undermined the ethic of individual accumulation of property that had to be inculcated into Native people in order to 'civilize' them. Government-run industrial schools, and government-supported residential schools run by churches, drilled Euro-Canadian ideals and various versions of Christianity into the minds of Indian children. Agriculture was central to assimilation: in theory, every reserve received equipment and instruction to enable it to feed itself, and to train future generations of Indian farmers.[15]

For most Aboriginal people, however, 'mingling with the white race' never happened. The government was as parsimonious as it was racist, so that the project of assimilation starved for lack of funds just as the Native people did. The Indian Affairs Branch occupied the lowest rung in Canada's Department of the Interior, a patronage-driven repository for the least-gifted relatives of Conservative politicians until 1896, and of Liberal politicians thereafter. The conversion to cultivation and husbandry, eagerly sought by most bands, was undermined by

Hanging Riel in effigy on Main Street, Winnipeg, Dominion Day, 1 July 1885. This scene explains as much about the reasons why so many Manitoba Métis moved west to the Saskatchewan River as do any of the detailed analyses of the land distribution to Métis in Manitoba. The banner to the right of the effigy reads 'Either shoot the wretch or have him HUNG.' On each side of the men hoisting the Riel effigy, young boys learn by example how to be males in the English-speaking Protestant Canada of the late nineteenth century. PAM N9582.

bureaucrats who provided plows without draft animals, seed that would not germinate, livestock that no white farmer would have allowed in his barn, and 'instructors' who ignored the people they were supposed to help. The plan for Aboriginal adaptation to agriculture failed because it was never sincerely attempted, not because Indians resisted it. Other assimilative schemes, however, were resisted or evaded. Native people preserved their identities and reconstructed them on their own terms, not the terms established by the bureaucrats. To fight against residential schools, pass laws, and rules preventing the practice of their religion,

Aboriginal people used what the historian Katherine Pettipas calls the 'predominant means of resistance': persistence.[16]

Would-be assimilators posed a less deadly threat to Aboriginal survival than poverty, malnutrition, tuberculosis, diphtheria, and whooping cough. Residential schools were breeding-grounds for disease; perhaps a quarter of their child inmates died from diseases contracted at school. Annual death rates on Prairie reserves in the 1880s ran as high as 62 per 1,000 at a time when Winnipeg's death rate was 16 per 1,000. Despite a high birth rate, Prairie Indian populations actually declined

Native parents camp by a residential school to visit their children, Birtle, Manitoba, 1904. According to the historian J.R. Miller, 'parents could disrupt the school by making unauthorized visits or by failing to return their children after holiday visits home'; children could, and did, 'misbehave, violate rules, refuse to learn, defiantly continue to speak their own languages . . . , run away, and . . . indulge in acts of arson against the property and violence against the staffs of the schools.' PAM N10264.

Native students at the Fort Qu'Appelle Industrial School, 1890s. This was a standard pose, repeated in photographs from every residential school, intended to show the success of the schools in 'civilizing' Native children. PA 182248.

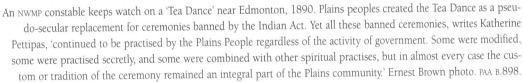

An NWMP constable keeps watch on a 'Tea Dance' near Edmonton, 1890. Plains peoples created the Tea Dance as a pseudo-secular replacement for ceremonies banned by the Indian Act. Yet all these banned ceremonies, writes Katherine Pettipas, 'continued to be practised by the Plains People regardless of the activity of government. Some were modified, some were practised secretly, and some were combined with other spiritual practises, but in almost every case the custom or tradition of the ceremony remained an integral part of the Plains community.' Ernest Brown photo. PAA B.898.

after the signing of the treaties that made them wards of the Canadian government. In 1896, the Sarcee reserve south of Calgary recorded 12 births and 30 deaths. There were 255 Sarcee in 1877 and 160 in 1924; 211 Plains Cree in the Keehiwin band in 1876 and 145 in 1908. These declines in Native populations help to explain the lack of urgency felt by white assimilationists: they simply assumed that soon there would be no Indians left to assimilate. Indian Affairs bureaucrats pressed

bands with declining populations to sell their lands, and hundreds of thousands of acres were sold—though never so many as white ranchers and farmers demanded.[17]

The ranching industry that sprang up in the southwestern corner of the North-West Territories in the early 1880s was a modern capitalist reworking of an ancient pastoral way of life. A growing urban population in Britain provided the demand for beef; railways and steamships provided the transportation; and

'Lady photographers "fixing" a War Dance'; drawn by Frederic Villiers for *The Graphic* (London), 14 Dec. 1889. Lady Stanley and her companion Miss Lyster photograph Blackfoot dancers on the Blood reserve during Governor General Lord Stanley's visit to the West. The drawing suggests that Villiers knew the images 'taken' by photographers were no more 'real' or 'true' than the work of graphic artists like himself. 'This barbaric fandango,' reported *The Graphic* with obvious disappointment, 'has lost the terrible significance which it possessed in the old days of primitive savagery, when the braves thus wound themselves up . . . to scalp or be scalped.' PAM N16239.

the Great Plains grew the cattle. The economics of the 'beef bonanza' were simple: after three or four years of eating almost-free grass,

a $5 calf became a steer worth ten times that. A rancher—or rather, his workers, the cowboys—branded the calves, stocked the range, let the cattle graze, then rounded them up and drove them to market. Ranching in its western North American form began in Texas in the late 1860s and spread north across the plains. But although the Canadian industry was identical to the American in terms of ranching technique, its corporate and social structures differed markedly. The US industry developed on an open range, outside any formal system of public land distribution, whereas the Canadian range-cattle industry was a product of federal intervention and promotion. After a brief free-range era in which small-scale stockmen raised beef to feed Status Indians, in 1881 the government amended the Dominion Lands Act to permit large-scale ranchers to take out 21-year leases on up to 100,000 acres at 1 cent an acre annually. Canadian ranch-owners needed not only capital but Conservative political connections: Macdonald's cabinet removed ranch leases from the purview of the Dominion Lands Branch and handed them out itself. Soon a ten-ranch oligopoly called the 'cattle compact' controlled two-thirds of all leased land; Senator Matthew Cochrane's 'ranche' alone covered 367,500 acres.[18]

In the United States, cattlemen's competition with each other, with sheep herders, and with 'sodbusters' over grass and water often led to violence: a dozen deadly range wars erupted between 1865 and 1893 in the American West. In Canada, the 'cattle compact' used government, rather than direct action, to gain and maintain control of the range. The Department of the Interior reserved watering areas for cattlemen, prohibited grazing sheep, and refused

Ranching in Alberta, near Calgary, 1880. If the legal and capital structure of the Canadian range cattle industry differed from that in the United States, the techniques were the same on both sides of the border, and in both countries cowboys were the industry's waged labour force. But the iconic cowboy of the US western myth never became a national archetype in Canada except in southern Alberta. Ernest Brown Collection. PAA B.114.

farmers' requests for homesteads in cattle country. American ranchers hired gunmen to protect their ranges; the NWMP smoothly performed that unpleasant chore for Canadian cattle magnates, adding another chapter to their legend. When disgruntled squatters gathered south of Calgary in April 1885 and threatened to join Riel, the Mounties dispersed them easily. The dexterity with which the Canadian state silenced resistance meant that there were neither range wars nor vigilantes on the Canadian ranching frontier.[19]

There is also some evidence that the grasslands fared better in Canada because of the government's policy of granting large long-term leases. Greater security of tenure encouraged ranchers to take care of their ranges, and

not to overstock or overgraze. Still, the short grass prairie of the North-West Territories experienced the same species-shifting that transformed the plains south of the forty-ninth parallel. Alien plant and animal 'invaders' supplanted native flora and fauna: domesticated stock replaced bison, pronghorn antelope, and elk; cheatgrass, sagebrush, and Russian and Canada thistle crowded out the grasses and forbs that were more palatable to wildlife. Wild carnivores were bad for the beef business, so ranchers massacred the remaining bears, wolves, coyotes, and foxes. But, however hard they were on the plains environment, the cattlemen made less destructive and thus more sustainable use of the semi-arid southwest corner of the

HALT!

'Halt!' CPR land sales advertisement, *c.* 1900. This particular image of an NWMP constable catching rustlers red-handed running off a stolen steer is fanciful, but the Mounted Police did in fact perform invaluable services for large-scale stockmen. By using the image to advertise its lands for sale, the CPR sent the message that, unlike the 'wild' US west, Canada was a safe haven for investment in ranching. PAA B.123.

total non-Indian population in Manitoba and the North-West Territories grew from 118,000 to 251,000 over the 1880s. But these respectable absolute numbers were embarrassing when compared with figures from Montana and North Dakota, which had grown from a combined non-Indian population of under 100,000 in 1880 to a total of 334,000 in 1890. Most galling, the US census showed that one in ten of these North Dakotans and Montanans, 32,085 in all, were former Canadians. Since the soil and climatic conditions were similar on either side of the border, differences in the development and dissemination of agricultural techniques and technologies adapted to those conditions cannot explain Canada's relatively slow growth. Rather, Canada's National Policy, in particular the protective tariff and the CPR monopoly, were blamed by angry nineteenth-century farmers, as well as classically trained twentieth-century economists.

The Canadian government would not bend its tariff or transportation policies to attract settlers. Instead, it tried to compete with the United States by liberalizing its homestead regulations and immigration policies. Homesteaders were allowed to make claims at the age of 18 rather than 21; they required only three years' residence to 'prove up' instead of five; and they had to actually live on the land for only three months of the year. Until 1889, they were allowed to 'preempt'— to purchase an adjacent quarter section at a guaranteed low price—when they received the title to their original 160 acres, or to sell their first homestead and file a claim on a second. These generous regulations allowed some of the families who arrived before 1890 to

Prairie West than farmers ever could have.[20]

Before 1900 there were so few farmers that they had their choice among the many parts of the Prairie West that were better suited to agriculture. Except during a brief settlement 'boom' that accompanied the construction of the CPR, the population grew at a gradual pace that frustrated both the Canadian government and the settlers themselves, most of them from Ontario. The census-takers counted 10,000 farms in 1881 and 31,000 ten years later; the

Edward Roper, 'A Settler's Home Near Carberry, Assiniboia [Manitoba]', *c.* 1887. In his book *By Track and Trail Through Canada* (London, 1891) Roper (1854–91) commented: 'There's a good deal more scenery wanted in this country, ain't there.' In this painting he creates some of his own by depicting a farm family transforming the prairie into a garden. NAC C-11030.

become successful commercial farmers: arriving early and acquiring cheap land accessible to transportation proved to be the most important determinants of the winners and losers in Prairie settlement.[21]

Determination to attract population to the Prairie West also made the Canadian government more generous regarding block settlement by ethnic groups than its US counterpart. Two communities of Mennonites (German Anabaptists from Russian Ukraine) were wooed and won in 1874 with promises of freedom from military service, subsidized ocean passage, and grants of reserves of eight and seventeen townships on the east and west sides of the Red River. To make the traditional Mennonite village structure possible in southern Manitoba, the Canadian government agreed to a 'hamlet clause': unlike other settlers, Mennonite families could live in a village away from their land, and earn title without fulfilling the residence requirements. Yet even though the US government refused to allow village settlement on homestead lands, another Mennonite community—one with enough capital—declined Canada's inducements and chose to settle in Nebraska; they bought contiguous sections of railroad land on which to recreate their village. Canada's difficulty in attracting immigrants suggests that Howard Palmer's history *Land of the Second Chance* is mistitled: 'Land of the Second Choice' would

Doukhobor women pull a plow near Swan River, Manitoba, 1899. Historians George Woodcock and Ivan Avakumovic describe breaking land with teams of women as 'an important symbolic event' in Doukobor group tradition, one that they had 'woven into their mystique of "Peace and Useful Toil"' (*The Doukhobors* [Toronto: McClelland and Stewart, 1977]). But photographs of Doukhobor women harnessed to plows shocked Canadians and mobilized nativist opposition against any government compromise that would allow the Doukhobors to prove up their homestead lands communally rather than as individual families. NAC C-681.

be a more accurate description of the region before 1900.[22]

Like the Mennonites, who were fleeing Czarist Russia's imposition of military conscription and state education, other minorities were simultaneously pushed to emigrate by conditions in their homelands and pulled by the liberality of a Canadian government eager to attract new settlers. In 1877, on a block grant on the west shore of Lake Winnipeg, Icelanders created their own 'Republic of New Iceland', complete with a constitution and an elected government. Canada ignored the tiny nation-state until it could be absorbed into an expanded province of Manitoba a decade later. In 1887, members of

the Church of Jesus Christ of Latter-day Saints (Mormons) moved north from the Utah Territory to evade US government attempts to enforce laws against polygamous marriage. The Macdonald government politely refused their request that polygamy be legalized in the North-West Territories, but took no action to enforce existing Canadian laws against it. The Mormons brought enough capital to buy railway lands, and the irrigation expertise they had acquired in Utah made them some of the most successful farmers in the territory. Only one experiment with a fugitive minority was a notable failure: the settlement of the dissident Russian sect called Doukhobors in ninety communal farming villages on blocks provided for them in the park belt of north-central Saskatchewan in 1899. The Department of the Interior denied the Doukhobors the privilege of proving up their lands collectively, and after repeated warnings their homestead entries were universally cancelled in 1907. Although some Doukhobors remained and proved up individual family farms, others moved on to the valleys of the Kootenay Mountains in British Columbia.[23]

Part of the Doukhobors' problem was timing: after 1900, the Prairie West suddenly became more attractive to other immigrants who were much more attractive to Canada, so that the government's settlement policies became less generous and less flexible. Ottawa had no intention of creating a multicultural West: its magnanimity was motivated by its anxiety to 'fill' the region with farmers, not by any enthusiasm for the cultural diversity brought by ethnic minorities. British Canadians, in the West and elsewhere, were even less accommodating of the newcomers than their governments were. They clamoured for cancellation of the Doukhobor homesteads, and rushed to file on them after the Doukhobors were forced off. The English-speaking Protestant Ontarians who formed the largest and most influential group of white settlers in Manitoba and the territories had no intention of allowing the Prairie West to become a 'multicultural mosaic'. Their creed was to acculturate and eventually assimilate ethnic minorities, and in their enthusiasm for this project they looked beyond immigrants from Europe to the bicultural basis of the Canadian confederation itself. For complex reasons, one of which was English-Canadian hostility, very few French Canadians migrated west. After 1889, English-

speaking Protestants began to ruthlessly assail the political and educational rights that the Manitoba Act and the North-West Territories Act guaranteed to French-speaking Catholics. By 1920 they had succeeded in eliminating those rights, just as English-speaking Protestants in Nova Scotia, New Brunswick, and Ontario had done.

What was striking about the Prairie West at the end of the nineteenth century was how much it had come to resemble the other English-speaking provinces. Manitoba, writes its historian W.L. Morton, was 'a British and Canadian province' by 1890, and the North-West Territories not much less so. Measured against the ambitions of 1870, and the success of the neighbouring American states, the first three decades of the Prairie West had been a disappointment to Canadian expansionists. But they had fundamentally altered the western interior. The region had been drawn into the web of industrial capitalism, and ways of life evolved over two centuries had been swept aside; the Indian and Métis people who were once central to that way of life had been forced to the margins. If the National Policy of the tariff and the railway monopoly had been less than satisfactory as a strategy for economic development, it had triumphed politically: the West had been integrated into the Canadian economy and severed from the American transportation routes that had linked it to the world before the policy was introduced. Most important, the forty-ninth parallel had been invested with meaning. By 1900 the once-fragile international boundary across the northern plains had become an ideological line drawn in people's minds, not just a line on the map. 'The forty-ninth parallel ran directly through my childhood,' remembered Wallace Stegner, born in Montana and raised in Saskatchewan. It was a boundary 'more potent in the lives of people like us than the natural divide of the Cypress Hills had ever been upon the tribes it held apart'.[24]

CHAPTER FIVE

The Twentieth Century
Belongs to the Canadian West:
1901–1921

*T*hirty years of disappointment ended in the late 1890s, and on their heels came twenty years of spectacular growth, two soaring decades that fulfilled the expansionists' long-awaited vision of western empire. A surging export-oriented wheat economy initiated this growth, but the numbers of people who moved west were the accepted measure of the region's progress. In 1901 census-takers enumerated 419,000 inhabitants in Manitoba and the North-West Territories; in 1921 they counted 1,956,082 in three Prairie provinces. With 757,510 people, Saskatchewan—created, along with Alberta, in 1905—had become almost overnight the third-largest province in the country. Manitoba and Alberta were fourth and fifth respectively, each larger than Nova Scotia or New Brunswick. From 5 per cent, the Prairie West had leapt to make up 22 per cent of Canada's population, and contributed an astonishing 45 per cent of the country's total population growth over a twenty-year period. Once the prospects for continuing development seemed assured, Prime Minister Sir Wilfrid Laurier liked to conclude his speeches with the promise that 'As the nineteenth cen-

tury was the century of the United States, so shall the twentieth century belong to Canada.' Appropriately, he first said this in the western 'gateway city' of Winnipeg, for it was the 'last, best West' that allowed him to hope that Canada could annex the century.

Laurier's Liberal government, first elected in 1896, basked in the glow of the western boom to win comfortable majorities in four consecutive federal elections. However, voters, like historians, sometimes confuse correlation with cause: the Liberal regime had little to do with the Prairie West's economic take-off. Laurier's development strategy duplicated that of Sir John A. Macdonald, and the fundamental elements of the National Policy—a protective tariff, public support of private transcontinental railways, the promotion of immigration and western settlement—all remained unchanged. Clifford Sifton, the Ontario-born Manitoban who became Laurier's dynamic minister of the Interior, was a strong Canadian nationalist who shared Macdonald's economic and political vision of the country.[1] The Liberal party claimed credit for the hundreds of thousands of immigrants who landed in Canada

Canada in 1906. Saskatchewan and Alberta were added to the map by what the Laurier government called 'autonomy bills'. However, like their neighbour Manitoba (which appears here with its pre-1912 northern boundary), Saskatchewan and Alberta differed from the other provinces in a very significant way: natural resources within their boundaries remained under the control of the federal government. NAC National Map Collection 16411.

during Sifton's tenure, but his Conservative predecessor, an Ontario-born Manitoban named T. Mayne Daly, had neither overlooked nor rejected any potential immigrants. The most significant administrative change after 1896 was that Liberal partisans replaced the Tory patronage appointees who had staffed the Department of the Interior.

Economic growth in the Prairie West was due not to a change of characters but to a change of circumstances: the end of a global depression, which increased European demand for grain, coincided with the end of agricultural expansion (at least in easily accessible regions) in the United States and Argentina. As a result, the stream of European out-migration was deflected away from those two countries, the usual magnets for immigrants in the

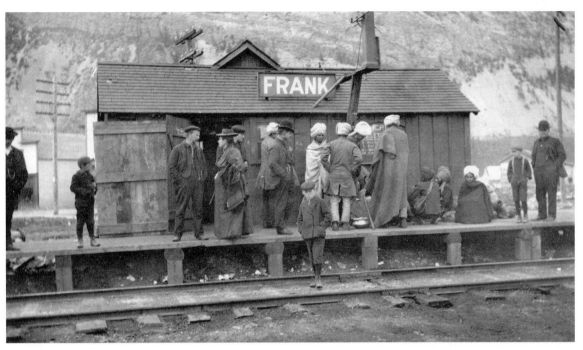

Euro-Canadians and Sikh mineworkers at the CPR station in Frank, Alberta, 1903. The racism directed at non-white immigrants exceeded the ethnocentrism directed at Eastern Europeans, and sustained Canada's exclusionary policies toward Chinese, Japanese, South Asians, and African Americans. NAC PA 125112.

Western hemisphere, and redirected towards western Canada. Until 1900, Canada had been a sieve rather than a container for European immigration: migrants had come to Canada but flowed right through to the United States. Native-born Canadians too had joined the southward hemorrhage: the US Census of 1900 reported 1,179,922 Canadian-born residents of the United States. Prairie prosperity persuaded emigrants from Maritime and Central Canada to move west within the country rather than to leave for the United States; they contributed at least as much as immigrants from outside the country to the post-1900 population surge.[2]

Canadian immigration policy at the beginning of the century was 'wide open', as opposed to 'selective' or 'restrictive', with one massive exception: Canada was to be a 'White Man's Country'.[3] To achieve the desired whiteness, governments systematically refined immigration laws to shut out people of colour. First new Chinese migrants, whose predecessors had done the dirtiest jobs pushing the CPR through the mountains, were shut out by an escalating 'head tax', which climbed to $500 in 1903—almost a year's wages for a worker. Next a so-called gentleman's agreement between Canada and Japan restricted Japanese migrants to a few hundred a year. Would-be South Asian migrants—most of them, like Canadians, subjects of the British Empire—were deterred by complicated legislation that required immigrants to arrive by a 'continuous

Delegates from the Chinese community meet with Calgary city commissioners, 13 Oct. 1910. As in the rest of North America, every Prairie city had a segregated 'Chinatown' of shops, restaurants, and laundries. When railway expansion forced the relocation of Calgary's Chinatown, no white neighbourhood wanted it to move nearby. 'They are undesirable citizens,' protested one alderman, and 'ought to be treated the same as an infectious disease or an isolation hospital.' The services the Chinese community provided, however, were essential to the city. By insisting upon their legal rights, and patiently enduring racist taunts, this delegation of merchants and laundrymen was eventually able to negotiate a new location for their businesses (Gunter A. Baureiss, 'The Chinese Community in Calgary', *Alberta Historical Review* 22, 2 [Spring 1974]). Glenbow NA-2798-6.

journey' when there was no shipping line that made such a journey possible. To screen out African Americans while encouraging the white American migrants that Canada sought, Immigration bureaucrats subjected the former to rigorous medical examinations.

As long as they had white skins, however, Canada welcomed immigrants from Britain, from every country in Europe (Canadians did not think of Britain as part of 'Europe'), and from the United States. New arrivals who came by sea disembarked at Quebec to receive a cur-

sory medical inspection. Each two-man team of immigration officials had a quota of 300 immigrants an hour. The 2 per cent who were refused were those with physical disabilities that, in the inspectors' opinion, made them likely to become a 'public charge'; they were deported immediately. Of the rest, more than half set out for destinations in Western Canada. These newcomers arrived as individuals or in families; no longer did they come as whole villages. Formal agreements to encourage group settlement ended once the Canadian

GERMANS ICELANDERS SCOTCHMEN ENGLISHMEN   AMERICANS FRENCHMEN   SCANDINAVIANS
BELGIANS   RUSSIANS   AUSTRIANS IRISHMEN

THE MAPLE LEAF   FOR EVER

CANADA

"NOW THEN, ALL TOGETHER"!

'Now Then, All Together!', 1904. In this cartoon from the Liberal election pamphlet *Laurier Does Things,* 'Jack
Canuck' conducts an international chorus of male immigrant stereotypes in 'The Maple Leaf Forever', English
Canada's unofficial anthem. Among the ethnic stereotypes not represented, presumably deliberately, were Italians,
Jews, and all non-whites. All the characters are male; there was no need to appeal electorally to women, who did
not have the right to vote. SAB R-A 12,402.

government no longer needed them to attract immigrants. Informal block settlement continued, however: Department of the Interior officials encouraged Ukrainian migrants from the Austro-Hungarian Empire—universally described as 'Galicians'—to choose homesteads in the park belt close to people with whom they shared a language. Their established Ukrainian neighbours would help impoverished newcomers through their first winter without any cost to the government, and their segregation averted friction with English-speaking Canadians who might not share Clifford Sifton's conviction that 'stalwart peasants in sheep-skin coats' made 'good quality' citizens for the Prairie West.[4]

'Only farmers need apply' was a supposed cornerstone of Canadian policy, but after 1906 more immigrants were actually 'navvies'—unskilled workers destined for railway construction, logging, and mining—than homesteaders or farm workers. Half or more of those who came were not 'immigrants' at all but sojourners, who sought work in North

'Jewish settlers Samuel and Hanna Schwartz with daughter Simma and her husband, Lipton District [Saskatchewan], c. 1903'. Given the virulent anti-Semitism of Ukrainian peasants, it seems particularly incongruous that this image of a Jewish family was used to illustrate 'the first permanent home' of Ukrainian homesteaders in Jaroslav Petryshyn's *Peasants in the Promised Land: Canada and the Ukrainians, 1891–1914*. SAB R-B 1781.

America while intending to return to Europe. Crude arithmetic makes it clear that not everyone stayed: official statistics reported 3.4 million 'immigrant arrivals' between 1901 and 1921—more than the total increase in the Canadian population over that period![5]

The ethnic pecking order set in place before 1900 proved durable. English-speaking Canadians, in particular Ontarians, stood at the top: as only one example, nineteen of the twenty-five members of Alberta's first legislature were Ontario-born. The status of immigrants from Britain varied with their place in the British class structure. British immigrants, especially the English, were not universally admired, but as subjects of the same King and Empire they did not have to wait long for naturalization: British men could vote after one year's residency. A broader British identity rapidly emerged among English, Scots, Welsh, and Protestant Irish immigrants as a way around economic competition from 'foreign' ethnic groups. They maintained strong group ties and built an extensive network of community institutions: Anglican and Presbyterian churches, clubs and lodges. Unlike the 'Galician' navvies, who were routinely discriminated against, British immigrants were deliberately favoured by certain large employers— the T. Eaton Company for women, the Canadian Pacific Railway maintenance shops for men.[6] Swedes and Norwegians, and Protestant Germans until the First World War, had 'honorary Anglo-Saxon' status because, in the racist idiom of the era, they were 'accustomed to the rigors of a northern climate, clean-blooded and hard-working'. At the bottom were the navvies and peasant homesteaders lumped together by the same writer for the *Manitoba Free Press* in 1905: 'those of serf-ridden Russia, the stiletto-carrying Dago, and the degenerate Central European.'

Many English- and French-speaking Canadians, in the West and elsewhere in the country, shared such opinions, and regarded Canada's wide-open immigration policies with feelings that ranged from anxious concern to outspoken ethnocentrism to outright racism. But the desire for inexpensive workers to speed economic development, voiced loudly by railway and resource companies, dictated that immigration should remain wide open. Sifton's successors, the Edmonton Liberal Frank Oliver from 1906 until 1911 and the Winnipeg Conservative Robert Rogers until 1917, pledged 'restrictive, exclusive and selective' amendments to the Immigration Act, but never actually implemented them. Annual arrivals peaked at 400,000 in 1914, a number equal to 5 per cent of the total Canadian population. The proportions of them who were navvies from Eastern and Central Europe increased as well. This polyglot population set the Prairie West

apart from the Maritimes, Quebec, Ontario, and even the other western province, the aptly named British Columbia. Prairie anglophones wanted desperately to assimilate these immigrants, but feared that they might be unable to do so. Prosperity, it seemed, might cost the Prairie West its Britishness.[7]

Prosperity poured forth in the wheat harvested from millions of newly broken acres of prairie soil. The 1.26 million acres sown to wheat in 1896 became 2.5 million in 1901, 4.5 million in 1906, and more than ten million in 1913. Yields per acre varied with the weather, but when sun and rain were kind, the size of the crop almost kept pace with the acreage planted: 63 million bushels in 1901, 108 million in 1906, 209 million in 1913, and the first 300-million-bushel crop in 1915. The Prairie West's golden bounty made Canada a significant world exporter of wheat, 114 million bushels of it in 1913. Wheat became Canada's fourth great export staple (cod, fur, and square timber had been the others), increasing from insignificance to 4 per cent of Canadian exports by value in 1901, 16 per cent in 1911, and 25 per cent by the mid-1920s.

Economic historians debate the reasons for this multiplying wheat economy. Kenneth Norrie jokes that 'the production of [scholarly] papers on the wheat boom will probably exhaust in the end all the surplus that the event ever created.' Increasing international demand produced a gradual increase in grain prices from the mid-1890s onward to 1912, which acted as an incentive to bring new land in Western Canada into production. Implement manufacturers, government researchers, and progressive farmers worked out technology and techniques to make possible

Breaking with a steam tractor, Pincher Creek, Alberta, *c.* 1910. Large-scale farmer-businessmen could hire steam tractors and crews to break their land, or even invest in the equipment themselves. The tank wagon at the left replenished the tractor's water. The slightly apprehensive woman tying her bonnet implies, falsely, that women had somehow been released from agricultural work. Glenbow NA-2382-9.

commercial grain production on the cold and arid prairies: barbed wire speeded fencing, chilled steel plows broke tough sod, new wheat varieties ripened earlier, 'binders' cut the crop quickly and bound it into sheaves before it froze. Probably most important were the cultivation practices developed to conserve moisture—collectively called 'dry farming'—in particular the technique of 'summer-fallowing': leaving a third or even half of improved acreage unsown so that it could retain enough moisture to ensure a crop in a dry season.[8]

'Dry farming' gave a horde of hopeful wheat kings the confidence to insist that the federal government end the range-cattle industry so that they could plow up the short-grass prairie for homesteads. The Liberals saw no reason to protect Tory cattle barons, and began to dismantle the ranching leaseholds. But the coup de grâce for ranching was the severe winter of 1906–7: early blizzards, -35°C temperatures, and no warm Chinook winds meant that an estimated fifty per cent of the cattle on the range froze or starved to death. The Two Bar Ranch near Gleichen, Alberta, lost 11,000 of its 13,000 head. Two years later journalist Howard Angus Kennedy reported that the short-grass prairie was 'dotted with homesteads . . . the arid immensities . . . are chequered with yellow fields of wheat, and the cowboy is a curiosity. The cattle-king has abdicated and the farmer reigns in his stead.'[9]

John Bolton breaking, Ranfurly, Alberta, 1906. As his wife and child look on, John Bolton proudly displays sod from the furrow he has just turned. Most farmers were like Bolton, with his oxen and walking plow. On large commercial farms, steam tractors did the breaking and custom threshers brought in the crop, but on smaller farms the family worked together and counted on neighbours to co-operate for harvesting. PAA A.10,688.

But not all the farm families who settled in the Prairie West were wheat kings and queens. Time of settlement, available capital, and ethnic background, as well as the differing economic opportunities offered by local environments, meant that rural society was not homogeneous: four different agricultural frontiers co-existed in the West. Some large-scale farmers did seem like cereal czars. The agrarian capitalist Charles S. Noble cultivated 30,000 acres of southern Alberta in 1917, when the average prairie farm was less than 300. An agrarian Henry Ford, he sped up his 160 farm workers and 300 work horses with time-and-motion studies, lived in a home with an indoor swimming pool, ran a real-estate agency, and distributed Reo automo-biles and Reeves steam tractors. Much more numerous, however, were the common folk of the countryside, near-peasant families like the Ukrainian settlers of southeastern Manitoba. Without capital or a capitalist ethic, these fam-ilies deliberately rejected prairie wheat lands for homesteads in the aspen park belt, where they found the wood and water they needed to practise almost self-sufficient agriculture. Between these extremes of agribusiness and peasantry were the families in the park belt and the river valleys who attempted diversified farming on mixed farms like the ones they had left in Ontario and elsewhere. Finally, on the prairie, there was the more aggressive frontier of the grain farmer, typical of districts like the

A sod house near Camrose, Alberta. Any illustrated history of the Prairie West must have an image of a 'soddy'. Sod houses required much more time and effort than frame and tarpaper construction, but saved the expense of buying and transporting construction materials. This house combines sod and frame construction, with sod wings added to the frame shack that was perhaps used to 'prove up' the homestead. Sod houses could last for decades, and were adapted as bunkhouses, sheds, or as shelters for stock after a family built a frame home. Glenbow NA-2507-26.

Vulcan area of southern Alberta. This kind of farming made a family part of a complex marketing system, but even grain-growing families met many of their needs from their own farms.[10]

Farm families combined subsistence and market approaches. Few thought of themselves as the small-business operators depicted by economic historians today. For most, the goal was independence, a farm that would support the family and could eventually be passed on to a new generation. Settlers did not set out alone into the unknown, but travelled west with family and friends. The Johnson family—Sam, Mary, daughter Verda and sons Ira, Arthur, and Morgan—left North Carolina for Alberta because Sam's brother Bud and two families of friends had preceded them. As Verda remembered it, 'They wrote home glowing accounts of this new country, saying what a wonderful place it was for the future of our young people.' The rural society that families like the Johnsons fashioned in the Prairie West before 1920 retained elements of traditional rural societies alongside elements of modern industrial society. Communities within the region shared the settlement experience, co-operated with their neighbours to harvest and to thresh, and took part in the rituals of local associational life.[11]

A prairie farm in winter, near Rapid City, Manitoba, *c.* 1895. The prairie winter was largely absent from propaganda to attract settlers. When it was mentioned, winter was explained away with phrases about the 'healthful climate', the lack of humidity, and the abundant sunshine. Readers who know the prairie climate will have noted many more images of the short summer than of the seven-month winter. This bias reflects both the economic and the physical limits within which the image-makers worked. Most of them wanted to present the region in ways that would persuade their viewers to become settlers—hence their almost universal desire to depict the Prairie West at its most attractive. At the same time, the northwestern winter deterred even those who deliberately sought out dramatic subjects: Paul Kane painted no scenes of buffalo struggling in deep snow because bitter cold made sitting by the hearth of a Hudson's Bay Company post infinitely more pleasant than sketching outdoors. Carl Nettekoven photo. PAM Rapid City—Farms 6.

The hardships that farm families faced are recounted in every local chronicle. Best remembered is the shock of the prairie weather: intense cold that turned water to stone, early frosts that cut down crops before they could be harvested, sheets of lightning that touched off prairie fires, hail that flattened a family's dreams as quickly as it levelled their grain. Such adversity meant that more than four of every ten homesteads that were claimed were never 'proved up'. But still new settlers came by the tens of thousands: there were 55,176 farms in Manitoba and the North-West Territories in 1901, and 288,079 in the three Prairie provinces two decades later. In 1911, 279,724 men—56 per cent of the census male labour force—worked in agriculture in the Prairie West; by 1921 the figure had increased to 369,107 workers (60 per cent).

Not all of these men were farmers or farmers' sons. One in five was a farm worker toiling for an agribusinessman like Charles Noble, or the single full-time hired hand working with a family who could afford him. Perhaps two-

'Hot Meals Served at All Hours', *c.* 1910. Threshers eat lunch beside their steam tractor and its tank wagon. By 1900, men eating lunch in the fields had become a common photographic subject. Many images show women serving them. But virtually none portray the massive effort required of farm women to prepare all that food. The absence of such images reflects photographic technology as well as culture: it was much easier to make a photo in a sunlit field than in a dark kitchen. SAB A8634(1).

thirds of these hired hands saw themselves as apprentices planting their feet on the first rung of an 'agricultural ladder'; and as long as homestead land was available, some of them did climb to independent farm ownership and start families. Another group of farm workers had no such prospects. Every August, when the wheat crop was ready, an influx of transients tripled the number of wage-workers in Western agriculture. Higher harvest wages attracted navvies from the resource industries as well as Eastern excursionists brought west on reduced fares by the railways. Transient workers were assigned the back-breaking task

of 'stooking': gathering eight or ten sheaves of grain into a weather-resistant conical pile until it could be threshed. Some of them would be kept on with the family for the less onerous task of threshing: after stooking, harvesters joked, 'Bringing in the Sheaves' was a picnic— 'no wonder there's a hymn about that.'[12]

Feeding a harvesting crew breakfast, dinner, and supper, with two 'lunches' in between, meant that women's day began earlier than men's and ended later. Setting a magnificent harvest-time table was part of the regional definition of womanliness: a farm wife who did not, observed the Prairie feminist Nellie

McClung, was 'almost as low in the social scale as the woman who has not a yard of flannel in the house when baby comes.' The harvest season only intensified the tasks that farm girls and women performed year round: although the Dominion Bureau of Statistics pretended that farm wives and daughters were not part of the agricultural labour force, virtually all of them did agricultural chores in addition to their domestic work. The field work that women did varied with their ethnic background. 'The average Ukrainian woman often contributes more to the farm than does the average hired man,' observed a British Canadian: 'she follows the family to the field where she may hoe or drive a gang plow, stook, etc.'[13]

Building a family farm in the West required so much hard physical work that the gender of the worker became less important than it had been in Ontario, Quebec, the Maritimes, or the 'Old Country'. In families without capital, men often 'worked out', away from the homestead, while their wives and children ran the farm. Some historians suggest that the western experience increased women's autonomy and reshaped constructions of gender; several go so far as to argue that the fact that the Prairie provinces (and the US western states) were the first to enfranchise women reflected a pioneering partnership between women and men that earned women political equality. Other historians maintain that the patriarchy continued undisturbed in the West, and that the 'cult of true womanhood', according to which women should be private, pious, pure, domestic, and submissive, was simply transplanted there. Certainly Western constructions of manhood left little room for women to expand their sphere. In practice, some family farms may

Mary McDonald displays a hawk she has killed, Carbon, Alberta, *c.* 1910. Children in the Prairie West may have faced fewer gender constraints than those elsewhere. Tasks for boys and girls, like those for men and women, remained strongly gender-linked, but circumstances on a Prairie homestead meant that gender-role distinctions were sometimes muted. Girls took on boys' tasks and acquired skills like hunting—although boys almost never took on girls' jobs. Certainly both boys and girls grew up with the farm child's view that farms needed protection from predatory wildlife. However, all the evidence suggests that the predators faced greater danger from the farms. Glenbow NA-2574-73.

have been partnerships, but legally the land, stock, equipment, and wife were the property of the husband. Farm wives and their husbands, says Veronica Strong-Boag, were not

'J. Cowell and Kodak, 1903', near Portage la Prairie, Manitoba. The hand-held camera with roll film, patented in 1888 by George Eastman, brought 'snapshot' photography to the masses. The amateurs who bought Eastman's Kodak cameras needed no chemicals or darkrooms, but mailed their rolls of film to the factory for developing. By 1900, few people were unable to afford a camera: the cheapest Kodak, the Brownie, cost about a dollar. Jack Cowell, who earned $25 a month as a farm labourer, bought a better model, the Kodak Combination (PAM, Cowell Reminiscences, MG8 B18). PAM John Cowell Collection 34.

'pulling in double harness': in fact, the wives were 'hauling a double load'.[14]

The rapid expansion of prairie agriculture spurred construction activity in every sector of the economy: entrepreneurs large and small invested in everything from grain elevators to false-front poolrooms. Railways determined where development would take place, but the relationship between railway construction and agriculture was reciprocal: new branch lines opened new farming districts, and the politicians who represented new farming districts demanded new branch lines. Politicians had much to say about where the railways would run, because not an inch of steel was laid without government assistance. The federal government had stopped land grants to railways in 1894, and the Prairie provinces, without control of the natural resources within their boundaries, had no land to give away. Instead, support was provided through cash subsidies and federal and provincial government guarantees of the principal and interest on railway bonds, to a total of $215 million between 1903 and 1915. By that year the Canadian Pacific had been joined by two new transcontinentals. The Grand Trunk Pacific and the upstart Canadian Northern Railway competed with the lordly CPR just enough to push freight rates modestly downward, to the delight of everyone in the region.[15]

Railways fuelled the coal-mining industry as surely as coal fuelled their locomotives. Coal was critical to the Prairie West's development: in the novel *The Foreigner* (1909), by the Winnipeg writer Ralph Connor (Charles W. Gordon), the young hero wins fortune and fair lady not by discovering gold but by finding a coal deposit. Southern Alberta provided the three million tonnes of hard steam coal that the railways burned every year; large-scale mines operated around Lethbridge, Drumheller, and Canmore and in the Crowsnest Pass. In addition, the demand for winter heating fuel led to the development of smaller coal mines in all three provinces: around Edmonton, near Estevan, and in Manitoba's Turtle

Dominion Exhibition poster, 1908. This poster for the precursor of the Calgary Stampede warns that the cowboys and Indians will soon be gone in the new Prairie West of the wheat boom; they will be curiosities to be stared at, relegated to exhibitions and fairs. Glenbow NA-1473-1.

Alberta Provincial Exhibition poster, 1910. Agricultural technology progresses from the single-shared walking plow to a sulky plow, to a steam engine pulling six plowshares, to a dirigible. One effect of the mechanization and commercialization of agriculture was to alienate women from the production process; in the last two images the woman vanishes along with the draft animals. Glenbow NA 1473-20.

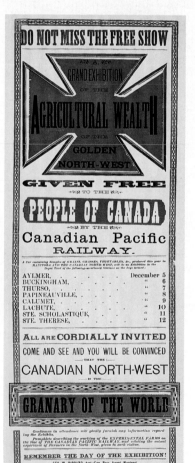

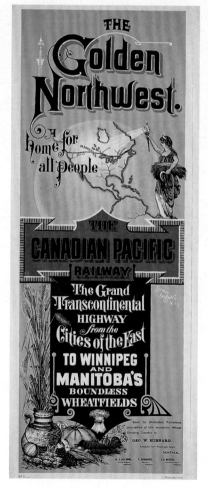

Laying track for a siding near Fort Macleod, 1897. NWMP Superintendent H.C. Forbes made this photo with his Kodak. Professional photographers paid little attention to railway construction workers, and posed them stiffly when they did; Forbes managed to show the crew actually laying steel. Glenbow NA-943-45.

Mountains. None of this coal found its way to markets in Central Canada, which imported its coal from Pennsylvania—much to the chagrin of Western coal operators.[16]

The image of a sod-house prairie frontier remains indelible in the popular memory, but building the commercial grain economy of the open plains rapidly aroused a voracious appetite for wood. A mile (1.6 km) of barbed-wire fence hung from 1,100 posts, and a mile of railway track sat on 2,000 ties; houses and barns, elevators and stations, consumed vast quantities of lumber. Until the 1890s, local sawmills processing white spruce from the

northern forests where the park belt met the Shield satisfied this hunger. Thereafter the Prairie lumber industry lost all but a fraction of its regional market to lumber shipped by rail from British Columbia, Ontario, and the United States. Instead of going to the local sawmill, farmers bought from retail lumber-yards, or they mail-ordered pre-designed and pre-cut buildings directly from mills in BC or Ontario. The rapid decline of local lumbering exemplified a persisting developmental dilemma for the Prairie West.[17] Although the expansion of the wheat economy increased demand for both producers' and consumers' goods

Prime Minister Wilfrid Laurier drives the first spike on the Alberta Central Railway, Red Deer, 10 Aug. 1910. Laurier's assistance to Western railways was much more than merely ceremonial. His government sponsored the creation of two new transcontinentals, private railroads built in large part at public expense. Glenbow NA-404-1.

manufactured in Central and Maritime Canada and in British Columbia, it stimulated comparatively little secondary manufacturing development within the Prairie West itself. There were the obvious industries that processed farm products—flour mills and meat-packing plants—as well as breweries and dairies serving local markets; Winnipeg had a garment industry, harness-makers, and iron and steel fabrication works. But manufacturing employed only about five per cent of the region's male waged labour force in 1911 and 1921, and over that decade the total numbers of women working in manufacturing actually declined.

The Prairie West was, not surprisingly,

Canada's most rural region. But as the wheat economy expanded, the population of the cities and towns that serviced agriculture actually increased faster than that of the countryside. In the Prairie West, however, unlike the rest of the country, urban growth came from migration into the region rather than from country-to-city migration within it. Railways brought the migrants and drew the map of a Prairie urban network. All three transcontinental railways ran through the regional metropolis of Winnipeg, the 'Chicago of the North', at the narrow end of the funnel through which wheat flowed east and manufactured goods flowed west. Between 1900 and 1915, the secondary contenders sorted themselves out: Regina and Calgary emerged on the southern route by the CPR line, Saskatoon and Edmonton alongside the Canadian Northern and the Grand Trunk Pacific. As Winnipeg's commercial élite had done in the 1880s, the 'boosters' of these cities made their own Faustian bargains to attract the transcontinentals. Calgary bribed the CPR to win freight yards and the Ogden railway maintenance shops; Saskatoon built a bridge for the Canadian Northern; Edmonton offered the GTP cash and a tax exemption. If 'knockers' in these cities complained that the railways ruled the political and physical lives of their communities, the boosters had only to point to the stagnation of the Emersons, Battlefords, and Fort Macleods—hopeful metropoli that had died when the main lines passed them by.

The five large cities performed major transport, service, and financial functions, and after 1905 Regina and Edmonton joined Winnipeg as provincial capitals. Smaller cities on the important rail lines became sub-regional supply

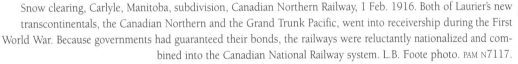

Snow clearing, Carlyle, Manitoba, subdivision, Canadian Northern Railway, 1 Feb. 1916. Both of Laurier's new transcontinentals, the Canadian Northern and the Grand Trunk Pacific, went into receivership during the First World War. Because governments had guaranteed their bonds, the railways were reluctantly nationalized and combined into the Canadian National Railway system. L.B. Foote photo. PAM N7117.

centres—Brandon, Moose Jaw, Medicine Hat, Lethbridge, Prince Albert—while a few larger towns like Dauphin, Estevan, Yorkton, and Red Deer sat alongside smaller railways, or branch lines of the transcontinentals. Small towns were literally railroaded into existence: railway companies established three-quarters of the towns incorporated in Alberta. The locations for towns were determined both by locomotives'

need for coal and water and by the distance a farm family could cover in a day with a team and wagon: the result was that no two towns were more than twenty miles apart. In these almost-identical towns, the railway station and grain elevator anchored one end of a main street that boasted a general store, a hardware merchant, a blacksmith who sold farm implements, a hotel, a weekly newspaper, and one branch

Facing above. '40,000 Men Needed in Western Canada', Soo Line poster, 1911. The Prairie wheat economy had massive short-term labour needs at harvest season, needs that the railways helped to meet by transporting harvest 'excursionists' from Atlantic and Central Canada at greatly reduced fares. In 1911 the Soo Line, which ran into southern Saskatchewan from Minneapolis–St Paul, brought 5,000 harvest hands from the United States. NAC C-56088.

Facing below. CPR posters. Except for those operating on the very largest scale, farm families combined subsistence and commercial strategies to sustain and reproduce themselves. Thus these posters promise that 'the granary of the world' offers 'a home for all people' as well as 'agricultural wealth'. CPR Archives.

Smith's Coal Mine, near Edmonton, *c.* 1900. Prairie coal-mining companies ranged from tiny operations like this one to large, vertically integrated corporations. Photographs of coal miners were almost always ritually posed around the pithead, and images of miners actually working underground are rare: what photographer wanted to face the technical problems and the danger of working in a mine? We can only guess at the identity of the well-dressed man leaning on the post at the left and his relationship to the miners; it is tempting to suppose that this image illustrates class divisions, but there is no other evidence to substantiate such speculation. PAA B.1632.

bank as evidence of the town's place as an outpost of a world capitalist economy; the Canadian Northern allowed its banker, the Bank of Commerce, the pick of the Main Street lots in the towns it established. Local businesspeople boosted their up-and-coming towns with the same enthusiasm as the boards of trade of Calgary, Saskatoon, or Winnipeg, albeit on a smaller scale. As in the cities, unrestrained confidence and unqualified faith in a boundless future characterized the urban commercial élite of the 'Land of Golden Opportunity'.[18]

The boom that created the boosters also created a working class. Twenty-five thousand women worked as domestic servants, cleaning and cooking for the élite. Workers in the building trades constructed the West's towns and cities: carpenters, bricklayers, painters. Miners dug coal in each province. Railway workers numbered in the tens of thousands, from highly skilled locomotive engineers (today's counterparts would be airline pilots),

The Burns meat-packing plant, Calgary, *c.* 1905. The manufacturing sector of the Prairie West's economy was relatively small, and concentrated in the industries (such as meat packing and flour milling) that transformed the products of Prairie agriculture. Glenbow NA-2351-4.

firemen, brakemen, telegraphers, and machinists in the maintenance shops, to section-men and freight-handlers. Thirty or forty thousand transient 'blanketstiffs' laboured at seasonal jobs in railway construction, logging, and agriculture, and when winter put an end to their working year they congregated in the cities. Those who belonged to unions were divided among the craft unions of the skilled trades, the militant industrial unions like the United Brotherhood of Railway Employees, or the revolutionary Industrial Workers of the World—the only labour organization that reached out

to the unskilled 'blanketstiffs'. Most workers were not organized, but Prairie élites feared their potential should they unite. Clifford Sifton's famous speech welcoming the 'stalwart peasant' as a 'good quality' immigrant had a seldom-quoted second part: 'A Trades Union artisan who will not work more than eight hours a day is . . . very bad quality.' Élites took steps to assure their political dominance. In Calgary and Winnipeg, businessmen shut the working class out of government by hedging the municipal franchise with property qualifications, and by granting themselves votes

Boaters and bathers on Wascana Lake, in front of the new Saskatchewan legislature, Regina, 1913. The smiling swimmers in the foreground of this staged photograph are the cast of 'Hanky Panky', a touring show playing in Regina. Saskatchewan's new legislature is under construction in the background across the lake. All the Prairie provinces constructed expensive legislative buildings that befitted the unrestrained economic optimism of the era, each massive stone structure a 'bizarre conjunction of pristine and gleaming temple architecture and treeless prairie', as the historian Dan Ring remarks: 'The legislative buildings not only symbolized the importance of the capital cities but were also tangible links to the pageantry and ceremony of the British Empire' (*The Urban Prairie, 1880–1960* [Saskatoon: Mendel Art Gallery, Fifth House, 1993]). SAB R-B764.

in every ward of the city in which they owned property. An Independent Labour MP, the British-born printer Arthur Puttee, represented Winnipeg in the Commons from 1900 to 1904; beyond that success, however, labour had little power in Prairie electoral politics before 1920.[19]

The electoral politics of the three provinces shared other similarities as well. The Canadian two-party system was rapidly set in place in the region after 1900, with no distinction between provincial and national wings within each party: the people involved were the same, and their connections were intimate. British-Canadian in leadership and laissez-faire in economics, the Prairie Conservative and Liberal parties virtually duplicated one another: they were 'two versions of the same class and cul-

An immigrant woman and her children, Winnipeg, *c.* 1909. The imposing Canadian Pacific Railway station overshadows a recently arrived immigrant who waits on the curb with her four young children and her belongings. The small cream can in front of her probably holds water to drink on the journey. This photograph appeared in *Strangers Within Our Gates* (Toronto, 1909), compiled by J.S. Woodsworth, superintendent of the Methodist Church's All People's Mission in Winnipeg. 'Perhaps the largest and most important problem that the North American continent has before it today,' wrote Woodsworth, 'is how incoming tides of immigrants of various nationalities and different degrees of civilization may be assimilated and made worthy citizens. . . . Western Canada has this problem in an even more perplexing form and to a greater degree than has the East.' The United Church of Canada-Victoria University Archives, Toronto, 93.049p/3111n.

tural loyalties', as the historian Gerald Friesen puts it. Their laissez-faire ideology abhorred social legislation but did not preclude public spending to foster private development. Both parties promised to assimilate European immigrants, but once in power they wooed the foreign vote and incorporated ethnic leaders into political machines well-oiled by patronage. Partisan newspapers made no pretence of objectivity, and got their rewards through government printing and advertising when their party won office. There was one *sine qua non*: each party listened carefully to the provincial farmers' organizations: the Grain Growers' Association in Manitoba and Saskatchewan and the United Farmers in Alberta. At their behest, a Conservative government introduced a public telephone system in Manitoba, and Liberal

Labour Day Parade, Winnipeg, c. 1905. On a sunny Labour Day early in the century, the trade-union parade moves slowly south along Main Street towards Portage Avenue, watched by packed crowds on both sidewalks. PAM N10342.

governments established a co-operative elevator company in Saskatchewan and a farm loan board in Alberta. The Saskatchewan Liberals went so far as to co-opt three farm leaders—W.R. Motherwell, C.A. Dunning, and George Langley—directly into the provincial cabinet.[20]

These similarities aside, each province developed its own distinct political pattern. Manitoba elections were the most hotly contested, decided by two or three per cent of the popular vote. Conservative Premier R.P. Roblin, who governed continuously from 1901 to 1915, spiced his campaigns with protests against federal control of natural resources and demands for the northern extension of Manitoba's boundaries. The Tory machine, primed with every drop of graft that Minister of Public Works Robert Rogers could squeeze from government contracts, eventually went too far even for that easy-going era: a kick-back scandal over the

All People's Mission Kindergarten, Winnipeg, 1904. Inspired by the social gospel, middle-class Methodists created urban missions to provide for the temporal as well as the spiritual needs of the immigrant poor. This kindergarten, taught by Annie Kelly and J.K. Lothrop, no doubt provided practical assistance to families with both parents in the waged labour force. However, the similarities between this photograph and the one on p. 62 suggest that the Protestant churches' attitudes towards the urban working class did not differ greatly from their attitudes towards Native people. PAM N13261.

construction of the legislative buildings knocked the Conservatives from office in 1915, to be replaced by a Liberal government led by T.C. Norris.

Liberals got a head start in Saskatchewan and Alberta because it was a federal Liberal government that had founded the new provinces and picked the first premiers. Laurier rejected Frederick Haultain, leader of the territorial campaign for autonomy, because

Haultain had insisted that the Territories become a single province with control of natural resources. Walter Scott, a former Liberal MP and the editor of the Liberal Moose Jaw *Times*, was appointed premier of Saskatchewan, and A.C. Rutherford, a Liberal member of the Territorial Assembly, was chosen to govern Alberta. In Saskatchewan, Scott's Liberals narrowly prevailed over Haultain's Provincial Rights Conservatives in the first provincial election by gerrymandering the constituencies and stuffing the ballot boxes. In contrast to the Manitoba Conservatives, the Saskatchewan Liberals built a twenty-four-year dynasty on close federal–provincial connections: every employee of the federal Department of the Interior canvassed Saskatchewan voters in a continuous Liberal election campaign. The machine became more efficient over time: after narrow victories in the provincial elections of 1905 and 1908, in 1912 the Liberals crushed the hapless provincial Conservatives, and until 1929 routinely won three-quarters of the seats in the legislature.[21]

The Alberta Liberals, on the other hand, squandered the lead that Laurier had given them. The Liberal party won the first two provincial elections with more than sixty per cent of the popular vote, but although its initial success was more spectacular, it never entrenched itself in Alberta as it did in Saskatchewan. The Conservative opposition retained a geographical base in the old ranching area of the southern prairie, and mining communities provided a base for various Labour and Socialist candidates. Unlike the Saskatchewan Liberals, who spread the good things of government around geographically (Regina got the capital, Saskatoon the provincial university, Prince Albert the penitentiary), the Alberta Liberals blatantly favoured their northern base. They outraged Calgarians by establishing the University of Alberta in Strathcona, directly across the river from the legislature in Edmonton. Like the Manitoba Conservatives, the Alberta Liberals were tainted by scandal: Premier Rutherford resigned in 1910 over an aborted railway project that had been promoted with public money. His succes-

sor, A.L. Sifton, won close victories in 1913 and 1917—the last elections Liberals have thus far won in Alberta.[22]

The success of the two-party system concealed stresses that could not easily be accommodated within it. Liberal or Tory, neither provincial governments nor federal MPs could do much about the national policies that troubled Prairie voters, who increasingly now described themselves as 'Westerners'. After 1910, projects for change gathered force. A reform impulse that had originated in Britain and the United States found a receptive audience in the Prairie West, where a decade of unrestrained growth had left social problems that could be seen in the city slums; where schools weren't turning immigrants' children into Anglo-Canadians fast enough; and where politics were dirty and machine-ridden. Prairie farmers were experiencing the worst effects of the Canadian variant of industrial capitalism. The tariff that protected Eastern manufacturers added 30 per cent to the cost of their farm implements. They bought wood from a 'line' (or chain) lumber dealer who fixed prices through the Western Retail Lumberman's Association, delivered their grain to a 'line' elevator of the Northwest Elevator Association, and borrowed money from (or were refused money by) a branch of a Central Canadian bank. Farmers doubted that competition really determined the freight rates of the railways, whatever the federal Board of Railway Commissioners told them. 'If you put a banker, a railwayman and an elevator agent in a barrel and roll them down a hill,' went a Western joke, 'there will always be a son-of-a-bitch on top.'

The reformers were 'middle-class' men

and women (this was something new: in the past, women had been expected to remain at home, in the private sphere) of Ontario, British, or US background and Protestant faith. Some historians suggest that their efforts were inspired by the 'social gospel' of Christian concern for the victims of rapid industrial development. Others explain their activism as the product of 'status anxiety' over perceived threats to the dominance of their ethnic and class values. Marxist historians argue that reformers perpetuated capitalism by limiting its excesses and legitimating its domination through reforms that actually helped élites to control the working class. The inventory of improvements that reformers sought and achieved can be used to support each of these interpretations. Urban reformers wanted a rudimentary welfare state with better public health protection, regulation of working conditions for women and children, and provincial 'mother's allowances' for widowed or deserted wives with families to raise. Organized farmers wanted curbs upon the power of capital, and debated whether control could be best achieved through regulation or public ownership. Reformers saw liquor not as a symptom of urban poverty but as its cause, and drinking as the most disturbing manifestation of immigrants' foreignness: prohibition would solve both problems. To make the public schools effective agents of assimilation, education had to be made universal, compulsory, and unilingual. Political reforms would guarantee that the (right) people ruled; through 'direct legislation', upright citizens would themselves initiate bills, ratify them in referenda, and recall elected politicians who did not do what 'the people' wanted. However,

in the 1910s and 1920s a popular municipal reform called 'commission government' was to take power from working-class voters in several Prairie cities and place municipal government in the hands of non-elected experts.[23]

Women's suffrage was both an end in itself and a means to achieve further reforms. First-wave feminism combined two superficially contradictory ideologies: 'maternal' feminism argued that women were more moral and virtuous than men, and would use their votes to nurture society just as they nurtured their families; 'equal rights' feminism insisted that women and men had the same inherent democratic rights. Historians have spilled far too much ink debating which ideology better characterizes Prairie feminism. This false dichotomy never troubled Western suffrage leaders like Nellie McClung, Violet McNaughton, and Louise McKinney, who used both maternal and egalitarian arguments for suffrage; however, because suffragists intended to use their votes to reform politics and society, maternalist arguments did have a stronger appeal in the Prairie West than elsewhere. What is significant is that women gained the vote because they worked for it through a regional network organized in Political Equality Leagues, the Woman's Christian Temperance Union (WCTU), and the women's 'auxiliaries' of the farm movement. In January, March, and April 1916, Manitoba, Saskatchewan, and Alberta became the first Canadian provinces to enfranchise women.[24]

Another reason why women's suffrage came first in the Prairie West was that women's votes augmented the electoral power of native-born Canadians against newcomers: English-speaking women were a larger percentage of

The Door Steadily Opens

 Dick Hartley, 'The Door Steadily Opens', *Grain Growers' Guide*, 21 Sept. 1910. A woman with a broom marked 'Woman Suffrage' forces her way into the 'smoke-filled room' of male politics to sweep up 'special privilege', 'white slavery', 'combines', 'drink', and 'monopoly'. SAB R-A369(2).

the population than 'foreign' women, who were always outnumbered by men among the immigrant population. In fact, nativism tinged every item on the reform agenda. In the name of reform, Manitoba in 1916 and Saskatchewan in 1918 abrogated the educational rights of linguistic minorities, making public schools unilingual and attendance at them compulsory; French was treated as a foreign language and eliminated, along with German and Ukrainian.

Between 1914 and 1918, the Prairie provinces also voted themselves 'dry' in prohibition referenda, regulated the wages and hours of women workers, established mother's allowances, and passed public health acts. Not coincidentally, the reformers' greatest success came when the First World War welded English-speaking Westerners together in patriotic fervour. Just as Canada's soldiers would clean up Europe and eradicate 'the national sins which are responsi-

A Woman's Christian Temperance Union group in Regina, 1908. The WCTU's political and social activism went well beyond supporting prohibition of beverage alcohol and 'maternal feminism'. Louise McKinney, later one of the 'famous five' who fought the 'Persons Case', is standing on the right. Glenbow NA-1399-1.

ble for this awful carnage,' said Louise McKinney, president of the Alberta WCTU, reformers would clean up their region.

The Prairie West became the bulwark of Canada's war effort. Enlistments were disproportionately high, reflecting both the large numbers of British-born in the population and the recession that had struck the region in 1914. English-speaking Westerners explained the Great War both as a patriotic duty to Canada and the Empire and as a struggle for democratic principles, but their conduct was anything but democratic. Outraged by the indifference of non-British minorities to their crusade, they enthusiastically supported the wartime internment of Ukrainian immigrants who posed absolutely no threat, and welcomed the disenfranchisement of naturalized 'enemy aliens' in the wartime federal election of 1917. Forty-one of the Prairie West's 43 parliamentary seats went to the Unionist Conservative–Liberal coalition in that election, and 70 per cent of its votes; the seven Labour candidates who opposed the Union govern-

Drinking in the Chevigny store in Plamondon, Alberta, *c.* 1915. Men like Alexandre Bourassa, Frederick Bourassa, Arthur Bourassa, and Benoit Plamondon were the targets of English-speaking Protestant reformers. PAA A 7781.

British Empire Day Parade in Gladstone, Manitoba, 23 May 1915. The Boy Scouts and Union Jacks point to the strength of British ethnic identity in the Prairie West. Note the false fronts on several buildings, creating the illusion of second storeys. The writer Wallace Stegner described his own hometown as a 'false-front Athens' (*Wolf Willow* [New York: Viking, 1966]). PAM N1258.

Cree volunteers for the Great War, The Pas, Manitoba, 1914. Native people didn't vanish after 1900; 3,500 Aboriginal men served in the First World War, out of a total Aboriginal population of about 100,000. All were volunteers, because Native people were exempt from conscription. At home, reserves donated money to the Red Cross. Despite such contributions to the war effort, however, several reserves had their lands leased, against their wishes, to white farmers for 'Greater Production' campaigns. PAM, Campbell, John A. series IV 2.

ment's conscription policy all lost resoundingly.

Although their support for the war effort never flagged, English-speaking Westerners soon turned against the Union government they had helped to elect. They criticized its fumbling attempts to ration food and coal and its failure to deal with wartime inflation; they resented the government propaganda urging Prairie farmers to plant wheat to feed Canada's allies even as Ottawa was cancelling military exemptions for farmers' sons and refusing to lower the tariff on the farm machinery necessary to increase production. Like the Liberal and Conservative governments that had preceded them, the Unionists seemed to govern for Central Canada and to ignore the West. This seemed doubly unfair, given that the West was contributing 'far more than the East in proportion to its population,' as President Henry Marshall Tory of the University of Alberta put it. The West had devoted itself to 'what could be put into the war,' wrote an Edmonton editor; 'what could be got out of the war has been all too prominent in Ontario's calculations.' Thus the war that had begun as a great English-Canadian national quest ended

Internment camp at Castle Mountain, Alberta, 1915. The war legitimated pre-war prejudices against immigrants. 'Enemy aliens', most of them ethnic Ukrainians, faced internment as subjects of Canada's enemy Austria–Hungary. Glenbow NA-1870-6.

by intensifying the Prairie West's emerging sense of regional grievance and advancing the gradual process by which the people who had come west as the colonizers came to see themselves as the colonized.[25]

The Great War also unleashed a force far more frightening to the federal government than regional alienation: a working class with a heightened awareness of its power. Wartime labour shortages and the temporary end to European immigration meant steady employment for working people, increasing both the numbers of unionized workers and the militancy of their unions. The industrial insurgencies that exploded in Western Canada in 1918 and

1919 took place in the context of a much broader working-class upheaval that encompassed Eastern Canada, the United States, Britain, and much of Europe. But international class solidarity intersected with the specific circumstances that distinguished the West from the rest of Canada: resource industries in which working conditions were measurably harsher and more dangerous; a stronger industrial, as opposed to craft, union experience; capitalists notorious for their willingness to use violent means to crush those unions. When radical trade unionists from Manitoba, Saskatchewan, Alberta, and British Columbia assembled in Calgary for a Western Labour Conference in

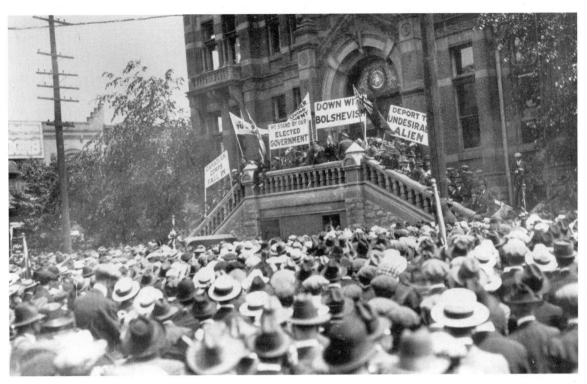

Anti-strike veterans rally at Winnipeg City Hall, 4 June 1919. The diverse banners of the anti-strike veterans suggest the complicated intersections of ethnicity, class, and region that make understanding the Winnipeg General Strike so difficult. 'Down with Bolshevism' and 'Deport the Undesirable Alien' echoed the rhetoric of the Winnipeg élites determined to crush the general strike. But other banners in the same parade shouted 'Down With the High Cost of Living', a demand that suggested sympathy with the objectives of the strikers. PAM N12296.

March 1919, they not only declared their solidarity with revolutionaries in Russia and in Germany, but declared their independence of the Ontario-based Trades and Labour Congress of Canada. The Calgary conference founded a movement to organize all working men and women (although most of the delegates themselves were men) into 'One Big Union' to fight 'the inevitable class struggle'. The OBU appealed across the ethnic divisions within the Prairie West's working class: the only 'alien enemy' was the capitalist. This bold attempt was barely under way when a conventional labour dispute in another Prairie city burgeoned into the most prominent event in Canadian working-class history.

The Winnipeg General Strike climaxed Canadian labour's year of revolt. For forty-two days in May and June of 1919, national and international attention focused on the Manitoba capital: the *New York Times* devoted six editorials to what it called 'an attempt at revolution' that had 'paralyzed a large part of the West'. The strike began on 15 May as an attempt by building and metal trades unions to gain a collective agreement; within two days

Strikers tipping the streetcar, Winnipeg. This image has been reproduced so often that J.M. Bumsted (whose own book on the Winnipeg General Strike also reproduces it) writes that 'the photograph of the tram at this moment has become one of the icons of the strike.' Yet the photograph has been subjected to little serious analysis as a visual source for what happened on 'Bloody Saturday'. Rather than an angry crowd determined on a showdown with authority, the picture suggests that the workers' protest was astonishingly calm, especially given the midnight arrests of their leaders. The well-dressed women and men in the foreground could be attending a garden party—and working-class men would not have brought along their wives and daughters if they anticipated or intended violence. The strikers' discipline, organization, and firm resolve were likely what made the General Strike so terrifying to bourgeois Winnipeggers, and what prompted the government violence that led to bloodshed. PAM N2762.

some 30,000 Winnipeg workers, most of them not union members, had walked off their jobs. Sympathy strikes took place in twenty-five Western towns and cities, in five towns in northwestern Ontario, in Toronto, and in Amherst, Nova Scotia. A 'Citizens Committee of 1,000' of the Winnipeg élite and the federal government acted resolutely to repress the insurgency. They condemned the strikers as 'alien Bolsheviks' out to replace the Union Jack with the red flag, and locked up the strike leaders—eight of them British-born and one from Ontario. When crowds gathered at Portage Avenue and Main Street on 21 June to protest the arrests, they were ridden down by North-West Mounted Police armed with baseball bats; when the strikers fought back with stones, the Mounties opened fire with their service revolvers. Two strikers died and dozens were wounded on 'Bloody Saturday'. That night and for the next five days, khaki-clad militia patrolled the streets with machine guns mounted on automobiles contributed by wealthy Winnipeggers. On 26 June, the strikers formally acknowledged defeat.

These facts are not in dispute: what is contested is their meaning. The government's account of the Winnipeg General Strike as the first stage of a Bolshevik revolution designed by the OBU did not long survive 1919. According to the currently sanctioned academic interpretation and the official public memory, the Winnipeg General Strike was about collective bargaining and decent working conditions. But this limited perspective does not explain why 30,000 workers, most of whom had no direct connection to the labour dispute that triggered the strike, spent six weeks off work to support it: surely these people hoped for more profound social change. The revolt of 1919 was national, not simply regional; the elaborate pains that the federal government took to defeat the strike demonstrate this. Yet it took place in Winnipeg, not in Hamilton or Montreal or Halifax. Today, proudly burnished, the General Strike rests on display in the Prairie West's pantheon of regional protest movements.[26]

CHAPTER SIX

Harsh Realities of Region: 1921–1939

*B*etween 1870 and 1900, Canadians made the northwestern interior of the continent into the Canadian Prairie West. Over the next two decades, many of the people who lived there came to think of themselves as 'Westerners' and of the place where they lived as part of a region distinct from the rest of the country. They contrasted their dynamic West against 'the Effete East', defined as 'the worn-out, exhausted Eastern Provinces' in the *Western Canadian Dictionary* published in 1913 by Winnipeg journalist John Sandilands. 'The Westerner who jokingly refers to the East in this fashion seldom means it,' Sandilands added; 'he has a warm corner in his heart for some well-remembered spot 'way back in Ontario or in the Maritime Provinces.'[1] The years that followed distinctly chilled this warmth, however. The Great War heightened feelings of Western identity: after a half-century within Confederation, the region 'came of age' just as Canada itself did within the British Empire. The decades of discord between the two world wars sharpened this sense of region.

The census of 1921 provided clear demographic evidence of regional differences. The statistics suggested that most of the Prairie West's population could no longer remember Ontario or the Maritimes: barely sixty per cent had been born in Canada, and more than half of the Canadian-born had been born in the West itself. Ethnically, Manitoba, Alberta, and especially Saskatchewan were much more heterogeneous than the rest of Canada. British Canadians, a clear majority in every other province save Quebec, were a bare majority in Manitoba and Alberta and only a plurality in Saskatchewan; in the Prairie West, French Canadians made up only about six per cent of the population, less than Germans (about ten per cent), Ukrainians (just over eight per cent), and 'Scandinavians' (just under seven per cent). Equally striking was the size of the group born in the United States: almost eight per cent of the Prairie population, as compared with barely two per cent in the rest of Canada. With 118 males for every 100 females, the Prairie West was much more 'masculine' than Canada as a whole, and the region had a larger percentage of its population—almost half—in the active years of adulthood between twenty-one and forty-five. Even though Winnipeg was

Canada's third-largest city, in 1921 the Prairie West was still more rural than the rest of the country: the region had gained 56,000 farms, while farm families were leaving the land in every other province but British Columbia. As had been intended, the National Policy had built a specialized regional economy in Manitoba, Saskatchewan, and Alberta: seven of every ten workers were directly engaged in agriculture, and most of the rest earned their living by transporting agricultural products or supplying the needs of farming communities.

On the eve of the Great War, in the summer of 1914, Prairie farmers had begun to debate the idea of independent political insurgency. The *Grain Growers' Guide*, a newspaper read in two-thirds of English-speaking farm homes, warned 'the financial centers of Quebec and Ontario' that 'the people of the Prairie Provinces are no longer satisfied to be herded into a legislative corral and plundered by the Barons of Special Privilege.' An Alberta farmer put the matter more bluntly: 'If a bunch of pigs were having a hog congress, would they elect a butcher to represent them?'[2] The war and the formation of the Union government temporarily diverted this non-partisan political revolt: nine farmers' candidates were elected as supporters of the Unionist coalition in the federal election of 1917. But the postponement only meant that the Prairie agrarian insurgency that poured forth anew in 1919 could not easily be channelled back into the two-party system. This agrarian movement fed off the social-reform ethos of the era, but it had deeper ideological roots in the critique of industrial capitalism articulated by the American Populist Party and its Canadian counterpart the Patrons of Industry, which flourished

briefly in Ontario and Manitoba during the 1890s. The insurgent farmers were neither socialists nor petit-bourgeois small businessmen envious of more successful ones (or at least most of them weren't), although some historians attempt to squeeze them into these categories. Farm families drew their values from the community self-reliance and co-operation that were part of their traditional rural culture. They were anti-corporate and anti-monopoly, rather than simply anti-capitalist: they envisioned an equitable democratic capitalism, built on co-operation, in which the people whose labour generated wealth would enjoy the full benefit of all they produced.[3]

In June 1919, frustrated by another refusal to lower the protective tariff, the nine Western farmers elected to Parliament in 1917 gave up on the Union government and created the National Progressive Party. Two new independent farmer-MPs soon joined them, endorsed by massive majorities over Liberal and Conservative candidates in by-elections in Saskatchewan and Alberta. The Progressive call for a 'New' National Policy went out to all Canadians, not just Westerners: the party stood for the nationalization of railways, public utilities, and coal mines; for 'greater democracy in government' through women's suffrage, reform of the Senate, and use of the initiative, the referendum, and the recall; for an immediate reduction of the protective tariff that had 'fostered combines and trusts' and 'built up a privileged class at the expense of the masses'. In the federal election of December 1921, Progressives not only won 39 of the 43 seats in the Prairie West, with more than half of the popular vote; they also took 24 seats in rural Ontario, two in British Columbia and one in

Progressive Party supporters, Moose Jaw, Saskatchewan, December 1921. Progressive campaigners pull a buggy carrying R.M. Johnson, the victorious Progressive candidate in Moose Jaw. On the wall of the building, one banner calls Progressivism 'The People's Movement' while another calls it 'The People's Party'—the official name of the American Populist party of the 1890s. The Progressive 'movement' never established an effective political 'party', however, because too many agrarian insurgents rejected political parties as a problem to be overcome, not an institution to be perpetuated. Note that, despite the active involvement of women in the agrarian movement, and despite the support of the Progressive Party for women's suffrage, there are no women in the photograph. Moose Jaw Public Library Archives/73-96.

New Brunswick, becoming the second-largest group in the House of Commons. This success at the federal level was paralleled by similar upheavals in several provinces: in 1919 Ontarians chose a United Farmers government to replace the Conservatives, in 1921 and 1922 Albertans and Manitobans elected United Farmers to succeed the Liberals, and in Nova Scotia the Farmer–Labour Party became the official opposition in 1920.[4]

The Progressive movement never fulfilled its democratic promise, and before long it dissolved in division and defeat. The federal Progressive Party never functioned effectively in the Commons; its principal accomplishment, a renewal of the regulated 'Crow's Nest Pass' rate

Arch Dale cartoon from the *Grain Growers' Guide*, 15 Dec. 1915. The political strength of Prairie regionalism in the inter-war period reflected the intersection of the agrarian critique of monopoly with the Prairie West's perception that the economic cards of Confederation were stacked against it. Agrarianism reinforced regionalism to provide a base for the succession of Prairie third parties that expressed Western discontent. SAB R-A19422.

for shipping grain, fell light-years short of the bright promise of the New National Policy. Some twenty Prairie MPs rejected the concept of party discipline and refused to be constrained by the timidity of the party's two leaders, T.A. Crerar until November 1922 and Robert Forke until 1925. This was a prudent decision on their part. Both Crerar and Forke were thinly disguised capital-L Liberals who sought no more than to nudge Mackenzie King's minority Liberal government toward a lower tariff; both

men ended up as Liberal appointees to the very Senate they had pledged to reform. Other crypto-Liberal Progressive MPs drifted back with them. After the federal election of 1926, only twenty Progressives were left in Parliament, eighteen of them from the Prairie West. The United Farmers government in Ontario was defeated in 1923, and in Nova Scotia it was the Conservatives, not Farmer–Labour, who used Maritime regionalism as the path to electoral success during the 1920s.[5]

The United Farmer governments in Alberta and Manitoba and the federal Progressive MPs from the West, on the other hand, endured into the 1930s because in the Prairie West agrarian revolt blended with regional discontent. With the single significant exception of the Winnipeg Grain Exchange, the adversaries that the Western Progressives confronted—railways, tariff-protected manufacturers, banks—all had their headquarters outside the region, beyond the reach of provincial governments, under federal political jurisdiction. The intersection of agrarianism and regionalism that sustained the Progressives, writes political scientist Roger Gibbins, 'established the dominant feature of prairie regional politics—the rejection of the major national parties in favour of indigenous third party vehicles of western discontent'.[6]

The working class of Western cities and towns fitted awkwardly into the evolving pattern of regional agrarian protest. Working-class voters divided their support between the moderate candidates of the Independent Labour Party and more outspoken radicals of a brighter red hue. Both moderates and radicals won seats in the Alberta and Manitoba legislatures, and moderates sometimes co-operated electorally with the United Farmers in particular constituencies. But Labour MLAs had very different relations with the two United Farmers provincial governments. The United Farmers of Manitoba, led by Premier John Bracken, allied themselves with the Winnipeg business élite and kept Labour at arm's length; the United Farmers of Alberta, on the other hand, led by Herbert Greenfield until 1925 and John Brownlee until 1934, did occasionally rely on Labour members' votes to govern. Three

Labour members from Prairie federal constituencies became fixtures in Ottawa: J.S. Woodsworth and A.A. Heaps from Winnipeg, and William Irvine from Calgary, who ran as a joint Labour–UFA candidate. When the Progressive federal caucus splintered, the three coalesced informally with the 'Ginger Group' of Progressive MPs most dedicated to the producer ideology that lay at the centre of their movement. The contrasting relationships of working-class representatives with the progressives showed that Western farmers were not monolithic.

Wealthier, well-established English-Canadian farmers had been the slowest to endorse independent political action; their limited objective was to eliminate the tariff and lower the freight rates that cut into their profits. The medium-scale and small-scale farmers who struggled to survive—'actual dirt farmers', as they called themselves—were the ones who had pushed the farmers' organizations towards political insurgency; accordingly, they were committed to using democratically elected governments to achieve the broader agrarian agenda. The question of a compulsory government board to market the wheat crop best demonstrates the divergence between the two tendencies. The first Canadian Wheat Board had been created by federal fiat to sell the 1919–20 crop in an erratic international market. Uniquely Canadian in concept and operation, the board gave farmers an initial per-bushel payment, sold the wheat crop for the highest prices it could get, and then distributed the additional earnings to the producers on a pro rata basis. This experiment delighted Prairie producers, who liked both the orderly marketing it made possible and the $2.62 a bushel they got for

Clearing the Right of Way

Arch Dale, 'Clearing the Right of Way', *Grain Growers' Guide*, 12 Jan. 1921. New technologies like farm trucks and automobiles changed the objective material conditions of Prairie farm families, but their producer ideology, which denied tribute to 'speculators & middlemen', remained deeply ingrained. The automobile aided immeasurably in the campaigns to organize the three Prairie wheat pools. SAB R-A19,419.

their wheat—more than most US farmers received that year. Nevertheless, the Conservative federal government of Arthur Meighen disbanded the Wheat Board and restored the supremacy of the Winnipeg Grain Exchange; and the King Liberals continued the open market for wheat, over protests from many Prairie farmers. But not all Western spokesmen protested the federal government's ideological loyalty to the free market: Progressive leader T.A. Crerar, Manitoba premier John Bracken, and UFA president Henry Wise Wood were

prominent among those who opposed a government-controlled wheat marketing board.[7]

Denied a state-run board, the tens of thousands of Prairie producers who wanted one created their own by establishing three massive farmer-owned co-operative provincial wheat pools. In Saskatchewan, pool organization was spearheaded by a grass-roots rival to the Saskatchewan Grain Growers that called itself the United Farmers of Canada (Saskatchewan Section) (in fact, there were no other sections). The pools duplicated as far as possible

The trading floor of the Winnipeg Grain Exchange on its fiftieth anniversary, 1937. The Prairie wheat pools charged that the private grain trade had attempted to destroy them through a 'deliberate bear raid' in April 1925. They accused traders on the Winnipeg Grain Exchange of attempting to drive the price of wheat below the pools' promised payment to members, in order to prompt the pools' bankers to call their loans and thus break them. Whatever the truth of the allegation, the incident confirmed the belief of most Prairie farmers that a stabilized wheat market would never be realized unless the pools or a government wheat board had total control of the crop. PAM N9874.

the design and operation of the Wheat Board: participating farmers signed contracts promising to deliver all the wheat they produced to the pools, which eliminated 'middlemen' by marketing the grain directly though the Central Selling Agency, based in Winnipeg. By the 1925–26 crop year, more than 140,000 of a possible 240,000 farmers had signed pool contracts, covering 52.2 per cent of the Prairie wheat crop. For the next two decades, the wheat pools fought a propaganda war over wheat marketing with the Winnipeg Grain Exchange, a war that made pool farmers ever more certain that private grain traders were part of a conspiracy to fleece them; they never gave up their campaign for a '100% cent compulsory pool': a federal wheat board that would put the Grain Exchange 'speculators' out of business.[8] Finally, in 1943, they won.

Both producers and speculators coped with

hard times for the first half of the 1920s. In the summer of 1920, the North American economy went into a deep recession that continued into 1924. Prices for grain and beef tumbled to less than half their wartime peaks, and the effects of deflation in agriculture reverberated throughout the Prairie economy: railways carried less freight, miners dug less coal, real-estate boosters sold fewer urban lots. The federal government took over the bankrupt Grand Trunk Pacific and Canadian Northern Railways and gradually cobbled them into the Canadian National Railways system, to the relief of the Prairie provincial governments, which had guaranteed $60.7 million in GTP and Canadian Northern bonds. More businesses failed between 1921 and 1923 than in any three-year period of the 1930s depression; among them was the Winnipeg-based Home Bank, whose 71 branches locked their doors in the faces of angry depositors in August 1923. The Home Bank had moved its head office to Manitoba from Quebec just before the war. Its collapse raised disturbing questions about the Prairie West as the 'Land of Golden Opportunity'.

Prairie cities never regained the momentum of the pre-1914 boom during the interwar period. The Winnipeg Board of Trade continued to open its meetings by chanting 'Winnipeg, Winnipeg, Gateway of the West/ Always growing greater, never growing less', but that optimism would have rung hollow to the thousands of unemployed war veterans seeking work. They signalled the beginning of a chronic urban unemployment problem throughout the region. With an occasional exception to prove the rule—for example, the automobile assembly plant that General Motors built in Regina in 1928 and the

Stoney Indians outside the Banff Springs Hotel, 1922. Established in 1885, Banff National Park followed the model of Yellowstone National Park in the United States. The federal government and the CPR co-operated to attract wealthy tourists to Banff, and colourfully costumed Plains Indians with full headdresses were part of the West that tourists expected to see reinvented for them. The Banff Springs Hotel evolved from the original building designed in 1886 by New York architect Bruce Price, and continued the French château style that Price had initiated. 'It is perhaps ironic,' writes architectural historian Janet Wright, 'that this exotic architectural type, . . . interpreted by an American architect, should have emerged in the popular imagination as typically Canadian' ('Fit for a King', *Horizon Canada* 5 [1987], 2048-52). Harry Pollard photo. PAA P.81.

Winnipeg garment industry—the Prairie West's urban industrial economy remained closely linked to agriculture. Winnipeg had its

Saskatchewan's Premier J.G. Gardiner and his children with the family auto in Banff National Park, 1928. The automobile triumphed over the train for personal transportation. The new 'car culture' became a largely masculine preserve. SAB RA-6029.

own special problems. The General Strike, grumbled its élite, had drawn a 'red circle' around the city and discouraged investment. The opening of the Panama Canal meant that wheat from Alberta and western Saskatchewan could be shipped west by rail and exported to Europe by sea. Thus it was Vancouver, rather than any Prairie city, that reaped the benefits of investment in grain-handling infrastructure. Branch offices of Montreal- 'or Toronto-based companies dominated Prairie cities, branch offices run by managers whose career paths would eventually lead them to Central Canada. Such men lacked the 'booster' zeal that had once united Prairie urban élites.[9]

The evolution of professional hockey illustrates the economic predicament of Prairie cities. Until 1927, professional teams from the West competed annually against teams from Central Canada's National Hockey League for the Stanley Cup, and cup finals became occasions for fervent expressions of regional identity. After the Canadiens de Montréal swept to victory over the Calgary Tigers, the *Calgary Herald* longed for a 'plainsman' champion to put 'the effete East' in its place, but Lord

Chevrolets on the line at the General Motors assembly plant in Regina, 1938. The short and troubled history of GM's Regina factory illustrates the perplexing path to economic diversity in the Prairie provinces. Opened in December 1928, the plant assembled Pontiacs and Chevies until the Depression forced it to close in August 1930. It was reopened in 1931 to take advantage of new high tariffs—probably the only Prairie industry to benefit from R.B. Bennett's protectionist policies. During the Second World War the plant produced munitions, but it closed for good in 1946. SAB R88,340.

Stanley's silverware spent more than six decades outside the Prairies. The NHL put franchises in Boston, New York, Detroit, and Chicago, cities where a single team could draw as many fans as all four Prairie teams in the Western Hockey League. Teams like the Saskatoon Sheiks and the Regina Capitals couldn't hope to match the salaries that NHL teams offered their star players. In 1926 the Edmonton Eskimos lost Eddie Shore, the Saskatchewan farm-boy who was the best defenceman in the game, to the Boston Bruins; the WHL didn't survive the year. By the end of the 1920s, every proud Prairie city had been reduced to minor-league status, its professional team a 'farm' for players waiting to be promoted to 'head office' in the NHL.[10]

For Prairie agriculture, the first half of the 1920s was a foretaste of the 1930s. International protectionism, best exemplified by the 1922 Fordney-McCumber tariff in the United States, impaired export trade. De-

The Saskatoon Sheiks and their mascot, 1927–28 season. During the inter-war period, Prairie cities were relegated to the minor leagues of sports, and of economic development in general. NAC PA-38585.

pressed grain prices coincided with drought in southwestern Saskatchewan and southeastern Alberta, the heart of the dry triangle that Captain John Palliser had reported and that expansionist optimism had denied. Thousands of families abandoned their farms in this dryland disaster: 'after toiling for eleven of the best years of our lives,' wrote one farmer to Saskatchewan's Premier W.M. Martin, 'my wife and my family find ourselves going up the road without the proverbial sack on my back.'[11] The total number of farms in the Prairie West actually decreased, from 256,000 in 1921 to 248,000 in 1926. Most of the families that evacuated the dry belt started over

again, however: over the next five years, 42,000 new farms were established, to make a total of 288,000 in 1931. The homesteaders' dream of independence refused to die. New generations clung to it throughout the agricultural crisis of the 1920s and even into the 1930s, long after any reasonable person—any 'rational economic actor', in economic historians' terms—would have realized that starting a farm was a bad business decision. For most families, the decision to remain on the land was not a 'business' decision at all.

The new farms were in the northern reaches of the park belt, in the Carrot River Valley of Saskatchewan, or in Alberta's Peace River coun-

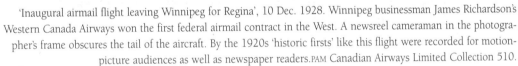

'Inaugural airmail flight leaving Winnipeg for Regina', 10 Dec. 1928. Winnipeg businessman James Richardson's Western Canada Airways won the first federal airmail contract in the West. A newsreel cameraman in the photographer's frame obscures the tail of the aircraft. By the 1920s 'historic firsts' like this flight were recorded for motion-picture audiences as well as newspaper readers.PAM Canadian Airways Limited Collection 510.

try. The overloaded wagons of migrating families pointed to the new direction of Canada's future, no longer west but north. In the 1920s, the economic frontier of the 'last, best West' moved from the prairie and park belt to the Precambrian Shield. The airplane facilitated the exploitation of northern resources. Each Prairie province can claim at least one aviation milestone: Alberta, Canada's first air transport company, incorporated in Edmonton in May 1919 by W.R. 'Wop' May; Saskatchewan, Canada's first licensed pilot, Regina's Roland Groome, in July 1920; Manitoba, the first commercial flight into Canada's North, Frank Ellis's trip from

Winnipeg to The Pas in October 1920. Railways remained indispensable to industrial development, however: the CNR built a line north into the Peace River country, and the long-sought Hudson Bay Railway to the northern Manitoba port of Churchill was completed in April 1929. Manitoba found US investors eager to extract resources from its piece of the Shield: a New York company mined and smelted the copper and gold deposits at Flin Flon, on the Manitoba–Saskatchewan border, and the American-owned Manitoba Pulp and Paper Company made newsprint at Pine Falls. Electricity generated by northern rivers pow-

The Manitoba Pulp and Paper Company, Pine Falls, 1927. When this US-owned paper mill was opened in 1926, the natural resources of the Prairie West were still administered by the federal government. It seems a cruel irony that the Prairie provinces negotiated the right to manage those resources themselves in 1930, the year that the Great Depression devastated resource prices, deferring investment for two decades. PAM Foote Collection 744.

ered these new industries as well as cities such as Winnipeg, making coal the fuel of the past. More than 200 coal mines continued to operate across the Prairie West, but the Alberta Coal Commission reported in 1925 that the province's mines were producing barely half their potential output, leaving miners under-employed or out of work altogether. Alberta had plenty of the fuel of the future: in October 1924, Royalite No. 4 gushed out of the Turner Valley, the first of more than a hundred wells that were to make the province Canada's lead-ing oil producer. Calgarians called the valley 'Hell's Half Acre' because the sky to the south was so often lit up by flames as unused natural gas was burned off. The pyrotechnics notwith-standing, the Alberta oil and gas industry was far from export markets, and several decades away from providing any major economic stim-ulus to the provincial economy.[12]

Despite economic difficulties, and over nativist opposition, the flow of immigrants that had been cut off by the war resumed in the mid-1920s. The sources of the flow had

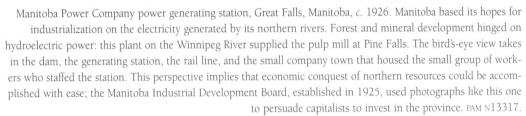

Manitoba Power Company power generating station, Great Falls, Manitoba, *c.* 1926. Manitoba based its hopes for industrialization on the electricity generated by its northern rivers. Forest and mineral development hinged on hydroelectric power: this plant on the Winnipeg River supplied the pulp mill at Pine Falls. The bird's-eye view takes in the dam, the generating station, the rail line, and the small company town that housed the small group of workers who staffed the station. This perspective implies that economic conquest of northern resources could be accomplished with ease; the Manitoba Industrial Development Board, established in 1925, used photographs like this one to persuade capitalists to invest in the province. PAM N13317.

shifted, however: many fewer migrants came from Britain, and very few from the United States, while a majority came from Central and Eastern Europe. Shut out of the United States by a quota system introduced in 1924, they once again made Canada their land of second choice. In deference to nativist opinion, the Canadian government designated Central and Eastern European migrants 'non-preferred'.

But corporate greed had more influence in Ottawa than citizen prejudice: the government allowed the Canadian Pacific and Canadian National railways to recruit immigrants in Europe without the supervision of the federal Department of Immigration and Colonization. Most of the newcomers transported to western Canada by the railways—Poles, Ukrainians, Mennonites, Czechs, German-Russians,

A Polish family harvesting potatoes on their Manitoba farm, *c.* 1928. Canadian National Railways photographers took thousands of such photographs to demonstrate the economic success of the 'non-preferred' immigrants that the railway company illegally recruited in Eastern Europe: Poles, Ukrainians, Mennonites, Czechs, German-Russians, Hungarians. NAC C-16926.

Hungarians—went to the Prairie West, to do pick-and-shovel work in the resource industries, to harvest grain, and to start small farms on quarter-sections purchased on time from the railway companies.[13]

Ethnicity remained a deep social cleavage despite the tentative attempts of the Farmer's Union and the wheat pools to construct cooperative bridges across ethnic barriers. The Saskatchewan Pool recruited in German, Ukrainian, French, and Hungarian, but the proportions of farmers from ethnic minorities who signed up remained low because relatively few of them were commercial grain growers with wheat crops to market. The farmers' political parties were slightly more willing to nominate candidates from ethnic minorities than were the Liberals, and much more so than the Conservatives: every history of Ukrainians in Canada records the name of the first Ukrainian-Canadian MP, Michael Luchkovich, elected as a United Farmers of Alberta candidate in

'A building bee helping Teodor Chruszcz', Athabasca district, Alberta, *c.* 1930. This family of Ukrainian immigrants, helped by their neighbours, worked together to carve a pioneer farm out of the northern fringe of the park belt. Families like this one lived near-peasant lives, breaking with oxen and harvesting with cradles, at a time when large-scale grain growers were buying the first gasoline tractors and combine harvesters. Families continued to build new farms even into the 1930s. The dream of an independent life on the land took many decades to die. CNR photo. NAC C-24880.

Vegreville in the 1926 federal election. But the farmers' movement was not immune to the nativism prevalent among other English-speaking Westerners. Ukrainian-Canadian pool organizer John Stratychuk endured taunts of 'bohunk' and 'goddamn foreigner' when he spoke at pool meetings in British-Canadian districts in Saskatchewan.[14]

Ethnic diversity made the Prairie West polyglot, but it could not make it pluralistic. In Saskatchewan, the Ku Klux Klan flourished briefly by linking racism and anti-Catholicism with regional resentment of an immigration policy made by large corporations in Central Canada. To counter the nativists, the CPR cynically tried to sell the concept of a 'Canadian mosaic' by sponsoring a series of ethnic festivals. But English-Canadian Westerners would have none of it. They remained determined to force the newcomers into the mould of Anglo-

Ukrainian Farmer's Co-op, Fisher Branch, Manitoba, *c.* 1940. The values of the 'moral economy' associated with rural communities lived on in the co-operative institutions that they built together. PAM N5590.

The cover of the newspaper of the Saskatchewan Ku Klux Klan, 1929. The Klan migrated from the United States in the 1920s and adapted easily to Saskatchewan and Alberta. The Union Jack replaced the Stars and Stripes, and French Canadians and Catholic immigrants replaced African Americans as the 'other' against whom 'Canadianism' had to be defended. In 1930, the hooded 'Knights of the Invisible Empire' marched in the streets of Regina to celebrate the defeat of the Liberal government, which they blamed for the 'Bohunk invasion' of immigrants from Eastern Europe. The Conservatives closed the gates to immigrants that summer, and by the mid-1930s the Klan had vanished as fast as it had sprung up. SAB R-A 6901.

conformity: a multicultural 'mosaic' in which minority ethnic groups would preserve their languages and cultures remained the farthest thing from their minds. Non-English-speaking immigrants were made painfully aware that their languages and cultures were to be shed as rapidly as possible. The public schools, made unilingual and compulsory during the war, were charged with the task of 'Canadianization': assimilation to the language and customs of the majority.[15]

Still immigrant ethnic identities persisted. But they were not static transplantations from the 'Old Country', they were identities relocated to, and reconstructed within, Western Canada. Ethnic minorities acculturated to English as necessary, but spoke their mother tongue at home: according to census reports, in Saskatchewan 70 per cent of Germans and more than 90 per cent of Ukrainians continued to do so in 1941. They married within their own communities, in their own churches, they belonged to ethnic fraternal societies, and they maintained distinctive residential and occupational patterns. Why did the minority ethnic identities crudely measured by these demographic characteristics persist in Canada's Prairie West longer than they did in the US West? Several explanations are compelling: the fact that in Canada most immigrants lived in rural areas; that they tended to settle in formal and informal 'blocks'; that wide-open immigration continued longer. Some historians suggest, in defiance of the evidence, that British-Canadian Westerners might have been less nativistic than Americans, and that they lacked a clearly defined Canadian identity for the newcomers to assimilate to. On the contrary, abundant oppression of and discrimination against immigrants by British Canadians seems to have done the opposite of what the assimilationists intended. Immigrants from Galicia and Bukovyna, for example, arrived

'CPR festival—June 1928—German settlers from St Andrews, Man.' The Canadian Pacific Railway attempted to defuse nativist reaction to immigration by promoting 'festivals' to celebrate what its public relations director, John Murray Gibbon, called the 'Canadian Mosaic'. As part of its publicity campaign, the railway hired Winnipeg's best commercial photographer, Lewis B. Foote, to photograph this German dance ensemble. L.B. Foote photo. PAM N1978.

with little sense of themselves as Ukrainians. Once they were in Canada, however, unilingual education, internment camps, and disenfranchisement helped the small Ukrainian nationalist intelligentsia to shape a national consciousness: it was in Western Canada, not Ukraine, that their struggles transformed them from peasants into Ukrainians. Eventually immigrant communities negotiated their own relationships with Canada and the dominant British-Canadian culture: Polish and Ukrainian dancers were featured in the official Manitoba celebration of the Coronation of King George VI in 1937. They demonstrated that being 'ethnic' did not preclude being 'Canadian', that identities were not simple either/or dichotomies. In the inter-war Prairie West, immigrants themselves were inventing the Canadian 'multicultural mosaic' three decades before governments discovered and sanctioned it.

The spectacular failure to assimilate immigrants demonstrated that the Prairie social reformers' projects were being derailed in the

'Nations', Smoky Lake, Alberta, *c.* 1935. The girls and boys riding the General Garage float in the Dominion Day parade in this Ukrainian-Canadian town northeast of Edmonton sported stereotyped costumes of a dozen national groups. Contrast this photograph with the cartoon on p. 75: these children represent a much more diverse Canada, which includes men and women and people of colour. Govinchuk photo. PAA G308.

1920s, and leaks in the prohibition dam provided further evidence. 'Moonshiners' made fiery grain alcohol without fear of the law: the Alberta Provincial Police estimated that only one still in ten was ever detected. Bootleggers sold the booze to local Prairie consumers, and 'rum-runners' ran 'hooch' into North Dakota and Montana aboard touring cars called 'Whiskey Sixes'. The immigrants that prohibition had been supposed to control instead seemed to control prohibition: in southern Saskatchewan, bootlegger Sam Bronfman quietly laid the foundations of his Seagram's empire, and in Coleman, Alberta, Florence Lessandro shot an APP constable as he struggled to subdue Emilio 'Mr Pick' Picariello, 'emperor' of the Crow's Nest Pass liquor trade. Prohibition, the *Winnipeg Tribune* complained, had attracted 'criminals of a desperate type' to the Prairie West, leading to a 'reign of lawlessness and criminality'. Legal liquor, urban businessmen argued, would attract tourists from the United States, trapped in national prohibition by constitutional amendment; Winnipeg, mused Mayor Ralph Webb, could advertise itself as 'the city of snowballs and highballs'. In referenda in 1923 and 1924, all the Prairie electorates voted their provinces 'wet' again. Rural British-Canadians remained faithful to the dry cause, but working-class and ethnic minority

A flag ceremony at a Saskatchewan school, 1920–22. The teacher who made this photograph, Robert England, taught for two years at Slawa School in rural Saskatchewan. England organized a Boy Scout troop to inculcate British-Canadian values into his pupils, the children of Ukrainian immigrants, whom England called 'Ruthenians' in the scrapbook in which this image was preserved. NAC-PA 127070.

voters were overwhelmingly wet. Like pre-war prosperity, however, the western barroom did not reappear: only government stores sold liquor, and in dingy parlours in hotels across the West, beer flowed from kegs to male customers in the bleakest surroundings imaginable.

The beer parlours were off-limits to women, and many Westerners would have been happy to say the same of public life in general. But there were notable political successes once women had the right to vote: in Calgary, women Labour candidates repeatedly won municipal office with the solid support of working-class women's votes, and they made a difference in city politics. Edith Rogers was

elected to the legislature in Manitoba, and in Saskatchewan Sarah Ramsland won office in a by-election as the widow of Liberal MLA Magnus Ramsland; both women were universally known by their husbands' initials—'Mrs R.A. Rogers' and 'Mrs M.O. Ramsland'—rather than their given names. The Alberta government appointed Emily Murphy and Alice Jameson as police magistrates, and Nellie McClung, Louise McKinney, and Irene Parlby all won legislative seats, McClung as a Liberal, McKinney for the Nonpartisan League, and Parlby as a United Farmer. With Emily Murphy and Henrietta Muir Edwards, McClung, McKinney, and Parlby added up to the 'famous five' plaintiffs in

The Women's Labor League, Winnipeg, 1922. Women's Labor Leagues (they rejected British spelling) sprang up across Canada amidst the working-class militancy that followed the First World War, pledging to support both women in the waged labour force and women in the home. They supported equal pay for equal work and campaigned for the eight-hour day. This group poses self-consciously with a relief bundle destined for the families of striking Cape Breton Island coal miners. Their solidarity with their Nova Scotia counterparts suggests that the 'limited identities' of gender and class transcended regional divisions. PAM N9343.

the 'Persons Case', a legal challenge to determine whether women were included among the 'persons' the British North America defined as eligible for appointment to the Canadian Senate. Their case went to the Judicial Committee of the British Privy Council in London, where in October 1929 their Lordships decided that all Canadian women were 'persons'. When the first woman senator was chosen, however, Prime Minister Mackenzie King deliberately snubbed the five in favour of an Ottawa society matron who was unconnected with the suffrage movement, but was the daughter and wife of Liberal MPs. 'Eastern women,' Murphy complained to McClung, seemed to dismiss the 'famous five' as 'coal-heavers and plough-pushers from Alberta'.[16]

With its mixture of regional feeling and middle-class condescension to working-class and farm women, Emily Murphy's comment

Mary Malofie feeding geese and chickens, Fisher Branch, Manitoba, June 1926. Girls and women on Prairie farms had important roles in the production process. Money earned from the poultry they raised and the cows they milked made up a significant proportion of the modest cash incomes of the majority of farm families, and usually gave them a say in the allocation of those resources. Malofie photo, PAM N5482.

suggests some of the issues that ultimately divided Prairie women. From city or country, from whatever class or ethnic background, women shared a gendered position as, in Nellie McClung's phrase, the 'unpaid servants of men'. Just as the discourse of the social reform movement assigned British-Canadian women the role of society's nurturers, nationalist males in ethnic minority communities assigned their wives, daughters, mothers, and grandmothers a special role as the conveyors of identity through language, food, music, and

dance; historian Frances Swyripa describes Ukrainian-Canadian women as literally 'wedded to the cause'. Beyond these commonalities, however, Prairie women were divided by large gulfs of class and ethnicity. A Calgary women's group's proposal that the Alberta government establish residential schools to teach Ukrainian girls to keep house to English-Canadian standards suggests the width of those gulfs. All women in farm families milked cows and fed chickens, but few if any English-Canadian farm wives ever had to scatter

The 'Dust Bowl' south of Regina in the 1930s. The Saskatchewan Wheat Pool commissioned photographs like this one to dramatize the scarcely believable drought conditions in 'Palliser's Triangle'. Sent to observe the situation first-hand, Minister of Labour Gideon Robertson reported to Prime Minister R.B. Bennett: 'One could never believe the desolation in southern Saskatchewan did he not see it himself. The whole country for more than one hundred miles in extent . . . is a barren drifting desert' (NAC, Bennett Papers, 1 July 1931, vol. 778). SAB R-A 15077-1.

lumps of manure by hand over fields that they had plowed themselves, as Ukrainian women sometimes did. English-Canadian feminists sincerely felt strong bonds with their immigrant sisters, but much of their agenda was not relevant outside their own ethnic constituency. Still, like other Westerners, Prairie feminists dreamed. 'Through co-operative effort we envisaged a new Heaven and a new earth . . . with our neighbours and friends in Saskatchewan and Manitoba,' remembered Susan Margaret Gunn, president of the United Farm Women of Alberta. 'Then along came the devastating thirties and we were flat on our backs.'[17]

The Great Depression erased the fragments of the Western dream that had survived the 1920s. Canada was the country hardest hit by the international economic collapse, and the Prairie West was the hardest-hit region of Canada. Images of blowing dust and gritty families fleeing drought in battered Fords will forever define the 1930s in public memory. In fact, though, the true 'Dust Bowl' was largely confined to Captain Palliser's infamous triangle, and half the wheat crops of the 1930s were above average. The Prairie West's problem was not so much ecological disaster as price deflation: a bushel of wheat that had earned a farmer $1.27 in 1928 was worth thirty cents in 1932. Families gave up on farms in the drought areas, but they didn't give up on farming: farms in the Prairie West increased by 12,000 between 1931 and 1936. People stayed on the farm because the rest of the economy was in such desperate condition. Half the

The Daynaka family moving north to a new farm, Edmonton, May 1933. Glenbow ND-3-6434.

urban population of the Prairie West was on unemployment relief at some time during the 1930s, and in the countryside farm wagons lined up at railway sidings to receive free windfall apples from Ontario and salt cod from the Maritimes. 'No one will starve,' promised Premier J.T.M. Anderson of Saskatchewan; but, significantly, that was all he promised.[18]

R.B. Bennett, the Conservative prime minister whose term coincided with this crisis, was a Calgary lawyer who had made millions during the Western boom. In 1930, Bennett's government hiked the protective tariff, cut off immigration, voted to assist the provinces with relief payments, and waited for business to improve. When it did not, he offered more of the same in 1931, 1932, and 1933, and when Communist Party membership increased dra-

matically, Bennett promised 'to put the iron heel of ruthlessness on propaganda of that kind'. The Depression's most tragic victims, unemployed single men, became the Communist Party's greatest success and Bennett's greatest failure. Denied relief in the cities, the single unemployed beat their way across the West in empty boxcars, looking for work that didn't exist: the hungry, hollow-eyed faces beneath their peaked caps aroused near panic in some respectable citizens. The government isolated the men in relief camps as far as possible from cities and put them to work clearing bush and building roads for twenty cents a day and their meals.[19]

From their inception, the camps were rocked by protests. In Saskatchewan, for example, an RCMP inspector who fell from his horse

'Welcome to Nordegg [Alberta], Tim Buck', 1935. Communist Party of Canada general secretary Tim Buck toured the country in triumph after his release from Kingston Penitentiary, where he had been imprisoned under section 98 of the Criminal Code, which had made the CPC illegal. R.B. Bennett professed to believe that Buck was poised to overthrow his government. Glenbow NA-2635-93.

was dragged to death as he charged demonstrators. The Relief Camp Workers' Union (RCWU) organized by the Communist Party of Canada co-ordinated such spontaneous outbreaks into a concerted campaign against the work-camp system. In 1935 the RCWU led campers from Western Canada on what became known as the 'On to Ottawa' trek to demand 'work and wages' from the government: 1,800 of them had rolled into Saskatchewan on top of 100 boxcars when the RCMP was ordered to halt the trek at Regina. On the evening of 1 July, as the trek leaders addressed a rally in Market Square, police whistles

shrilled at the fringes of the crowd: from four furniture vans, steel-helmeted constables rushed into the square, 'waving baseball bat batons overhead'. The trekkers fought back with sticks, rocks, and bottles from eight until midnight; when the 'Regina Riot' was over, the city was a shambles and a plainclothes policeman was dead. Thirty-nine trekkers and Regina citizens were treated for injuries, half of them gunshot wounds inflicted by police revolvers.

The Dominion Day bloodbath was a Pyrrhic victory for the Bennett government. The prime minister made a belated attempt to emulate US president Franklin Roosevelt's

'On-to-Ottawa' trekkers climb off a freight in Calgary, June 1935. The trekkers moved across the country with almost military discipline, and won the sympathy of every Prairie town and city in which they camped. But the discipline that won the hearts of ordinary citizens struck fear into those of R.B. Bennett and his cabinet. SAB RB-3485(1).

New Deal, introducing an unemployment insurance act and legislation to protect farmers from foreclosure, and reinstating the Canadian Wheat Board on a voluntary basis. But in the Prairie West, as elsewhere, the electorate swept the Conservatives from office in October 1935. They were replaced by Mackenzie King and the Liberal party, who closed the federal relief camps but whose only response to the continuing crisis was a Royal Commission on Dominion–Provincial Relations. As far as Prairie premiers were concerned, the federal–provincial crisis of the Great Depression was not about the constitution but about cash and how to provide it to unemployed workers and destitute farm families. The King government's distaste for state activism and its faith in the free market went beyond Bennett's: the Liberals even tried to abolish the newly re-established Wheat Board. They stopped only for fear of the political problems this would cause in the Prairie provinces, where the Liberals were being challenged by two new third parties: Social Credit and the Co-operative Commonwealth Federation.

As its name implied, the CCF was a Depression-induced federation of pre-existing farmer, labour, and socialist parties, among them the United Farmers of Alberta, the Saskatchewan Farmer–Labour Party, and the

Demonstration at Market Square before the 'Regina Riot', 1 July 1935. Most of the 1,800 trekkers were not party members, but their leaders made no secret of their communism. Communist Party sponsorship of this demonstration is suggested by the formalistic slogans and the high quality of the lettering on the banners. SAB R-A27560-1.

Independent Labour Party of Manitoba. The phrase 'co-operative commonwealth' dated from the 1880s, and had originally been given currency by the American Populist Henry Demarest Lloyd, but Winnipeg MP J.S. Woodsworth, the Federation's chairman, described the CCF as 'a distinctly Canadian type of socialism'. Never an exclusively Prairie movement, the CCF tried to cross boundaries of region, ethnicity, occupation, and gender. Its program, the 1933 'Regina Manifesto', echoed Marx only in its title. The manifesto promised that 'no CCF government will rest content until it has eradicated capitalism', but proposed to replace capitalism with democratic 'socialized planning' rather than proletarian revolution. Financial institutions, railways, and power companies would be nationalized, but the owners of the expropriated property would be compensated, not executed. The CCF promised an end to 'insane protectionist policies', a national labour code like that of the US New Deal, unemployment insurance, and universal health care.

CCFers were not the only ones who thought the movement's national prospects were good. The capitalist class was frightened and attacked viciously: students at Notre Dame College in Wilcox, Saskatchewan, were threatened with expulsion for CCF activity. One political economist seriously predicted that 'the CCF could probably within the decade force the Liberals and Conservatives into a permanent union.' But a movement including so many farmers should have known better than to measure the crop until the grain was in the bin. The party's Saskatchewan wing became the official opposition to Jimmy Gardiner's Liberal government in 1934, but despite winning 8.8 per cent of the national popular vote and 20 per cent of the vote in Manitoba and Saskatchewan, in the federal election of 1935 only seven CCFers, two each from Manitoba and Saskatchewan and three from BC were returned. In Alberta, where hopes had been highest, the CCF was crowded out by the only truly new party to capture a Canadian provincial capital during the 1930s.

The election of a Social Credit government in Alberta in August 1935 was the most sensational Canadian political event of the 1930s: a *New York Times* correspondent rushed to Edmonton and reported that 'bankers and businessmen . . . are scared.' The Depression alone does not explain the emergence of Social Credit, for Albertans had already turned away from the populist UFA before it began. Only a sixth of Alberta farm families still belonged to the UFA when it joined in the formation of the CCF, and Premier John Brownlee governed Alberta in direct contradiction to some of the social-democratic CCF principles that the UFA had endorsed. In the autumn of 1933, Brownlee was successfully sued for seduction by Vivian MacMillan, a junior provincial clerk; the scandalous trial

CCF picnic poster, July 1939. The CCF expounded its message of 'Humanity First' within the context of long-standing community traditions of agrarian political insurgency. The picnic, softball tournament, and dance were as important to rural people as the speeches by CCF luminaries. As the Second World War loomed on the horizon, CCFers were eager to pass the test of loyalty, as the Union Jack and 'God Save the King' suggest. Glenbow NA 2629-10.

doomed the premier and his government and created a political vacuum in a province where Liberals and Conservatives were considered suspect.

Social Credit was a plan drafted by a Scottish engineer named Major C.H. Douglas to reform capitalism according to what he called the 'A plus B Theorem'. 'A' represented what producers earned and 'B' stood for the cost of materials, bank charges, and other expenses; since 'A plus B' equalled the total cost of all goods produced, and since the producers received only 'A' as income, they would never have enough money to consume everything they made. To avoid depression, government had to wrest control of the financial system from bankers and place it in public hands; other property would remain private. The government would then set 'just prices' for all goods to avoid inflation and issue a 'national dividend' to citizens, who would be required to spend it to maintain consumption. Social Credit found its first Prairie audience in the Progressive MPs William Irvine and Henry Spencer; the man who peddled it to Albertans, however, was a portly evangelist named William Aberhart. Principal of a Calgary high school, Aberhart was also the president and radio spokesman of the Calgary Prophetic Bible Institute. His Sunday radio broadcast on CFCN had a higher rating than even comedian Jack Benny; an estimated 300,000 listeners tuned in. Aberhart preached dispensationalism, a theology that was critical of the Social Gospel: 'God never intended us to reform the world,' he liked to say. But when a colleague gave him a Social-Credit-made-simple book in July 1932, he became an overnight convert. Aberhart injected Social Credit into his radio sermons with catchy phrases like 'poverty in the midst of plenty', and soon won a larger congregation of the airwaves. Aberhart's disciples Edith Rogers and Ernest Manning wove a web of Social Credit study groups around Alberta, with the Prophetic Bible Institute at its centre.

Aberhart at first aimed to persuade the UFA to adopt Social Credit, and many among the UFA rank and file were willing. But its leaders were not. To rid itself of this nuisance, the UFA invited Major Douglas to Alberta in 1934 so that he could point out Aberhart's errors. The error was theirs, for the public preferred Aberhart's Social Credit to the genuine article. Whereas Douglas answered questions with theoretical digressions, Aberhart simply promised that every adult would receive $25 a month, with larger amounts for the handicapped. Frustrated by the UFA leaders' obduracy, Aberhart turned the Social Credit study circles into a political movement. Election rallies were picnics followed by revival meetings: after a martial hymn, Aberhart would blast the 'Fifty Big Shots' who in his view controlled the financial system. His platform was progressive, calling not simply for Social Credit but for a 'new social order', with educational reform, aid to agricultural co-operatives, state-supported medical care, and occupational health and safety legislation. No woman in Alberta would have to depend on a man for a 'meal ticket'; instead, women would be 'uplifted and made more independent'. Although he held 'no brief for our present capitalist system', Aberhart made it clear that traditional socialism was not the answer: Social Credit had 'all the advantages of Socialism, but eliminates its drawbacks'.[20] A record turnout of voters from the country, the cities, and the mining towns rolled up a Social Credit avalanche: 56 of the 63 seats, with 54 per cent of the popular vote.

During his first eighteen months in power, Aberhart caused the Mackenzie King government little trouble, for he did nothing to establish Social Credit. 'Seventy-five per cent of those who voted for me don't expect any dividend,' he told the *New York Times*, 'but hope for a just and honest government.' He provided exactly that: an increased minimum wage, educational reform, more generous relief, and aid to the co-op movement. As one Albertan wrote to the premier, 'You and the government have done more for the poor classes than any government of the past.' When Alberta legislated to reduce the interest on private debts and defaulted on a provincial loan, the *Financial Post* sputtered that the province was in 'the early stages of the Russian revolution'. But in fact Aberhart's only real concession to Social Credit purists was to issue $250,000 in 'prosperity certificates' to civil servants as part of their wages; when merchants refused to accept the 'funny money', the certificates were withdrawn.

Faced with a back-bench revolt among his MLAS, Aberhart began to reaffirm Social Credit's radical purpose. In 1937, the Credit of Alberta Regulation Act placed the banks under directors appointed by a Social Credit Board so that their credit policies would be shaped to suit Alberta producers. The Bank Employees Civil Rights Act made it illegal for bankers to take civil action against the province, and an amendment to the Judicature Act made it illegal to challenge the validity of provincial laws in court. To the consternation of Aberhart and his cabinet, the federal government swiftly disallowed this legislation. Aberhart chastised Prime Minister King for listening to 'plutocratic bankers' instead of 'democratic Albertans . . . seeking their economic freedom'. With a few cosmetic changes he re-introduced the legislation, along with the Accurate News and Information Act requiring newspapers to publish official refutations of stories critical of Social Credit policies. But Lieutenant-Governor J.C. Bowen refused to sign these bills, reserving

Premier William Aberhart on the platform, Calgary, August 1936. Social Credit, like the CCF, presented its message at picnics, wrapped its platforms in Union Jacks, and inherited a radical agrarian tradition. But Aberhart's acolyte Ernest Manning (sitting in the background) appropriated his mentor's movement in the 1940s for anti-progressive politics. Glenbow NB-16-206.

them for federal scrutiny, and after reference to the Supreme Court they were ruled *ultra vires* of the province.

Between 1937 and 1941 eight more Alberta statutes were introduced that would restrict foreclosures or reduce the interest rate on debts: all were disallowed. This swift federal action to crush threats to financial institutions stood in sharp contrast to Ottawa's unwillingness to deal with the economic crisis that had been crushing the Prairie West since 1930. At a public meeting to protest the disallowances, one voice in the angry crowd went so far as to shout 'give us a gun,' and there

Let's Be Calm

Arch Dale, 'Let's Be Calm', *Winnipeg Free Press,* 9 Jan. 1937. Cartoonist Arch Dale mixes metaphors as 'Roman' fireman John Bracken, the premier of Manitoba, attempts to arouse Emperor Nero—federal Finance Minister C.A. Dunning—to respond to the 1930s crisis in Western Canada. Western political leaders of all parties unsuccessfully sought national solutions to the Depression, and called repeatedly for the federal government to take more responsibility for the economic crisis. PAM N203.

were calls for secession. But Aberhart sternly warned that he would have 'none of that. . . . We have no desire to leave the home of our forefathers.' Instead, he pursued his struggle with Ottawa through such petty gestures as taking away Lieutenant-Governor Bowen's automobile, chauffeur, and secretary. Aberhart's impotence doomed Social Credit's imme-

Queen Elizabeth accepts flowers while William Aberhart looks on, Edmonton, 2 June 1939. An ardent anglophile and a British-Canadian nationalist, Aberhart wanted his own granddaughter to present flowers to the Queen when the Royal Tour reached Alberta. Prime Minister Mackenzie King (looking on smiling on the right) and the federally appointed lieutenant-governor, J.C. Bowen, Aberhart's bitter enemies, insisted that Dorothy Stacey, an Edmonton orphan, make the presentation. PAA Bl.473/3a.

diate plans to expand to the other Western provinces, and eased Mackenzie King's fears of 'a Social Credit empire . . . from the Great Lakes to the Pacific'. Within Alberta, however, the federal disallowances added another verse to the litany of regional grievances and helped to elect Social Credit governments long after the party's early radicalism had faded.[21]

The stunted policy initiatives of the Bennett and King governments in Ottawa played a minimal role in putting the Prairie West back on its economic feet. The Prairie Farm Rehabilitation Administration, set up by the Conservatives and gradually expanded by the Liberals, did its most effective work in the 1940s, after the Depression was over. Federal rural relief programs—or rather the provincial relief programs that the federal government partially financed—were no different from those offered to drought-stricken areas after the First World War. The Farmers' Creditors Arrangements Act of 1934 was introduced to forestall more radical action from the provinces, and it helped large national financial institutions at the expense of local unsecured creditors. Comparing the policies of Canadian governments with what the US New Deal did for the American West—and many Prairie Westerners of the 1930s did exactly that—demonstrated Ottawa's abject failure. Yet Westerners, however alienated, remained proud Canadians. 'I am Canadian born,' William Aberhart replied to the fringe that talked of Western secession; 'I have gradually imbibed that Canadian courage that impels us to stand for right no matter what happens.'[22]

CHAPTER SEVEN

Prairie Canada Recast: 1940–1971

$\mathcal{T}$he First World War had exacerbated class and ethnic divisions within the Prairie West and intensified a regional sense of distinctiveness within Canada. In sharp contrast, the six war years from 1939 to 1945 muted class and ethnic conflict and consolidated the Prairie West within Confederation. Government spending on the war effort gradually brought an end to the Great Depression. The Prairie militia units had been weakened by the economic crisis: in June 1939, as the King and Queen were escorted through one Western city by cavalry mounted on horses borrowed from a local dairy, each trooper rode in fear that someone in the crowd might shout 'MILK!' and halt his horse in its tracks.[1] But the tens of thousands of men and women who were still unemployed when war began in September faced the prospect of another hard winter, and military service offered a steady job. Prairie regiments quickly filled waiting lists with would-be recruits; some of those who eventually enlisted got their first decent suit of clothes from an army, navy, or air force quartermaster.

Mobilization stimulated the economies both of Prairie cities and of those small towns lucky enough to be close to training bases like Camp Shilo, north of Brandon, Manitoba. The British Commonwealth Air Training Program, which Canada enthusiastically welcomed, not only prepared pilots, gunners, and navigators at thirty-eight schools across the Prairies; it also provided thousands of jobs building airfields, hangars, and barracks, and looking after the trainees' needs. Today, museums in all three provinces remember the BCATP with grateful nostalgia. Edmonton, whose civic boosters had long billed their city as the 'Gateway to the North', suddenly found their boast made real when the United States plunged into the war in earnest in 1942. US personnel turned the Alberta capital into the administrative hub for construction of the Alaska Highway and the Canol oil pipeline project, and made it the most important stop on the Northwest Staging Route, the chain of airfields leading north to Alaska. Five flights a minute took off from Edmonton's Blatchford Field, which became the busiest airport in North America—so busy that the United States spent $7 million to construct a new airport at Namao, 16 kilometres north of the city.

Naval recruits parade in Edmonton, April 1943. One legend of Prairie history insists that the region provided disproportionate numbers of Canada's Second World War sailors. Survey histories of all three provinces restate the claim. John Archer writes of the 'surprisingly large contribution' Saskatchewan made to the Royal Canadian Navy (*Saskatchewan*, 249), and W.L. Morton asserts that 'the naval depot in Winnipeg, HMCS *Chippewa*, was swamped with the prairie lads who were drawn to the seas' (*Manitoba*, 444); James G. MacGregor is more circumspect, claiming only that 'scores of young prairie boys went to sea . . . on the cruel wintry Atlantic' (*A History of Alberta*, 277). Evidence contradicts the saga of disproportionate numbers of Prairie sea dogs; the largest absolute number of Prairie recruits became infantrymen, and it was the more glamorous Royal Canadian Air Force that attracted a disproportionate number of Prairie volunteers. Alfred Blyth photo. PAA Bl.525/1.

But although the war prompted an industrial boom in Central Canada, relatively little war-related manufacturing took place in the Prairie West despite incessant lobbying by the business élites of Winnipeg and Edmonton. The Prairie urban industrial economy remained stunted in 1946, just as it had been after the First World War.[2]

The impact of the Second World War on the Prairie West nonetheless differed profoundly from that of the First. The nativist outburst of 1914 did not recur in 1940, and nativist demands that all 'enemy aliens' be locked up failed to rally broad support from either public or government in the Prairie provinces. Hitler, Mussolini, Nazism, and

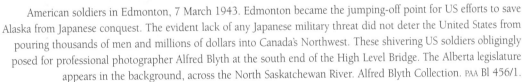

American soldiers in Edmonton, 7 March 1943. Edmonton became the jumping-off point for US efforts to save Alaska from Japanese conquest. The evident lack of any Japanese military threat did not deter the United States from pouring thousands of men and millions of dollars into Canada's Northwest. These shivering US soldiers obligingly posed for professional photographer Alfred Blyth at the south end of the High Level Bridge. The Alberta legislature appears in the background, across the North Saskatchewan River. Alfred Blyth Collection. PAA Bl 456/1.

Fascism were to blame for war, not German- or Italian-Canadians. German-Canadians in the 1940s were over 90 per cent Canadian-born and diffused among many different religious groups, virtually all of them hostile to Hitler and anxious to profess their loyalty to Canada. The small Italian community in the Prairie West was similarly anti-Fascist. Incidents did occur: Calgary's nativist mayor dismissed twenty-four Italian-born municipal workers in 1940. But the city hired them back two weeks later because there was no one else to operate the water and sewer systems. Ukrainian-Canadians were no longer seen as subjects of an enemy empire. The federal government exploited their intra-ethnic divisions to win support for the war, courting the nationalist Ukrainian Canadian Committee and repressing Ukrainian communists; the UCC went so far as to endorse a 'yes' vote in the 1942 national plebiscite on conscription. And even when two Alberta rural constituencies with large

Mechanics at No. 2 Air Observers School, Edmonton, 1943. The British Commonwealth Air Training Program provided opportunities outside the domestic sphere for Prairie women just as it did for men. The smiling, well-coiffed mechanic in the foreground was posed to reassure readers that working in a traditionally male skilled trade would not make a woman unfeminine, and to imply that women would return to their proper sphere at war's end. Alfred Blyth Collection. PAA Bl. 529/1.

Ukrainian populations departed from the pattern of Prairie unanimity and voted 'no', their audacity brought no reprisals from their English-speaking neighbours.[3]

The ethnic diversity of the Prairie people who volunteered as soldiers, sailors, airmen, and airwomen pointed to the change in the ethnic environment. In 1944 Pilot Officer Andrew Mynarski of Manitoba was awarded the Victoria Cross. Ukrainian-Canadians made up a tenth of the Winnipeg Grenadiers' garrison decimated by the Japanese at Hong Kong in December 1941, and one Ukrainian-language newspaper headline shouted 'Vidomstit [Avenge] Hong Kong'. There were so many Slavic soldiers that jokes suggested renaming a Manitoba Scottish regiment the Queen's Own Ukrainian Highlanders; no one laughed when they were slaughtered on the beaches of Dieppe in August 1942. 'These young men have with their blood purchased and guaranteed for us a permanent place of equality in this nation,'

Celebrating V-J Day in Smoky Lake, Alberta, 15 Aug. 1945. The Second World War speeded the integration of European ethnic minorities into the Prairie mainstream, in terms of outlook as well as material life. By 1945, these Ukrainian-Canadian children self-consciously waving Union Jacks and US flags did not appear discernibly different from their British-Canadian counterparts in other Prairie small towns. Gavinchuk photo. PAA G.1293.

promised Alberta Social Credit MP Anthony Hlynka. What historian Peter Melnycky says of Ukrainian-Canadians could be extended to other ethnic minorities: the war became 'a crucible in which Ukrainians continued to forge the character of their identity within Canada . . . , an experience which they shared with their fellow Canadians, yet to which they brought their own particular perspective.'[4]

Japanese-Canadians were denied entry to the wartime patriotic consensus. At the behest of white British Columbians, the Mackenzie King government interned 22,000 of them in 1942, separating men from women and children. Four thousand Japanese-Canadians kept their families together by agreeing to become indentured farm workers in the sugar-beet fields of Alberta and Manitoba. Most did not return to the Pacific coast when the war was over. The uprooting of Japanese-Canadians was assimilation's most conspicuous success, and whatever the scale used to measure ethnic integration—language retention, residential and occupational segregation, marriage patterns—

'A Japanese evacuee family, Dominion City, Manitoba', 1946. With the original caption above, this photo was used by the Department of Labour to show that Japanese-Canadian families paroled from the British Columbia internment camps were happy and prosperous on the prairies. The original caption continues: 'Mr. and Mrs. Yoshiya Fujita and family. . . . They are engaged in [sugar] beet work, but in winter time Mr. Fujita and one son go to the bush while other son works in a local garage and drives his own car.' NAC C45103.

all but two minorities became more a part of the Prairie mainstream after 1945. The Hutterites were significant exceptions to this trend towards integration. Pacifist Anabaptists, they refused any compromise with the war, and their successful communal farms scattered across Manitoba and southern Alberta made inviting targets for nativists. War legitimated the prejudices of peacetime: in Alberta, the Land Sales Prohibition Act officially limited

Hutterite expansion, but only increased the Hutterites' separation from their neighbours.

Although Native people had made substantial contributions to the war effort, they too continued to defy integration into Euro-Canadian society. About a third of the Native men eligible for military service enlisted; one Cree recruit from Saskatchewan explained to a British journalist that he had volunteered because his great-grandfather Mistawasis had

Hutterite schoolchildren, Stand Off, Alberta, 1971. Despite discriminatory legislation that hemmed in their colonies, the Hutterites have maintained their traditional political and social structures. Provincial governments require compulsory education using standard provincial curricula, but this has not eroded the Hutterites' ability to socialize new generations to their values, based on the principle of 'all things common'. Ed Spitieri photo. NAC PA 131086.

made an alliance with Queen Victoria in the 1870s. Because virtually all of them became infantrymen, their casualty rates were higher than those for the forces as a whole. Indian reserves, the poorest communities in the Prairie West, contributed to war charities: the Moose Lake Band of Manitoba donated furs worth $3,000 to the Red Cross. Such sacrifices shamed Parliament into a post-war reconsideration of Canada's Indian policy. A special committee heard forceful testimony from recently formed Native associations from Alberta, Saskatchewan, and Manitoba. In 1951 the government revised the Indian Act to repeal prohibitions against ceremonies and dances, and to grant bands greater administrative autonomy, including the right to spend band money on lawsuits to advance land claims. The explicit goal of Indian policy remained assimilation, but these amendments permitted Native people to develop new means of resistance, which they would use adeptly.[5]

'Cree children, members of the Lac La Ronge First Nation, at an Anglican Church Mission School', Saskatchewan, March 1945. Compare the caption above, which accompanied this image on display at the National Archives of Canada in 1996, with the text that originally accompanied the photograph: 'Sons and daughters of the Cree Indian trappers learn their "ABCs". . . . One of the largest of such schools in Canada, the boys and girls there are given an opportunity to study and take their places in a kind of life not otherwise possible.' Bud Glunz photo. NAC PA-134110.

Unlike the First World War, which had stimulated a wheat boom, the Second World War stimulated diversification and extensive federal intervention in agriculture. German tanks had conquered Canada's European wheat customers, so that, by 1941, 750,000 unsold bushels were crammed into Canadian elevators and the price hovered around 74 cents a bushel. Offered $4 an acre by the federal government to sow feed grains instead, farmers nearly halved their wheat acreage and doubled that sown to barley, oats, and rye. Much of this feed grain nourished 'pigs for Britain': between 1939 and 1943, the number of hogs on Prairie farms quadrupled to 4.5 million. Beef production increased more gradually because cattle took longer to raise, but regional diversification into cattle would have long-term significance when the US markets re-opened in 1945 and, with the end of rationing, domestic consumers began clamouring for beef. Wartime demand also brought

Threshing in Manitoba, 1948. There are surprisingly few close-ups like this one of farmers feeding sheaves into a small threshing machine. During the 1950s and 1960s, swathers and combines supplanted stooking and threshing machines. WCPI AO214-06836.

the modern specialized commercial dairy farm to the Prairies, while wartime restrictions on imports created captive domestic markets for beet sugar and oilseeds. Farmers in southern Manitoba joined the established growers of southern Alberta in planting beets during the war; in 1946, the federal government guaranteed Prairie beet producers the regional sugar market. Federal government price incentives similarly expanded production of sunflowers and flax, and initiated the production of rapeseed (renamed 'canola' in the 1980s to make it more palatable to consumers).

Some of this diversification was reversed when wheat markets reopened after the war, but Prairie agriculture never returned to its former near-complete reliance on the wheat crop. To use a metaphor much favoured by those who had unsuccessfully pleaded the case for diversified agriculture between 1900 and 1939, no more would the region's eggs all be in one basket. Park belt farms diversified more than those on the southern plains, and Alberta and Manitoba more than Saskatchewan: in 1965–66, wheat represented 65 per cent of all farm sales in Saskatchewan, but only a quarter

of those in Alberta and a third of those in Manitoba. Nor were the newly diversified farms the
self-sufficient units advocated by the propo-
nents of mixed farming. The Prairie farm families who survived into the 1950s and 1960s
were commercial farmers, and their success was
usually directly proportional to the degree to
which they made their farms into businesses.

The farm labour force decreased sharply,
even though—in contrast to 1917–18—the
federal government honoured its promise to
exempt farmers' sons and hired hands from
conscription. They enlisted by the tens of
thousands anyway, and those who did not had
no trouble finding jobs off the farm. Most of
the young men and young women who left the
farm for work or war never returned: between
1941 and 1946, the farm population of the
Prairie provinces decreased by over 150,000
and the region experienced a net out-migration of 146,000. To make up for those who
had left, farmers used their improved incomes
to replace horses with tractors and trucks, and
binders and threshing machines with swathers
and combines; by 1946 over half of all the census farms in the Prairie provinces reported
tractors, and 15 per cent reported combines—
double and triple the respective 1936 figures.
And because the largest farms were the first to
adopt the new machines, these statistics actually underestimate the percentage of the total
acreage that was worked with tractors and
combines. Despite these capital investments in
machinery, steady incomes enabled Prairie
farmers to reduce their overall debt burden by
almost half between 1942 and 1947.[6]

By the end of the Second World War most
Prairie farmers had become advocates of an
active role for the federal government in agri-

culture. The Depression had cured the more
conservative, business-oriented farmers of
their antipathy to government intervention;
like most urban businessmen, they had come
to recognize that such intervention could be
very much in their interest. Most of them supported the federal government's decision in
September 1943 to close the Winnipeg Grain
Exchange and make the Wheat Board the sole
marketing agency for their crop. The radical
farmers who clung to the agrarian dream
soldiered on in the United Farmers of
Canada–Saskatchewan Section and the Alberta
Farmers' Union, whose membership was concentrated in the smaller farms of the park belt.
No longer satisfied with simply a marketing
board, now they wanted indexed, govern-
ment-guaranteed 'parity' prices for all agricultural products.

But wartime agricultural change hastened
the radicals' demise and solidified the claims of
the farmer-businessmen that they alone spoke
for the Prairie farm community. Federal government policies directed a disproportionate
share of the economic benefits of war to larger
farmers. The Wheat Acreage Reduction program paid subsidies by the acre, and the government imposed quotas on the number of
bushels a farmer could sell to the Wheat Board,
which disadvantaged smaller farmers. Between
1941 and 1946, 37,000 small farmers—almost
ten per cent of all Prairie farms—had gone out
of operation despite the improved economy
created by the war, and those who remained
faced an ominous future. In September and
October 1946, the farmer's unions played their
last card: a 'non-delivery' strike. Union farmers
refused to market grain, livestock, or milk until
the federal government took action towards the

Farmers picket the stockyards in Saskatoon, 27 Sept. 1946. Members of the United Farmers of Canada (Saskatchewan Section) block a road during the non-delivery strike to prevent non-union farmers from marketing cattle and hogs. The strike was a desperate and unsuccessful gamble for the UFC (SS), which by 1948 was moribund. During the 1950s, however, progressive agrarianism was reborn in the Saskatchewan Farmers' Union under the dynamic presidency of Joseph L. Phelps. SAB S-B829.

establishment of a parity pricing system. Grassroots support came from small farmers in the park belt of Alberta and Saskatchewan, but the strike had no impact in Manitoba. Denounced by the Canadian Federation of Agriculture and not endorsed by the wheat pools, it petered out inconclusively without forcing significant government concessions. The marginal producers petered out along with their strike; the censuses of 1951, 1956, and 1961 provide a grim record of their decline and the ascendancy of the mechanized commercial farmer-businessman.[7]

Small farms disappeared in every Prairie province during these decades despite the best efforts of Saskatchewan's Co-operative Commonwealth Federation government. Voters swept the social-democratic CCF into power in June 1944 with 53 per cent of the popular vote and all but five of the 52 seats in the legislature. The landslide grew out of unique circumstances in Saskatchewan—an agrarian critique of capitalism, a discredited Liberal government, and the bitter legacy of the 1930s—but the election represented much more than one-

T.C. Douglas inaugurates the Interprovincial oil pipeline, 23 Oct. 1950. By the time the Saskatchewan premier symbolically turned this valve to send crude oil east, he and his government had abandoned their vision of public development of provincial resources. SAB R-B289.

dimensional regional protest. In 1943, having won 39 of 90 provincial seats in Ontario and passed the Liberals and the Conservatives in a national Gallup poll, CCFers dreamed that Saskatchewan was only the first step in their electoral march towards a democratic socialist Canada. The CCF *Program for Saskatchewan* made clear that it was 'not constitutionally possible to set up a complete co-operative commonwealth within the boundaries of a single province', but Premier T.C. Douglas promised

to go as far as he could toward 'a planned type of economy for the Province', and an expanded provincial welfare state complete with 'socialized health services'.[8]

In its first term in office, Douglas's government established eleven Crown corporations ranging from provincial electric power, telephone, and insurance companies (which succeeded), to companies that manufactured shoes, bricks, leather, and woollens (which eventually were closed or privatized). After this initial flurry of activity, the CCF government backed away from public ownership and turned instead to co-operatives and regulation of private enterprise. The first recommendation of the Economic Planning and Advisory Board, set up to perform the central planning envisioned in the Regina Manifesto, was that the CCF government do more to encourage private investment. After 1951, the Industrial Development Fund assisted private capital and co-operative enterprise to develop the province's potash, petroleum, and natural gas. In effect the Saskatchewan CCF permitted private development of resources to earn revenue to finance the Douglas government's notable achievements in social legislation: the Farm Security Act, which protected the 'home quarter' of every farm from foreclosure; the Trade Union Act, which outlawed union-busting and guaranteed collective bargaining; educational reforms, which placed students in poor and wealthy school districts on an equal footing; and the Saskatchewan Hospital Plan, the first cautious step towards publicly funded health care for all. The CCF managed government prudently; Finance Minister Clarence Fines balanced sixteen consecutive provincial budgets. If the CCF failed to deliver a social revolution, it satisfied the people of Saskatchewan: the party won renewed mandates in 1948, 1952, 1956, and 1960.[9]

But the national breakthrough never came. In the 1945 federal election, the CCF won a plurality of the fragmented Prairie popular vote—34 per cent to the Liberals' 31, the Conservatives' 21, and Social Credit's 14—and its 23 Prairie MPs were the largest group from the region. But 18 of the CCFers were from Saskatchewan seats and five from Manitoba: the party elected only five MPs in the rest of the country, and none at all in Alberta, despite earning a fifth of the popular vote. Nor did the party capture another Prairie provincial government. In Manitoba the Liberal–Progressives soldiered on after John Bracken's 1942 defection to lead the national Tory party, renamed at his insistence the Progressive Conservatives. But under Bracken's successors Stuart Garson (1942–48) and D.L. Campbell (1948–58), the Liberal–Progressives governed Manitoba without a hint of progressivism. To keep the provincial CCF at bay, Garson formed a coalition with the Conservatives and refused electoral redistribution to reflect population changes. In the 1945 provincial election, the Liberal–Progressives won 25 seats with fewer popular votes than the CCF, which won only 10![10]

Canada's first-past-the-post electoral system also helped Social Credit to retain its hold on Alberta. In federal elections in 1945, 1949, 1953, and 1957, Social Credit candidates won 75 per cent of Alberta's seats with less than 40 per cent of the popular vote. The provincial Social Credit government was almost beaten in 1940 by a 'stop Aberhart' coalition of Liberals and Conservatives determined to undo the radical legislation of his first term. That radi-

Ernest Manning throws the first rock at the International Oilmen's Bonspiel, 13 April 1953. 'As thin as Aberhart was fat and as measured in tone as Aberhart was bombastic, [Manning] proved a success with [the business] community,' writes Alvin Finkel. When he was a member of Aberhart's cabinet, business people had regarded Manning as a moderate member of a government they distrusted as radical. In his quarter-century as Alberta's premier, Manning fulfilled the faith that the business community placed in him by consistently taking its side against labour (Finkel, *The Social Credit Phenomenon in Alberta*, 84). PAA PA 1628/2.

calism faded in the 1940s, however. Challenged on the left by the CCF, Aberhart took care to distinguish Social Credit from socialism; on Aberhart's death in 1943, his successor, Ernest Manning, eagerly led the party to the right of the political spectrum. Some Social

Leduc No. 1, 13 Feb. 1947. Imperial Oil, a subsidiary of Standard Oil of New Jersey, carefully stage-managed the 'spudding in' of its first well in the Leduc field. Imperial's Vernon Hunter prepared a special show for the crowd of reporters who looked on as the oil roared from the earth; on his signal, workers 'switched the flowing oil to the flare line and lit the fire, [and] the most beautiful smoke ring you ever saw went floating skywards' (Hunter quoted in MacGregor, *A History of Alberta*, 287). City of Edmonton Archives EA-10-3164.

Manning's small-c conservatism congenial; the *Financial Post*, which in 1935 had denounced the Social Creditors as Bolsheviks, now praised them for 'nine years of good government'. 'Our main objective should be to defeat the CCF,' explained an oil company executive who endorsed Social Credit. Manning obliged by attacking the socialists with the same fervour that his mentor had directed against financiers. The strategy succeeded. In seven Alberta elections from 1944 to 1967, Manning's party averaged 51 per cent of the popular vote and over 80 per cent of the legislative seats.[11]

Oil wealth greased the political path for Social Credit. Alberta's petroleum potential had long been understood, but new discoveries dwarfed the oil booms of the 1910s and 1920s. On 13 February 1947, Imperial Oil assembled reporters just south of Edmonton to watch the gusher from its Leduc No. 1 well illuminate the winter twilight. The Leduc-Woodbend field sprouted 1,277 more wells, but the Redwater field soon overshadowed Leduc, and both were rapidly eclipsed by the Pembina field; by 1953 a ring of wells encircled the provincial capital. The timing could not have been better: Alberta's oil gushed in as the Canadian and US economies entered a long period of post-war expansion that would be dependent on fossil fuels. Even the natural gas that had once been burned off as a nuisance joined oil as exportable energy to be transported east and south by pipeline. But it was foreign capital, most of it American, that piped the gas and pumped the oil: wholly owned subsidiaries of the 'seven sisters' of the international oil cartel: Standard Oil of New Jersey, of New York, and of California (later Exxon, Mobil, and Chevron), Gulf, Texaco, Royal Dutch Shell,

Creditors, and many Social Credit voters, defected to the CCF, but after ten years the mass movement of 1935 had become an almost conventional political party. New supporters made up for the loss of the old. Businessmen who had loathed Aberhart found

'Roughnecks' at work near Minton, Saskatchewan, 1950s. This crew operates a Shell Oil drilling rig in the Estevan-Weyburn field. The Saskatchewan Government Photographic Service provided such photographs to show investors that Alberta was not the only Prairie province with oil reserves for sale. SAB Petroleum Industry AC-78.

and British Petroleum. Manning and his cabinet never considered giving the province an active role in oil production. Instead, the Alberta Petroleum and Natural Gas Conservation Board, which had been set up by Aberhart in 1938, regulated the major oil companies very, very gently, while the government sat back and collected royalties.[12]

The problem with this strategy was that it yielded only limited economic diversification and left little role for local entrepreneurs.

However solicitous the Manning government was for their welfare, giant foreign corporations had no particular interest in Alberta, and no commitment to foster development in the region other than to extract oil and natural gas and to pipe them to market. Oil and gas exploitation brought exploration and construction activity, and companies to manufacture steel pipe, but these depended on continuous expansion; beyond refineries and petroleum by-product plants, oil wealth left little perma-

Signing the International Nickel Company agreement, Winnipeg, 5 Dec. 1956. Beaming Premier D.L. Campbell points to the portion of northern Manitoba that he has just signed over to INCO president H.J. Wingate. 'The post-war period,' writes Robert Robson, 'witnessed increasing cooperation between government and industry in the resource field. Although government established the parameters of the relationship, it did so in deference to the resource industries' ('Wilderness Suburbs: Boom and Gloom on the Prairies', *Prairie Forum* 13, 2 [1988], 191). PAM N8966.

nent secondary manufacturing activity behind in Alberta. Ordinary Albertans and their government became rich with these passive policies, however; in the decade after Leduc No. 1, Alberta went from one of the poorer provinces in terms of per capita income to one of the most prosperous, and its government took in twice the national average revenue per capita—the entire difference the result of oil royalties. The Manning government spent this money on an excellent system of education, relatively generous health care and social ser-

vices, provincial parks and campgrounds, and smooth, black-topped highways, viewed with envy by Manitoba and Saskatchewan drivers through their gravel-chipped windshields.

The oil industry eventually expanded to smaller fields in Saskatchewan and Manitoba. Although neither province had the vast pools that lay beneath Alberta, each had mineral meal tickets of its own. The Manitoba government turned that province's nickel, a metal critical to Cold War re-armament, over to mining multinationals. International Nickel's cor-

United Steelworkers picket INCO, Thompson, Manitoba, 1964. INCO's agreement with Manitoba called for the creation of a community that 'the Province . . . , the Company and its employees will be proud of', but in Thompson,
as in other company towns, class conflict could not be imagined away. NAC PA 120680.

porate city of Thompson sprang from the Canadian Shield in 1957 to house the largest integrated nickel mining, refining, and smelting operation in the world; signifying the power relations of resource development, the instant city was named after INCO chairman John F. Thompson rather than Northwest map-maker David Thompson. The Saskatchewan government laid out its own company town, Uranium City, to service Eldorado Mining and Refining, the federal Crown corporation that provided the uranium for nuclear reactors and Cold War bombs. An unsuccessful oil-drilling crew serendipitously discovered that Saskatchewan sat atop vast deposits of potash (60 per cent of world reserves), a mineral indispensable to fertilizer production. The Potash Company of America launched the Saskatchewan potash mining industry in 1958, and eight other mines were in production by 1970. The exploitable natural endowments of Alberta, Manitoba, and Saskatchewan differed, but all three provinces agreed that (except for uranium, which was a federal monopoly) the public resources of the Prairie West would be developed by private foreign capital.[13]

As new primary-sector jobs appeared in

Farmer E.H. Fischer swathes his wheat with the Kalium potash plant in the background, Belle Plaine, Saskatchewan, September 1964. Prairie photographic archives contain many such images, which were intended to reassure rural people that agriculture could co-exist peacefully with the new extractive industries, potash and oil. In Alberta the photographers who made the images were hired by the oil companies; in Saskatchewan they were government employees of Saskatchewan Photo Services. Images conveying the same message are still being constructed, appropriately adapted to reflect the passage of time and a changing audience: today tourists to Alberta can buy postcards that show a red-and-black oil pumper operating amidst a field of golden canola. SAB 64-512-05.

metal and potash mining and in the industry, old ones disappeared. Coal production, crippled by the lack of markets outside the region, shrank still further as homeowners switched to natural gas or fuel oil for heating, and as the Canadian National and Canadian Pacific railways replaced their steam locomotives with oil-burning diesel engines: 8,500 Albertans dug coal in 1946, and only 1,146 in 1966. Railway employment plummeted as diesel engines reduced the need for operating and maintenance crews, and pipelines, highways, and air transport took over many of the railways' functions. Farming diminished both as an occupation and as a way of life. Between the 1951 and 1971 censuses, the numbers of workers in agriculture declined from 336,000 to 212,000, and from 35 per cent to 10 per cent of the Prairie labour force; the total farm population fell more sharply, from 953,000 to 599,000, and the number of farms dropped from 249,000 to fewer than 175,000. Geographer T.R. Weir summarized the situation bluntly: 'The farmer who lacks managerial skill, who regards farming as a way of life rather than a business, is sure to be eliminated in time.' On the surviving farms, fewer people used new machines to do more work: in 1971 the average Prairie farm had $75,000 worth of equipment. On grain farms a tractor, a truck, and a combine enabled a farm couple and their children to do the work that had once required a gang of harvesters, and on livestock farms mechanical hay-making equipment spat out square bales and simplified the once labour-intensive task of haying. A study of the Interlake district of Manitoba found the farm population decline to be greatest among young people: there were 30 per cent fewer families, but 46 per cent fewer children and 64 per cent fewer young adults.[14]

Young people who left the farm—those who remained in the Prairie provinces—sought opportunities in the region's rapidly expanding cities. In 1941 a quarter of the Prairie West's population had resided in the five big cities (Winnipeg, Regina, Saskatoon, Calgary, and Edmonton); in 1971 half lived there. Growth among the five was uneven. Saskatoon, and especially Regina, grew slowly. Oil money made Edmonton and Calgary into Canada's fastest-growing cities, vaulting from populations of under 100,000 in 1941 to 496,000 and 403,000 respectively in 1971. Winnipeg, monarch of Prairie cities, was dethroned. In 1941, more people had lived in Winnipeg than the other four large Prairie cen-

tres combined; in 1971, the 'Gateway to the West' was barely larger than Edmonton. The internal structures of the cities changed as well. Automobiles facilitated the centrifugal forces impelling cities towards their peripheries. Beginning in the 1950s in Edmonton, a new style of subdivision emerged; the self-contained neighbourhood unit soon became the model in Calgary, Regina, Saskatoon, and even Winnipeg, the only Prairie city with old neighbourhoods. These new developments, with their own shopping, education, and recreation facilities, decentralized cities that had once centred on their downtowns.[15]

'Two kids, a good wife, the big house in the new subdivision,' remembers a country-born Albertan who left the farm for Edmonton, 'to a kulak kid out of the Ukraine and no brains at all . . . we were on top of the world.'[16] Women were much more ambivalent about leaving the country or a city neighbourhood for a new suburb, but then so were women in every Canadian region: the Prairie West was rapidly becoming much more like the rest of Canada, which itself was becoming part of a wider North American world. The Second World War had reconnected the region with the rest of the country through the 250,000 men and women who served in the Canadian forces and the equal number who migrated to other parts of the country during the 1940s. After 1951, the demographic distinctiveness that had set the Prairie West apart from other regions of the country largely disappeared. The proportion of immigrants to Canada who chose the Prairie West as their destination fell from 50 per cent before 1930 to 15 per cent in 1946, and stayed at that level until 1966. By the latter year, more than nine in ten Prairie residents were

A billboard in the middle of the prairie announces the Calgary suburb of Glendale Meadows, 13 Aug. 1958. Prairie families participated eagerly in what Veronica Strong-Boag describes as 'the postwar experiment with . . . a spatial segregation that placed Canadian women in suburban homes and men in employment located elsewhere' ('Home Dreams: Women and the Suburban Experiment in Canada, 1945–1960', *Canadian Historical Review* 72, 4 [December 1991], 473). Rosetti's Studio photo. Glenbow, NA-5093-558.

Canadian-born, and almost eight in ten had been born in the region. Despite the 'baby boom', the Prairie West's rate of natural increase, once the highest in the country, slipped back to equal the national rate, and in the 1960s fell slightly below it. The ratio of men to women in the region also came to approximate the national average.

Three decades of population growth well above the national norm had ended in the 1930s, and the Prairie West grew at less than the national rate for the next three decades. Its population fell from 21 per cent of Canada's total in 1941 to 16 per cent in 1971, and migration reshaped all three provinces. In Saskatchewan, leaving the farm often meant leaving the province: Saskatchewan actually lost 7.2 per cent of its population in the 1940s, grew slowly in the 1950s, and in the 1960s increased at the glacial rate of one-tenth of one per cent. Critics of the CCF government made jokes—'Will the last person to leave

The Mayfair subdivision, Calgary, 18 June 1958. The Prairie West suburbanized more than any other Canadian region between 1951 and 1961. Suburban populations in the Prairie provinces increased 133 per cent over the decade, as compared with the national average of 110.7 per cent. Rosetti's Studio photo. Glenbow NA-5093-494.

Saskatchewan please turn off the lights?'—but the fact that Manitoba's governments did not fare much better suggests that the forces at work were beyond the control of the provincial state. Alberta, the Prairie success story, grew twice as fast as Manitoba, and more than three times as fast as Saskatchewan. In 1941 Alberta had less than a third of a total Prairie population of 2.4 million; in 1971 the 1,627,875 Albertans made up almost half the Prairie population of 3,542,000.[17]

The region also recast itself politically dur-ing the 1950s. Despite the very significant presence of third parties—first the Pro-gressives, and later Social Credit and the CCF—in seven federal elections from 1926 until 1953 the Prairie West never failed to return a substantial contingent of Liberal MPs: as many as 33 (in 1940) and never fewer than 14 (in 1945). The fact that the Liberals won all but one of those elections (in 1930) gave the Prairie provinces a voice within the Liberal caucus and strong regional spokesmen within the Liberal cabinet (Saskatchewan's James G.

Actor Gene Barry with old-timers, Calgary, 8 July 1959. Barry, star of the US television western 'Bat Masterson', was the featured guest at the Calgary Stampede. The 'old-timers' who surround him had lived in perhaps the most British place in Canada, as the Union Jack behind them suggests. Beginning in the 1950s, however, Albertans began to reinvent their past as a facsimile of the American West that 'Bat Masterson' represented. Glenbow NA-5093-712.

Gardiner, Manitoba's Thomas Crerar and Stuart Garson, and Alberta's J.A. MacKinnon). These ministers had clout: responding to pressure from Prairie farmers, for example, Gardiner and MacKinnon persuaded their colleagues to preserve the Canadian Wheat Board after the war ended, and to expand its role. The Conservative party, on the other hand, had rarely been a factor in Prairie politics. Manitoba's last Tory government had collapsed in corruption in 1915, Saskatchewan's single Conservative government had been chased out by the voters in 1934, and Alberta had never elected one. In federal constituencies Tories were regularly trounced by Liberals, CCFers, and SoCreds. Saskatchewan's John G. Diefenbaker, one of only three Prairie Tories elected to Parliament in 1940, joked that Conservatives in the region needed protection as an endangered species.

John Diefenbaker unveils the Taras Shevchenko statue, Winnipeg, 9 July 1961. Prairie constructions of 'multicultur-alism' had become perplexingly complicated by the 1960s. With Union Jacks waving in the background and Ukrainian-Canadian war veterans standing at rigid attention, a prime minister from Saskatchewan, pledged to 'unhy-phenated Canadianism', unveils a statue of Taras Shevchenko (?-1861), a former serf whose angry and melancholy poems are anthems of Ukrainian nationalism. Some 50,000 people attended the ceremony on the grounds of the Manitoba legislature and cheered an announcement by Premier Duff Roblin that the Ukrainian language would be taught in Manitoba high schools, as it already was in Saskatchewan and Alberta. Yet Prairie Westerners were hostile to attempts by later Liberal federal governments to accommodate French-Canadian nationalism. PAM N10382.

Chosen to lead a party that had been crushed in five consecutive federal elections, the lonely Saskatchewan Conservative engineered the most astonishing electoral reversal in Canadian political history. In the election of June 1957, the Conservative party eked out a narrow plurality and formed a minority government with little help from Diefenbaker's own region. Winning only 14 of 48 Prairie ridings, the Conservatives were out-polled by the CCF and the Liberals in Saskatchewan, and by Social Credit and the Liberals in Alberta. Over

Queen Elizabeth II attends a 4-H club fair, Tuxford, Saskatchewan, 22 July 1959. Her Majesty watches her footing as she inspects dairy calves with Alvin Hamilton (hands folded at right), Diefenbaker's minister of Agriculture. The Diefenbaker Conservatives earned the support of the Prairie voters by paying both symbolic and practical attention to their concerns. SAB R-A11470(7).

the next ten months, Diefenbaker built a nation-wide majority of unimagined proportions. In April 1958, Diefenbaker's candidates won 208 of the 265 seats in the House of Commons on 54 per cent of the popular vote. The most astonishing thing about this landslide was not the Conservatives' progress in Quebec, but the stunning transformation in Manitoba, Saskatchewan, and Alberta: the party doubled its popular vote from 28 to 56 per cent and took every seat but one, which went to the CCF.[18]

Diefenbaker's national charisma proved ephemeral, and he was out of power in five years. But his appeal endured in the Prairie West. Until the 1990s, the Conservatives remained the dominant party in the region's federal politics, and broke through in all three provincial political arenas as well. His appeal in the Prairie provinces endured, paradoxically, not because he massaged regional grievances, but because he linked populism and nationalism. Diefenbaker, writes his biographer Denis Smith, 'gave to the Prairies [a] sense of dynamic and central participation in nation-building'; his policies 'of national integration . . . typified the Prairie conception of Canada.' Among those policies was consistent attention to the economic well-being of Prairie agriculture, attention personified by his Saskatchewan colleague Alvin Hamilton, the minister of Agriculture. Diefenbaker and Hamilton proved that they were 'rogue Tories' by authorizing the Canadian Wheat Board to sell massive quantities of grain to China and the USSR, stealing a march on the US government, which refused to permit such trade with 'Red' enemies.[19]

In Manitoba, Duff Roblin, grandson of the Tory premier disgraced by scandal in 1915, duplicated Diefenbaker's national triumph at the provincial level. Roblin rebuilt a moribund rural Tory rump into a truly progressive Conservative party, searching out community leaders who had never thought of themselves as Conservatives to join him. Like Diefenbaker, he first won a minority; then in 1959 he gained a majority with almost half the popular vote—a margin of victory unheard of in Canada's most politically competitive province. With more enthusiasm from CCF MLAs than some of his own Conservative backbenchers, Roblin's government introduced Manitobans to modernity: a reformed educational system from elementary school to university, provincial hospital insurance, improved provincial social services, a crop insurance program, and (of course) paved highways to every hamlet. Their most spectacular project was a huge concrete channel that diverted the Red River's spring crests around Winnipeg to avert disasters like the great flood of 1950. Digging 'Duff's ditch' moved more earth than the Suez Canal; only infusions of cash from a co-operative federal government made the floodway financially possible.

The Conservative party's success in the Prairie provinces meant a corresponding decline for the region's Liberals. Nationally, the Liberals defeated Diefenbaker in 1963 to begin another twenty-year run in power; but in Manitoba, Alberta, and eventually even Saskatchewan, the party gradually evaporated electorally. The provincial Liberals in Saskatchewan had a last hurrah, however. In 1962 the CCF government honoured the last of its original campaign promises by enacting a universal public medical insurance plan, despite a bitter three-week physicians' strike.[20] 'Medicare' was soon emulated across the nation, but within Saskatchewan the confrontation with the doctors unified the once-dormant pockets of opposition to the government. Premier T.C. Douglas resigned in 1961 to lead the national New Democratic Party, an alliance of the CCF with the Canadian Labour Congress. But Saskatchewan farmers were suspicious of the union with labour. In 1964 Liberal leader Ross Thatcher, an apostate CCFer, rallied 'free enterprise' voters to defeat the CCF under its new leader, Woodrow Lloyd, by the narrowest of margins. Once in office, Thatcher fulminated against CCF 'socialism' and watered down CCF labour codes; although his government left the CCF's social programs in place, it cut budgets and increased medicare premiums. After gerrymandering constituency boundaries, Thatcher won re-election in 1967, again with a minuscule plurality of the popular vote.

The once-intimate relationship between the provincial and federal Liberals in Saskatchewan dissolved in rancour, however.[21] Thatcher was uncomfortable with L.B. Pear-

Hanging Woodrow Lloyd and Tommy Douglas in effigy, Regina, 11 July 1962. Supporters of the Saskatchewan physicians striking to oppose medicare organized a 'Keep Our Doctors' rally on the legislature grounds. The signs on the effigies of the two CCF premiers, illegible in the photograph, read 'Down with Dictators'; demonstrators called the CCF government 'Communists' and told them to go 'back to the Kremlin'. But the demonstration failed, both in the short and the long term: only 4,000 people turned up, not the 40,000 the 'Keep Our Doctors' committee had predicted, and by the end of the 1960s Saskatchewan's medicare was universal in Canada. SAB R-83980-2.

alienation from a federal government that seemed increasingly to ignore their interests and whose concern for Quebec seemed an affront to them. Westerners did not share Ottawa's concern with Quebec's demands for 'égalité ou indépendance', for example, and were cool to the solutions of the Royal Commission on Bilingualism and Biculturalism. In the Prairie West, French Canadians were but one ethnic minority among many, and the other minorities added their voices to the ancient English-Canadian antagonism regarding French-language rights. Meeting in Winnipeg, the Ukrainian Canadian Committee rejected national bilingualism in favour of English alone and biculturalism in favour of multiculturalism. Polls showed that seven out of ten Westerners opposed the modest attempts in Trudeau's Official Languages Act to implement the commission's recommendations, and in the House of Commons John Diefenbaker led fifteen Western Tories in opposition to the act, defying the decision of the federal Conservative caucus to support the legislation. On this issue and others, Prairie Conservatives began to transform themselves into spokesmen (and they were all men) for regional discontent, as opposed to the Central Canadians in their own party as they were to the Liberal government.

Few Euro-Canadian Westerners noticed the Trudeau government policy that was most oblivious to Prairie reality: its White Paper on Indian Policy. With confidence founded in ignorance, Indian Affairs Minister Jean Chrétien announced in June 1969 that, by 1975, Status Indians would be rapidly integrated 'to full social, economic, and political participation in Canadian life'. Special Indian

son's federal Liberal government (1963–68) and openly contemptuous of Pearson's successor, Pierre Elliott Trudeau. Thatcher both reflected and exploited Prairie voters' growing

Duncan MacPherson cartoon of the Grey Cup crowd, *Toronto Star*, 26 Nov. 1966. The Liberals' inability to wrest Prairie seats away from Diefenbaker's Conservatives cost Pearson majority governments in 1963 and 1965, and contributed to a sense of what commentators called 'Western alienation'. In the 1966 Grey Cup, however, Ron Lancaster and George Reed led the Saskatchewan Roughriders to their first-ever Canadian football championship by defeating the Hamilton Tiger-Cats. NAC 113548.

legal status would be abolished, the federal Department of Indian Affairs dissolved, and social programs for Indians turned over to the provinces; reserves would disappear, and Native people would become just another tile in Canada's ethnic mosaic. This reiteration of

Pierre Trudeau (left) and Ross Thatcher (right) unveiling a statue of Louis Riel, Regina, 2 Oct. 1968. During the 1960s, Prairie regionalist ideology appropriated Louis Riel from the Métis and French Canadians and transformed him into a powerful symbol of regional, rather than ethnic, protest. Ross Thatcher used the unveiling of Riel's statue to bash federal government policies with respect to the Prairies: 'Whether we realize it or not, we of 1968 face a situation which is similar in some respects,' Thatcher told the crowd in front of the Saskatchewan Legislature. 'If Riel could walk the soil of Canada today, I am sure his sense of justice would be outraged as it was in 1885.' Trudeau urged the majority not to forget 'the rights of the minority', and promised that 'should disturbances erupt, a remote and powerful government [would not] crush them in the name of law and order'. Given Trudeau's subsequent use of the War Measures Act against Quebec nationalists, his speech outdoes Thatcher's as a monument to political hypocrisy. SAB 68-574-06.

the century-old policy of assimilation was absurdly mistimed. Improved health standards and a very high birth rate had increased the Indian population by 91 per cent since 1945; in 1967, 91,246 Status Indians and an estimated 113,500 Métis were living in Manitoba, Saskatchewan, or Alberta. Although post-war economic growth had almost entirely bypassed them, Prairie Native people were well organized and determined both to improve their living standards and to retain their identities. Articulate Native responses such as the Indian Association of Alberta's 'Red Paper' demolished the White Paper's arguments and forced the federal government to back down; Prairie chiefs led the establishment of the National Indian Brotherhood, which insisted that Treaty obligations be respected and reinterpreted to meet the modern needs of Native people.[22]

Non-Native Westerners reacted with similar outrage to the Trudeau government's failure to recognize federal 'treaty obligations' to the Prairie resource economy. In 1968 a world glut reminiscent of the 1930s collapsed wheat prices and created surpluses that clogged the grain-handling system. With the spell-binding arrogance that characterized his shots-from-the-lip, Pierre Trudeau asked in Winnipeg: 'Why should I sell the Canadian farmers' wheat?' Other federal governments, Liberal and Conservative, had accumulated wheat and waited out surpluses; Trudeau's government imposed a quota on the amount that could be delivered to the Wheat Board and introduced the massively unpopular LIFT (Lower Inventories For Tomorrow) program, which offered farmers $6 for every acre not planted with grain. A 1970 federal task force on agriculture that calmly predicted the imminent demise of

The Indian and Métis Friendship Centre, Winnipeg, 1960. Native people moved to Prairie cities after 1950, just as Euro-Canadians did. The Friendship Centre was a tangible result of a series of conferences, begun in 1954, between Indian and Métis representatives and the Winnipeg Council of Social Agencies. The conference 'became an annual event which more and more Indians and métis attended,' wrote W.L. Morton in 1967, 'and which they came to control' (*Manitoba: A History*, 494). PAM Nan Shipley Collection 74.

thousands of 'inefficient' Prairie farms may have been good social science, but it was very bad politics. Angry and anxious, farm families wondered why the federal government wasn't doing something to ensure a future for what was not just their industry but their way of life.

The Prairie economy had diversified beyond agriculture since the 1940s, but the region remained resource-dependent, continuing to sell its resources in a world market and to buy manufactured goods from Central Canada at prices inflated by protective tariffs. The service sector provided jobs for the same percentage of the labour force in the Prairie provinces as it did in Ontario, but the Prairie manufacturing sector was less than half as large; 30 per cent of the Prairie labour force worked in the primary sector—twice the national average and three times that of Ontario. Nickel, potash, and petroleum, like

Indian Affairs and Northern Development Minister Jean Chrétien at York Factory, Manitoba, 11 July 1968. Chrétien has just accepted the transfer of York Factory from the Hudson's Bay Company to the Canadian government. Manitoba historian Ed Russenholt reads at his left. Closed by the HBC in 1957, what remained of the post became a National Historic Site. Chrétien's attempt, a year later, to shut down Canada's system of Indian reserves was spectacularly less successful. PAM Events 235/4 68-1396.

wheat, were only as strong as the world demand for them in markets that Prairie producers and their provincial governments— Liberal, Conservative, CCF, or Social Credit— had only the most limited ability to influence. In response to falling potash prices, the 'free enterprise' Thatcher government colluded with New Mexico, the other large North American producer, to restrict output; the nine Saskatchewan potash mines voluntarily curbed production at half capacity in 1970. Federal policy dictated that Prairie oil should supply only Ontario's needs, and that Canadian refineries in Quebec and the Maritimes should be supplied with crude oil brought from Venezuela by tanker. This meant that Western oil depended on export markets in the United States that were constantly under threat of US import restrictions. Like the Saskatchewan potash mines, Alberta oil wells in the late 1960s prorated production and pumped at roughly half their capacity.

Manitoba and Saskatchewan grasped at forestry 'mega-projects' in pathetic attempts to diversify their economies, but neither province had any thought-out development strategy. Forest industries faced the same unpredictable demand fluctuations as minerals, potash, and petroleum, and the subsidized mills would compete directly with each other for markets. The two provinces competed indirectly through the escalating bribes they offered to foreign entrepreneurs to develop the projects. (Given how little of their own capital these businessmen invested, 'entrepreneurs' seems a more accurate term than 'capitalists'.) Manitoba's Conservative government poured an initial $90 million into a complex called Churchill Forest Industries in the northern town of The Pas, and kept pouring until the total reached $138 million. Saskatchewan's Liberal government guaranteed $50 million in loans to a US-owned pulp mill in Prince Albert, and handed the company nearly a third of the province's northern forest at cut-rate royalties. Neither project came close to yielding the hoped-for economic results; instead, as the economic geographer Brenton M. Barr acidly observed, the projects were 'a flagrant example of the desperation with which some governments attempt to encourage regional development'. The future of the Prairie economy was obvious, Barr concluded bluntly: the 'basic function of the region will continue to be the supply of raw materials. . . . Prairie resource developments have not created general economic growth akin to that of the Southwestern United States or California. Rather their situation is more like that of Montana, North and South Dakota, Wyoming, Nebraska, and northern Minnesota. . . .'[23]

The three Prairie governments made no serious attempt to act in concert for economic development. The only functional trans-regional institution they ever established was the Prairie Provinces Water Board, set up in 1948. The Prairie Economic Council, set up in 1965, brought the premiers together for photo ops but produced no practical interprovincial co-operation. When Winnipeg Liberal MP James Richardson, a minister in Trudeau's cabinet, mused that the Prairie West might not 'really need three of everything', and hinted that political union might help solve some of the three provinces' economic problems, academics studied the possibility of creating 'One Prairie Province'. But provincial governments dismissed their message. Increasing regional alienation from Ottawa, it seemed, could not stimulate a corresponding enthusiasm for regional integration.

In July 1969, Canadians in other regions who had been oblivious to this alienation were informed by featured articles in three national English-Canadian magazines that a 'wind of discontent' was sweeping the West. 'I found a seething rage directed at central Canada and shared by an astonishing cross section of the population,' journalist Walter Stewart reported in *Maclean's*. He claimed that 'in farm kitchens and city living rooms, in business offices and union halls' he had heard the same message: 'Ottawa, Go to Hell.' 'Separatism could become a potent force across the Canadian West,' Stewart concluded ominously. Westerners were 'a long way from serious thoughts of secession,' Robert McKeown countered in *Weekend Magazine*, but they had developed 'a confident western identity' and were 'no longer content to have the remote East set

The Prairie Economic Council meets in Edmonton, 2 Sept. 1966. Premiers Duff Roblin and Ross Thatcher are second and third from the end of the table on the right, while Ernest Manning leans forward opposite them. The only importance of such meetings was to provide Prairie premiers with opportunities to pose as defenders of the region against the federal government. PAA PA 1080/1.

down the rules for them.' But in *Saturday Night* Arnold Edinborough laughed at Western grievances, lampooning them as petty complaints about 'French on cereal boxes' and 'dirty books' subsidized by the Canada Council. 'If there weren't the Easterners to blame for everything, the Westerner would have to blame himself,' he continued. 'When the present generation of farmers is gone, . . . urban development will bring an end to many of the things that now separate the East from the West.'

CHAPTER EIGHT

The New West and the Nation

Neither the commentators who feared Prairie separatism nor those who hoped that Western alienation would vanish with a younger urban generation turned out to be correct. When regionalism was repackaged for the 1970s and 1980s, young urbanites proved more receptive to it than the rural generation of the 1930s had ever been, although they found new forms through which to express it. After 1970, Prairie élites added new beads to the rosary of regional grievances. But the prayer that the Prairie West said on this rosary was not for independence; it remained a prayer for influence in Ottawa. 'The underlying significance of western separatism . . . is the opposite of what appears on the surface,' concluded journalist Peter Newman in 1970. 'In essence the West wants *power* of some kind at the centre—a more effective version of Canadian federalism.'[1]

Between 1969 and 1971, Prairie voters installed new provincial governments in Winnipeg, Edmonton, and Regina, each one determined to renegotiate its province's future within the Canadian confederation. In Manitoba the New Democratic Party leapt from third-party status to power by defeating a Conservative government that had turned its back on progressive politics. When Duff Roblin made an unsuccessful foray into federal politics in 1967, rural reactionaries regained control of the Conservative party and imposed a Minnedosa mortician named Walter Weir as premier; Weir soon buried himself and the party. The social democratic party had also changed since the CCF years: the NDP had moved towards the political centre but held both its rural support from the Manitoba Farmers' Union and its urban working-class base while attracting new support from acculturated ethnic minorities. Class intersected with ethnicity to produce an NDP victory in June 1969. Commentators joked about the 'kielbasa curtain' or 'perogy line' that divided Manitoba from northwest to southeast and ran right through the centre of metropolitan Winnipeg. NDP constituencies clustered north and east of this line, while those to the southwest were Tory blue; swing ridings along the line were hotly contested. Only five patches of Liberal red marked the map, for the Liberal party had obliged the NDP by moving to the

Alberta opposition leader Peter Lougheed competes in a hay-pitching contest with Premier Harry Strom, 7 June 1969. Such rituals helped Lougheed to assure rural Albertans that an urbanite like him was qualified to govern them. He pitched more hay than Strom in the contest, and his Conservatives won more seats than Strom's Social Credit party in the election that followed two years later. *Edmonton Journal* photo. PAA J 346.

irrelevant right, promising to undo the Roblin educational reforms and return to the 'little red schoolhouse' of yesterday. NDP leader Ed Schreyer, a rural Roman Catholic of non-British background who professed a fuzzy amalgam of liberalism and social democracy, represented the new Manitoba, in which the traditional outsiders had used the NDP to supplant traditional insiders.[2]

In Saskatchewan, Allan Blakeney led the NDP back to power over Ross Thatcher's increasingly strident right-wing Liberal govern-

ment. Farm income had fallen to 1942 levels, and farm families blamed federal Liberal agricultural policy; Blakeney toured rural Saskatchewan in a rented bus, waving the report of the Federal Task Force on Agriculture as proof that Liberals in Ottawa and Regina intended to wreck the family farm. The NDP promised more than rural revitalization, however: it would 'stop any further sellout of resources' and use the provincial state to wring more revenue and economic development from the province's pulpwood and potash than the Thatcher

Liberals had been able to. 'The whole ethos of the Prairies,' Blakeney told a journalist, 'is one of cooperation, of using government as an instrument. . . . The tradition here is not one of fear of government but, rather, of the use and control of government.' The electorate agreed. In June 1971, the NDP crushed 'Boss Ross' Thatcher, winning 45 of 60 seats.

Peter Lougheed, the leader of the Alberta Conservatives who evicted Social Credit two months later, resembled Manitoba's Duff Roblin more than he did Blakeney or Schreyer; an urban businessman and the scion of an old Tory family, Lougheed was a truly progressive Conservative who built his party from literally nothing through long, exhausting effort. The six seats that Lougheed's candidates won in 1967 to become the official opposition made up the largest Tory caucus in Edmonton since 1917. In 1968, Social Credit Premier Ernest Manning anointed Municipal Affairs Minister Harry Strom to succeed him, but Strom could not halt Social Credit's ossification. In August 1971, the Conservatives won the votes of baby-boomers, new migrants to the province, and urbanites to form a majority government with 49 of 75 seats. But Social Credit retained 42 per cent of the vote, and the NDP managed 12 per cent; it was the provincial Liberals that were exterminated, with 1 per cent of the popular vote.[3]

In Alberta, Manitoba, and Saskatchewan the determination to use provincial control of resource development to effect economic diversification provided a common theme. After visiting all three provincial capitals, Ontario journalist Peter Desbarats explained that each Prairie government 'now sees the day approaching when exploitation of its non-renewable resources will have to be accompa-nied by rapid industrial development'. In Alberta the 'Lougheed team' rejected Social Credit's passive management of Alberta's oil and gas, acting as the political voice of a new home-grown class of entrepreneurs and pro-fessionals—John Richards and Larry Pratt called them 'Alberta's *arriviste bourgeoisie*'—who wanted to use resource development to build a stronger, more diversified provincial economy that they themselves would control. Unlike Manning, Lougheed had a Harvard MBA and a plan: the provincial state would be an active partner in resource industries, and when necessary the government would roll up its sleeves and go into business itself. As the new premier told a Toronto journalist, 'though we want to encourage the private sector, if they can't do the job—or won't—this government will.' Lougheed's government created the Alberta Energy Company, a quasi-public cor-poration with $75 million in government cap-ital and the participation of private sharehold-ers, and invested $200 million to buy 10 per cent of Syncrude, a huge project to extract oil from the Athabasca tar sands. The Conserva-tives even spent $36 million to buy Pacific Western Airlines and move its headquarters to Calgary. The most spectacular venture of all, however, was the Alberta Heritage Savings Trust Fund, started with $1.5 billion in capital, up to 65 per cent of which was to be invested in enterprises that would diversify Alberta's resource-based economy.[4]

The New Democrats in Saskatchewan aggressively raised resource rents, and were uninhibited about using public enterprise as a development tool. The Blakeney government launched ten joint ventures in uranium min-ing, nationalized the Prince Albert pulp mill, increased potash and oil royalties, and created a provincial oil company, SaskOil, to search for gas and petroleum when foreign oil companies stopped exploration to protest the increased royalty. In November 1975 the throne speech announced a more controversial policy: nationalization of 'some or all of the producing potash mines in the Province'. Attorney General Roy Romanow explained the government's reasoning: government ownership was 'the only measure by which we can ensure that control of such a vital resource will remain in Regina and not Houston, Chicago and Toronto'. Over challenges from the US potash companies and the federal government, eventually the public Potash Corporation of Saskatchewan acquired 50 per cent of the province's production capacity. Unlike the Lougheed government in Alberta, the Saskatchewan NDP took on the Trudeau government and the US-based resource corporations without the general support of the province's business class, long estranged from the 'socialists'. The US Senate paid Saskatchewan the ultimate compliment of comparing the province's potash policies to the oil policies of the Organization of Petroleum Exporting Countries (OPEC), the international cartel.

In Manitoba the counterparts to oil and potash were more modest: minerals and hydro power. The Schreyer government invested heavily in northern hydroelectric development through Manitoba Hydro, the provincially owned electric utility. In 1974–75, for example, $480 of the $622 million allotted to capital spending went to build dams and transmission lines. Under Schreyer Manitoba also created two new departments, of Northern Affairs and of Renewable Resources, and raised min-

eral royalties and corporate taxes. The NDP government was unwilling, however, to nationalize the northern mining industry, no matter how fervently back-benchers and party members demanded that it do so. The only resource operation it nationalized was the Churchill Forest Industries complex, taken over because its owners were bankrupt.

The timing of the Prairie governments was excellent: they initiated their new resource strategies just as world prices for potash, uranium, wheat, and especially energy moved sharply upward. OPEC colluded with the major oil companies in 1973 to create a shortage that quadrupled the price of a barrel of crude oil. The resource boom increased Prairie per capita incomes, and the provinces realized new revenues, but the three governments, two of them NDP and the other Conservative, found themselves in conflict with a Liberal government in Ottawa determined to shield Central and Atlantic Canada from the increased world prices for energy. The federal government froze oil prices below world levels in 1973, and in 1974 spent revenue from a federal oil export tax to subsidize imports of foreign oil for Quebec and the Atlantic provinces. Prime Minister Trudeau and his cabinet draped these policies in the Maple Leaf rhetoric of nationalism, but they reflected simple political calculation: the Liberal caucus had 115 MPs from Ontario and Quebec, 13 from Atlantic Canada, and three from the Prairie West.

Premiers Schreyer, Blakeney, and Lougheed co-operated with NDP Premier Dave Barrett of British Columbia to resist these federal attempts to deprive their provinces of the resource revenues that, according to the British North America Act, should belong to them.

'Western premiers hang tough in gang-up on Ottawa' ran the headline in Southam newspapers, with the lone Conservative premier described in a photo caption as 'Alberta's Lougheed—Man with money muscle'. Asked by journalist Nick Hills if 'the poor' in other regions weren't 'in worse shape than the people of the prairies', Blakeney replied: 'We are not trying to rob region-Peter to pay region-Paul. . . . We just want certain penalties removed and genuine inequities abolished.' Lougheed added that Canada needed 'a national industrial strategy' that would 'concentrate largely on growth potential areas . . . and they are largely in the west.' The Prairie premiers at first avoided regionalist rhetoric; at a national energy conference in Ottawa in January 1974, Lougheed turned Trudeau's patriotic rhetoric inside out, speaking of 'sound *national* energy policies . . . simultaneously 100% Albertan *and* 100% Canadian' and 'a New Confederation' built on federal–provincial co-operation. He provided the sound-bite the reporters had longed for, however, when in the winter of 1974 the federal government threatened to tax natural gas exports: such a tax would be 'the biggest rip-off of any province that ever occurred in the history of Confederation.' 'Alberta must use those resources for the long-range goal of diversification. . . . Oil doesn't last forever.' He also pointed out that 'many of the things that Quebec would like to see in terms of their jurisdictional and revenue-sharing responsibilities are almost exactly the feelings that I and my colleagues have.'[5]

But Lougheed was no separatist, and as journalist Peter Desbarats reported, 'in Western Canada the emotional attachment to confederation is probably stronger than in any other part of the country.' There were Western separatists, however, almost all of them in Alberta. Milt Harradence, a millionaire Calgary lawyer, former Alberta Conservative leader, and president of the Independent Alberta Association (IAA), was always good for a quote to titillate readers in Central Canada. In his view Prime Minister Trudeau was 'a crypto-Communist', Peter Lougheed was Trudeau's dupe, an 'almost socialist' who had 'forsaken almost every traditional Conservative principle', and unless Westerners chose independence they faced, 'a hell of a future as . . . hewers of wood and drawers of water.' In 1974 the IAA released *The Cost of Confederation*, which claimed that being part of Canada cost Albertans $1.4 billion a year—and ignored the fact that an abrupt drop in oil, meat, and grain prices would confound any such calculation. But although it appropriated Prairie protest, Western separatism was confined to an ultra-right fringe. For one thing, argued political scientists Larry Pratt and Garth Stevenson, it lacked 'a significant intellectual component and a leader like René Lévesque'. For another, as the *Calgary Herald*'s Bill Gold pithily put it: Alberta had 'five separatists with $100,000 each, while in Quebec there are 100,000 separatists with $5 each'.[6]

However much provincial governments in other parts of the country might sympathize with the Prairie provinces' position on resource revenues, the federal–provincial confrontation took on a vivid East-versus-West colouring. Its bombastic nadir came when a bumper sticker appeared in southern Alberta that read 'Let the Eastern Bastards Freeze in the Dark'. No longer ignored, the Prairie

Duncan MacPherson, 'The Marriage Broker', *Toronto Star*, 24 Oct. 1974. Central Canadians vilified Peter Lougheed and Albertans as 'blue-eyed Sheiks'.NAC 112480.

West—specifically Alberta—now seemed to be heartily resented by Central Canadians. 'Blue-eyed Sheiks' was a common sobriquet, but the most frequent comparison was to Americans. Albertans, said Trudeau adviser Ivan Head, 'look to Texas and Oklahoma as the source of values, ideas, and life-styles, turning their backs on Canadian history and heritage. If they became more Canadian,' he fatuously continued, 'they would have even more influence in Canadian affairs.' Albertans were de-scribed in the primitive stereotypes that Canadians usually reserved for the United States. 'What could Alberta possibly want? *More*,' read the headline for a *Maclean's* cover story. Journalist Suzanne Zwarun depicted Albertans as *nouveaux riches* on 'a wildcat kind of shopping spree', and devoted two paragraphs to a Calgary shop that stocked $50,000 worth of gold faucets and sold sculptured toilets that cost $1,000 each. Its customers, Zwarun claimed, would 'equip a house with,

Duncan MacPherson cartoon, *Toronto Star*, 19 Nov. 1974. The Toronto cartoonist escalated regional name-calling by depicting the 'Western provinces' in league with the US 'Petroleum Industry' against 'Canada'. NAC C 112956.

say, seven or even nine bathrooms, a perhaps Freudian obsession in a society so recently removed from the frontier'; and because of 'the quirky sense of democracy that Albertans display, the domestic help also have their own brushed gold faucets.'[7]

Central Canadian commentators were appropriately appalled by such crass materialism. 'What does "Canada" mean if Canadians in one spot exploit provincial rights and an accident of nature to grow ever more rich at the expense of Canadians who are already much poorer than they are?' asked *Toronto Star* columnist Harry Bruce in a fulmination about 'oil parasites' and 'sour . . . provincial meanness'. Alberta's ingratitude was astounding, for 'in the Thirties . . . you know who bailed her out, don't you? Yes, it was the federal government.' Who did Albertans think they were? 'Alberta hasn't much past anyway. . . . We invented her, really. . . .' Bruce and other Canadians outside the Prairie region helped to 'invent' a new West by defining it as the 'other' to their constructed 'Canada': Ontario and Quebec. Using data collected during June and July 1974, political scientist Jon H. Pammett concluded that Saskatchewan, Manitoba, and Alberta displayed the highest degree of 'regional consciousness' in the country. The three Prairie provinces were 'the best-defined regional unit in Canada', although more Prairie residents characterized themselves as living in the 'West' than the 'Prairies'. In other provinces, including Quebec, the sense of region was much less sharp; many Ontarians, Pammett noted, thought of themselves simply as residents of 'English Canada'.[8]

Inside the Prairie West, people were also at work reinventing their region to distinguish it from 'the East'. Every summer urbanites dressed up to celebrate a West that never existed. Jack Ludwig, a Westerner-moved-to-Toronto who was sent back by *Maclean's* to cover the 1975 Calgary Stampede, was astonished at how things had changed: not only did people gamble publicly in the Frontier Casino, but 'now Western gear swathes woman, man and child in blue denim. Farm boys wear cowboy boots, cowboy hats, string ties.' The Stampede was the biggest and best-known of the civic festivals dedicated to Westernness,

but Buffalo Days in Regina, the grotesquely named Louis Riel Day in Saskatoon, and myriad small-town events commemorated an imaginary past more modestly. Edmonton's Klondike Days celebrated a mythic link to the Yukon gold rush of 1898: brochures promised that tourists would see 'bank holdups, a stagecoach robbery, sheriff's posses and beard-growing contests occur right before your eyes'.[9]

Prairie intellectuals made their contributions to regionalism. When the University of Alberta Press republished a facsimile edition of John Sandilands' 1913 *Western Canadian Dictionary and Phrase Book* in 1977, the cover carried a new subtitle—'*Picturesque Language of the Cowboy and Broncho-Buster*'—and featured a sketch of a Marlborough-man style cowboy. A study of *The Harvests of War: The Prairie West, 1914–1918* (1978) by a young Manitoba historian named John Herd Thompson exposed the 'injustices' suffered by Manitoba, Alberta, and Saskatchewan during the First World War because of 'the unfair application of laws that were fashioned for eastern conditions'. A new West needed such histories to give university and community-college students a 'usable past' of their region. J. Arthur Lower's textbook *Western Canada: An Outline History* and John Conway's polemic *The West: The History of a Region in Confederation*, both published in 1983, earnestly explained how the Western provinces had 'reached maturity and no longer needed parental guidance from the federal government'. Neither approached the erudition or the graceful prose of Gerald Friesen's *The Canadian Prairies: A History*, which appeared in 1984. Yet all three volumes made clear that whatever their historic grievances, Westerners were, in Lower's words,

'Klondike Days' in Edmonton, mid-1970s. A leering 'gambler' pays a 'saloon girl' for a pitcher of beer as Edmontonians, like many other Prairie Westerners, invent a new and more exciting 'Wild West' past for themselves. City of Edmonton Archives, A85-141.

'above all, Canadians, but . . . Canadians who intend to protect and control their own economic, cultural, social and political destinies'.

This redefinition of 'the West' ignored or skated around the rapid and continuing erosion of the objective characteristics that had once differentiated Manitoba, Saskatchewan, and Alberta from the other seven provinces. Prairie people, urban and rural, ate the same processed foods, drank 'national' beers from Labatt's or Molson's, and watched the same US television programs that English-speaking Canadians watched all across the country—except on Saturday, when all regions and both linguistic groups tuned in 'Hockey Night in Canada'. Demographically, Prairie people became less distinguishable from the rest of Canada with each passing year as the cities grew and the countryside emptied out. Despite generally good grain prices during the 1970s, operating costs increased faster; 2,500 farms a year disappeared, and those that remained became larger and more mechanized. For smaller farms to survive, women and men needed waged jobs off the farm; the 1981 census reported that the percentage of farm family members with off-farm

A National Farmers' Union demonstration at the Alberta Legislature, 9 Nov. 1974. The question on the boy's picket sign had become more than rhetorical by the mid-1970s: farming as business was supplanting farming as a way of life. The members of the National Farmers Union, writes Grace Skogstad, 'demonstrated a readiness to engage in highway blockages, mass rallies, food giveaway programs, and sit-ins in government buildings' in their struggles to preserve family farming (*The Politics of Agricultural Policy-Making in Canada* [Toronto: University of Toronto Press, 1987], 28]). *Edmonton Journal* photo. PAA J.1579/3.

unsustainable. As huge 'inland terminals' replaced local grain elevators, and semi-trailers hauled the crops instead of branch-line railways, rural service centres died. And once the grain-handling facilities went, the local hotel, the newspaper, the school, clubs, teams, and churches followed.[10]

There was no consensus on how to cope with these changes. The illusion that 'the Prairies' were a regional unit obscured the division between farming as a business and farming as a way of life that, although it was as old as Prairie farming itself, was now widening. Wilf Edgar of Red Deer spoke for the agribusinessmen in an interview with *Time* in April 1974, shortly after his return from wintering in his Hawaiian condo: 'A lot of misfits have dropped out of farming. They just couldn't keep up with the challenges.' The Edgars were doing just fine, thank you, with revenues of $300,000 the year before and a farm 'conservatively valued' at $1.3 million. The National Farmers Union (NFU), founded in 1969, spoke for farm families in more modest circumstances; rooted in the producer ideology of agrarian radicalism, it challenged the complacency of the established provincial farm organizations. At the same time, those organizations faced challenges from groups organized around specific commodities, such as the Canadian Cattlemen's Association and the Palliser Wheat Growers Association, whose agendas were no different from those of any business lobby group. Although their membership was numerically small, the Palliser Wheat Growers attacked the Canadian Wheat Board, the marketing agency that Prairie grain growers had struggled for decades to create; their complaints, the NFU noted, coincided with the

jobs, once lowest in the Prairie provinces, now approximated the Canadian average of 40 per cent. The rural associational life that had been the cultural base of the agrarian movement decayed as depopulation and distance made it

Northern Alberta demonstration in support of the American Indian Movement occupation of Wounded Knee, Edmonton, 10 March 1973. These Native marchers identified with the 250 armed AIM members in South Dakota who were defying US federal marshals at the site of the infamous 1892 massacre by the US Cavalry. The following summer, the Ojibway Warrior Society occupied Anishnabe Park, just east of the Manitoba border in Kenora, Ontario. Unlike the Wounded Knee confrontation, however, the Anishnabe occupation ended without bloodshed; in general, Aboriginal resurgence in the Canadian Prairie West took non-violent forms. PAA J-959/3.

arrival in Canada of the giant US grain-trading companies Cargill and Continental, which hoped to make millions from the Wheat Board's abolition. The federal government's decision in 1973 to confine the board's monopoly to wheat, and to put oats and barley on the open market, was opposed by a substantial majority of farmers. Even though the fraction belonging to the Palliser Wheat Growers had favoured the open market, Wheat Pool farmers construed the change as further evidence that the federal Liberal government was the captive of Eastern interests. The Saskatchewan Pool demanded that Otto Lang—one of two surviving Saskatchewan Liberal MPs—be fired as minister responsible for the Wheat Board. Some farmers inked in black dots to separate the letters on their POOL baseball caps; they said the new acronym, P.O.O.L.., stood for 'Piss On Otto Lang'.[11]

The Indian Association of Alberta protests provincial health-care policies, Edmonton, 24 Jan. 1979. The Indian Association emphasized confirming and reinterpreting treaty rights as the best way to win the better material conditions that would make cultural survival possible. *Edmonton Journal* photo. PAA J.4427/2.

By the 1980s, the demographic distinction that most set the Prairie West apart from the rest of Canada was its large minority of Native people. More than half of Canada's Status Indians lived in the Prairie provinces, making up about six per cent of the population there in 1981, as compared to less than three per cent of the country as a whole. Their numbers continued to rise until by 1996 Status Indians constituted 11 per cent of the populations of both Manitoba and Saskatchewan. The April 1974 *Time* cover story that disclosed the opu-

lence of 'American' Alberta also pointed out that 'Lougheed has not tilted the provincial cornucopia in the direction of Alberta's 80,000 treaty [Status] Indians and Métis, who still live in extreme poverty. . . . [They] endure an 80-90 per cent unemployment and school dropout rate, and at least 50 per cent of them still live in substandard housing without electricity and water.' Prairie First Nations demanded their share, with some success. They had long been leaders in the pan-Indian resurgence movement, and helped to shape the

Law Courts under construction, Edmonton, 1970s. During the urban construction boom, Calgarians and Edmontonians joked that the 'hammer-headed crane' was the provincial bird of Alberta. *Edmonton Journal* photo. PAA J-416.

National Indian Brotherhood into the Assembly of First Nations in 1980. Sociologist Linda Gerber explains their prominence as a function of the ways in which 'prairie Indian bands differed from their counterparts in the rest of Canada'; they were 'remarkably cohesive, well-developed at the community level, and relatively likely to retain the use of native languages.' Métis expressed their own politics of identity through the Métis National Council, despite its name an organization formed to represent Métis to the provincial governments of the Prairies specifically. But if Native organizations made Native problems visible, non-Native Westerners resented their new presence. Opinion polls suggested that the attitudes of Prairie residents towards Indians were very different from those of Canadians outside the West; whereas 65 per cent nationally supported 'many' or 'all' Native land claims, in the Prairie West more than half believed that 'few' or 'no' such claims were valid. A 'sympathy index' created by two social scientists in 1980 suggested that Prairie residents were the Canadians least compassionate towards Native people.[12]

Once the Assembly of First Nations had achieved recognition of Aboriginal rights in the amended Canadian Constitution in 1982, it set Native self-government as its goal. Not surprisingly, with the exception of Manitoba's NDP premier Howard Pawley, Western provincial governments were cool towards the proposal. When the Trudeau government met with Native leaders and the ten provincial premiers in March 1984, premiers Don Getty of Alberta and Grant Devine of Saskatchewan joined with British Columbia to postpone any serious discussions. Given the Western provinces' large proportion of Canada's Aboriginal population—300,000 of the 375,000 Status Indians represented by the Assembly of First Nations lived between the Great Lakes and the Pacific—non-Native Westerners would have been the people called upon to make the concessions required for Native self-government to become possible. Like official bilingualism, Native self-government was resented by many Prairie Westerners who felt that it was being 'shoved down their throats' by a Central Canada incapable of understanding their circumstances.

Meanwhile, the Prairie West had aroused Central Canada's ire by escaping the worst effects of the long recession of the 1970s. The centre of prosperity was no longer Manitoba, but Alberta. The westward shift of power was underscored by the decline in the cost of a seat on the Winnipeg Grain Exchange (renamed the Commodity Exchange), from $25,000 in 1929 to $4,000 in the 1980s. Winnipeg remained the Prairie city with the largest manufacturing labour force, processing agricultural products and making goods for the regional market, but Edmonton loomed as its successor. Edmonton Economic Development, the municipal department of boosterism, took pride in the city's 'Little Ruhr Valley' along the North Saskatchewan River, the site of refineries, fertilizer factories, and petrochemical

Facing above. Workers maintain a potash mining machine at the Duval Mine near Saskatoon, August 1976. This 52-tonne 'continuous mining machine' dug five tonnes of potash-bearing ore every minute. The capital-intensive technology of the new staple industries meant that very little direct employment was created in the Prairie provinces. Total employment in potash mining and refining was only about 4,000 when this photo was taken. L. Melit photo. SAB 76-1098-62.

Facing below. Combines harvesting in southern Saskatchewan, September 1968. Unlike the ominous prairie depicted by nineteenth-century artists and photographers, the prairie of modern image-makers 'is no longer alien or forbidding; indeed, it is mostly as manicured, trimmed, combed, and accessorized as are we ourselves' (Joni L. Kinsey, 'Not So Plain: Art of the American Prairies', *Great Plains Quarterly* 15, 3 [Summer 1995], 197). Bruce Weston photo. SAB 68-467-50.

Overleaf above. The Prairie Economic Council, Regina, 13 Jan. 1972. Peter Lougheed, Allan Blakeney, and Ed Schreyer co-operated much more effectively than their predecessors. Journalist Jack Ludwig reported that the two New Democrats, Blakeney and Schreyer, got on well with the Conservative Peter Lougheed. Lougheed's right-wing opponents described him as 'almost socialist', wrote Ludwig, while 'Ed Schreyer and Allan Blakeney compliment him with the sobriquet "Red Tory"' (*Maclean's,* July 1975). D. Varley photo. SAB 71-1482-26.

Overleaf below. A Native drummer at the Northern Saskatchewan Games, La Ronge, August 1980. Native people have adapted for more than three centuries without losing their identity. L. McDowell photo. SAB 80-1236-R5-32.

plants. More than factories, however, the high-rise office building symbolized the urban Prairie West of the late twentieth century as surely as the false-front hotel had a hundred years earlier. There were more cranes 'in the Calgary sky than you can find at a bird sanctuary, and office towers continue to climb,' boasted the *Calgary Herald* on 10 March 1981. 'Calgary exhibits the spirit of new power, new wealth and initiative characterizing Western Canada,' wrote historian J. Arthur Lower in 1982; 'in a few years Calgary will displace Toronto as the financial centre of Canada.'[13]

The new class of indigenous entrepreneurs that sprouted in the 'oil patch' certainly thought so, as did the lawyers and accountants and the provincial civil servants who looked out for oil's interests. The Lougheed government reserved a slice of the petroleum pie for independent regional companies, which could obtain oil and gas exploration rights with small investments. Small Canadian-owned companies did most of the actual drilling on contract,

and provided the oil industry with most of the services and supplies it required.[14] There was one multi-billion-dollar Canadian petroleum giant: the Alberta Gas Trunk Line Company. Renamed 'Nova—an Alberta Corporation', it expanded from humble gas transmission into a vertically integrated oil and petrochemical conglomerate; nation and region alike were proud of its ability to compete with the multinational oil companies, and Nova became the corporate counterpart to the myth of the self-made man. Its president, Bob Blair, was chosen 'Man of the Year' by *The Globe and Mail Report on Business* in 1977, and was the only capitalist to be depicted as a hero in Friesen's *The Canadian Prairies*.

The images of a wealthy Prairie West and an indigent Eastern Canada were considerably overdrawn. In the three decades between 1950 and 1980, per capita incomes in Manitoba exceeded the national average exactly twice, and in Saskatchewan only four times; even the 'oil sheiks' of Alberta earned more than the national average in only eighteen of the thirty

---

Facing above. A farm woman greases a cultivator, Saskatchewan, September 1980. Modern farm women, like their great-grandmothers, continue to play an important role in the production process. Bruce Weston photo. SAB 80-1628-03.

Facing below. An oil pumper silhouetted against the Alberta sky, *c.* 1980. Photos of industrial development by Prairie boosters have changed since the early twentieth century. In 1905, such images proudly featured belching smokestacks; in 1980, boosters attempted to depict development while showing as little actual industrial activity as possible. Glenn Sitler photo. City of Edmonton Archives ET-11-61.

Overleaf above. Governor General Edward Schreyer and elder Dan Weasel Moccasin in a chieftain ceremony, 20 July 1979. Images of the King, the Queen, or the Governor General meeting with Native leaders are often clichés, but this pose is at least less formal than the one on p. 50. Schreyer, a former Manitoba NDP premier, accepted Pierre Trudeau's invitation to become governor general after his defeat in 1977 by the Conservatives under Sterling Lyon. Although his appointment did nothing to reconcile the Prairie West to the Trudeau government, the Manitoba NDP-did return to power in 1981, led by Howard Pawley. Sue Brun photo, *Calgary Herald.* Glenbow NA-2864-35765.

Overleaf below. Ukrainian-Canadian dancers at Alberta '75 Celebrations, 15 Nov. 1980. When Alberta and Saskatchewan observed the seventy-fifth anniversary of their provincehood in 1980, 'multiculturalism' had become an officially sanctioned part of the commemoration. *Calgary Herald* photo. Glenbow NA-2864-41891 #32A.

A Canadian Union of Public Employees picket during a nursing-home strike, Parkland, Alberta, 18 Jan. 1978. In all three Prairie provinces, thousands of women entered the waged labour force in public-sector service jobs during the 1970s. Bitter Prairie winters, however, remained unchanged. PAA J.3823/4.

years. It was not until 1979 that Alberta became the first Prairie province in which per capita income had ever exceeded that earned in 'impoverished' Ontario. The new West's economy might no longer be exclusively agricultural, but the region still depended on resources exported to external markets; for all its new confidence and burgeoning culture, the Prairie West remained a producing hinterland to a consuming—and controlling—metropolis.[15]

The May 1979 federal election seemed to offer the Prairie West the voice it sought in Ottawa. For the first time since 1962, Westerners turned on their televisions at 8 p.m. Central and Mountain Time to find that the results remained in doubt; after the Liberal candidates met their usual grisly fate on the Prairies, the region presented the new Conservative leader, native son Joe Clark, with 38 MPs, enabling him to form a minority government. But Clark governed for only ten months before his government was defeated in the Commons over a budget that made major oil price concessions to Alberta and Saskatchewan. In February 1980 Pierre Trudeau was back with a majority, returned by Ontario voters determined to have cheap energy, but with less Prairie support than ever: only two of the region's 49 seats, both in Winnipeg. Trudeau's National Energy Policy, announced in October, unilaterally tripled the federal share of oil revenues in order to finance an ambitious program to Canadianize the petroleum industry. NEP incentives diverted oil and gas exploration away from Alberta and Saskatchewan, where the provinces legally possessed the resources, to federally controlled areas off-shore or in the territories. Alberta retaliated with two 5 per cent reductions in the flow of oil that it piped east, and relations between Ottawa and Edmonton came to resemble those between none-too-friendly foreign powers.

Like every Prairie boom before it, however, the expansion based on oil, potash, and grain came crashing down. What was cruellest about the 1980s recession was that all the commodities on which the region depended collapsed together: the final blow was the Chernobyl nuclear disaster in 1986, which blunted demand for Saskatchewan's uranium. Unem-

To the Victors go the Spoils...

2,306,479,597,031,261.04 BUSHELS OF UNSOLD WHEAT...

ROMANOW

NDP

WELCOME TO SASKATCHEWAN

Brian Gable, 'To the Victors Go the Spoils . . .'. Saskatchewan voters decisively rejected the provincial Conservatives for Roy Romanow's New Democrats, but this cartoon illustrates an enduring Prairie dilemma: the region's economy remains tied to primary products sold in export markets. *The Globe and Mail*, 23 Oct. 1991.

ployment rates and provincial deficits soared: even mighty Alberta was soon 'running on empty' as the price of oil fell from nearly $30 a barrel to less than $10. Nova Corporation lost $82 million in 1985; its shares tumbled from $14 to $4.30, and the mantle of industrial genius slipped from Bob Blair's shoulders.[16]

Political casualties followed the economic ones. The Saskatchewan NDP government went down first, defeated in 1982 by Grant Devine's Conservatives. Manitoba's New Democrats lasted longer, but eventually succumbed to the provincial Conservatives under Gary Filmon. Alberta's Conservatives survived, chastened by a reduced popular vote and the annoyance of

a 16-seat NDP opposition, but Peter Lougheed's activist development strategy was left in ruins, as were the family strategies of Albertans who had bought real estate high and were forced by their creditors to sell low. In the 1984 federal election, the Prairie provinces scarcely stood out on an electoral map that Brian Mulroney turned Tory blue in every region. At last the Prairie West would have a voice in Ottawa— seven voices, in fact, from seven Prairie ministers in Mulroney's cabinet.

Recovery from the economic collapse was painfully slow, despite federal assurances that Prairie resource industries were now priorities. The sign that a *Globe and Mail* reporter saw over a beer cooler in an Alberta saloon in 1987 spoke for the hundreds of thousands of ordinary Prairie people who bore the brunt of the recession: 'Please God, let there be another oil boom. I promise not to piss it all away this time.' But unlike the 1970s, the 1980s saw no consensus on development or diversification. Both levels of government threw money at agriculture, especially in 1986, when the Devine government in Saskatchewan faced re-election and, with the assistance of the federal Tories, paid out an estimated $3 billion to grain farmers. But larger farmers gobbled up the subsidies, just as larger farms continued to gobble smaller ones. Bill Uruski, Manitoba's NDP Agriculture minister, estimated that the largest 30 per cent of farmers got 70 per cent of the federal grants, and an academic assessment confirmed his judgement: 'current programs,' two agricultural economists concluded, 'favour farmers with large amounts of land and less need for subsidies than many other farmers.'[17]

The Conservatives liked their businesses big. Following the lead of the Mulroney government, which had declared Canada 'open for business' to foreign capital, Tory premiers Grant Devine in Saskatchewan and Don Getty—the former Edmonton Eskimo quarterback to whom Lougheed had handed the ball—in Alberta, adopted the prevailing free-market approaches that commentators called 'neo-conservatism'. Under Devine rule, Saskatchewan sold off all or part of virtually everything that the Blakeney NDP government had built: SaskOil, the Potash Corporation, the provincial pulp mill. Only one export increased in volume: people. By 1991, 69,000 of them had left the province. Alberta imitated the Manitoba and Saskatchewan give-aways of

the 1960s, handing over the largest untouched boreal forest in North America to conglomerates, and blessing them with government-funded infrastructure, grants, and guaranteed loans. Both provinces' benefactions to the private sector were aided by federal grants from the Western Diversification Fund set up by the Mulroney government.

The Prairie West's thirty-year electoral love affair with the federal Conservatives lasted less than a decade once the Tories actually gained power. Brian Mulroney's party was re-elected in 1988 on its twin pillars of strength in the Prairie West and Quebec, but the partners in this cross-regional Conservative compact shared little but enthusiasm for provincial rights and for the 1987 free trade agreement with the United States. The alliance quickly fell apart when Prairie Tory voters perceived Quebec to be Mulroney's favoured child. Prairie premiers supported both of Mulroney's attempts to incorporate Quebec into the Canadian constitution, the Meech Lake Accord and the Charlottetown Accord, but opinion polls and the 1992 referendum on the Charlottetown Accord showed that the people in their provinces emphatically did not.

The heavy majorities against the Charlottetown Accord in Manitoba, Saskatchewan, and Alberta represented more than a reflexive regional rejection of Quebec. Some 'No' voters were expressing working-class unhappiness with the erosion of federal social programs implicit in the transfer of federal power to the provinces; some wanted a more precise constitutional definition of Aboriginal rights; and still others were feminists angered by the Accord's failure to address the status of women. Similarly, although the meteoric rise of Preston Manning's Reform party in the federal elections of 1993 and 1997 might seem to reflect a simple Western rejection of Mulroney's attempts to accommodate Quebec, the political developments of the 1990s suggest that easy 'East versus West' or 'Prairies versus Quebec' dichotomies, however much they might appeal to advocates of 'deconfederation', don't really explain very much. The pattern of Reform's success in the federal election of 1993 suggests that the Prairie West no longer exists as a region in federal politics. The only thing that Manitoba, Saskatchewan, and Alberta did in concert was to emphatically reject the Conservative party; however, given that the Tories elected only two members nationally, that hardly qualifies the Prairie West as distinct. Preston Manning's candidates won 22 of 26 seats in Alberta, but only four of 14 in Saskatchewan and one of 14 in Manitoba. In the latter two provinces the NDP remained electorally viable, and in all three the Liberals won significant numbers of seats for the first time in four decades: 12 in Manitoba, and five in Saskatchewan, as well as the four Edmonton seats that Reform failed to capture in Alberta.

Reform, like the Progressives in the 1920s and Social Credit in the 1930s and 1940s, benefited from Canada's single-member district-plurality electoral system, which hands large numbers of seats to small parties that concentrate their votes in one or two regions—a system that first exaggerates, and then exacerbates, regionalism. There also can be no doubt that Manning intends his party to be a national force, not a regional or provincial one. Its slogans, from 'The West Wants IN' to 'Building the New Canada' and its emphasis on the reform of federal institutions, like the 'Triple-E Senate'—Elected, Equal, Effective—suggest that Reform is squarely in the Prairie political tradition identified a half-century ago by W.L. Morton: 'revolt against, and . . . rejection of, the political and economic controls, but not the institutional foundations, of the nation.' Prairie Westerners—if they have ever existed as a unified group—continue to want to reshape Canada in their own image, even as their own images of themselves face constant renegotiation.[18]

Some things seem not to change. As these words are being written, a new boom is sweeping 'the West'. Once again *The Globe and Mail* writes that 'Canada's economic centre of gravity is rapidly moving west,' although it qualifies the comment by amalgamating Alberta with British Columbia to construct 'the West' and erases Saskatchewan and Manitoba, which 'have contributed virtually nothing to the West's latest rise as an employment powerhouse'. In *Maclean's*, Peter C. Newman gushes over Canadian Pacific's decision to move its headquarters formally from Montreal to Calgary; soon, he predicts, 'Western Canadians will recognize their one-time exploiter as a welcome and creative player in the West's inevitable march to economic greatness.' No matter how many times 'Next Year Country' fails to be what Canadians wish it to be, the myth of West as Hope resurfaces. Balladeer Ian Tyson invites Torontonians to go west in a lyric only slightly altered from the language that Clifford Sifton's Department of the Interior might have used a century ago: 'gas up your old Chevrolet and head 'er way out west/to the Land of *Golden Opportunity*./You'll get a first-hand education, how the cowboy rocks and rolls/And that old Alberta moon thrown in for *free*.'[19]

NOTES

Introduction: Imag[in]ing a Region

1. Ramsay Cook coined the term 'limited identity' to describe the sub-national identities of ethnicity, class, gender, and region in 1967, and J.M.S. Careless popularized it in a much reprinted article entitled '"Limited Identities" in Canada', *Canadian Historical Review* L, 1 (1969), 1–10.

2. Patricia Nelson Limerick, *The Legacy of Conquest: The Unbroken Past of the American West* (New York: Norton, 1987).

3. Richard White, *It's Your Misfortune and None of My Own: A History of the American West* (Norman: University of Oklahoma Press, 1991), 617.

4. J. Robert Davidson, 'Turning a Blind Eye: the Historian's Use of Photographs', *BC Studies* 52 (1981–2), 16–38; Jim Burant, 'The Military Artist and the Documentary Record', *Archivaria* 26 (1988), 33–51.

5. Peter Robertson, 'More than Meets the Eye', *Archivaria* 2 (1976), 33–43.

6. Susan Sontag, *On Photography* (New York: Farrar, Straus and Giroux, 1977); John Tagg, *The Burden of Representation: Essays on Photographies and Histories* (Amherst: University of Massachusetts Press, 1988).

7. Lilly Koltun, 'Not the *World of William Notman*', *Journal of Canadian Studies* 30, 1 (1995), 125–33; Koltun, 'Pre-Confederation Photography in Toronto', *History of Photography* 2, 3 (July 1978), 249–63.

8. Bryan D. Palmer, review of Elaine Bernard et al., *Working Lives: Vancouver, 1886–1986*, in *BC Studies* 73 (1987), 52–67.

1: 'Ever . . . useless to cultivating man'

1. William Westfall, 'On the Concept of Region in Canadian History and Literature', *Journal of Canadian Studies*, 16, 2 (Summer 1980), 3–15.

2. John Warkentin, *The Western Interior of Canada* (Toronto: McClelland and Stewart, 1964), 3–4; David A. Gauthier and J. David Henry, 'Misunderstanding the Prairies', in Monte Hummel, ed., *Endangered Spaces* (Toronto: Key Porter, 1989), 183–93; J.O. Wheeler, 'Geographical Regions', *The Canadian Encyclopedia*, 2nd edn (Edmonton: Hurtig, 1988), 884–9.

3. Irene M. Spry, ed., *The Papers of the Palliser Expedition, 1857–1860* (Toronto, Champlain Society, 1968).

4. Richard Glover, ed., *David Thompson's Narrative 1784–1812* (Toronto: Champlain Society, 1962) 164–5.

5. Kane's narrative is reprinted in J. Russell Harper, *Paul Kane's Frontier* (Toronto: University of Toronto Press, 1971), 143; George J. Mitchell, ed., *Man: User and Modifier of Canada Plains' Resources*, a special issue of *Prairie Forum* 9, 2 (Fall 1984).

6. Butler is quoted in R. Douglas Francis, *Images of*

the West: *Changing Perceptions of the Canadian Prairies, 1690–1960* (Saskatoon: Western Producer Prairie Books, 1989), 53–4.

7. J.G. Nelson, *Man's Impact on the Western Canadian Landscape* (Toronto: McClelland and Stewart, 1976), especially 67–8.

8. Catlin quoted in Joni L. Kinsey, 'Not So Plain: Art of the American Prairies', *Great Plains Quarterly* 15, 3 (Summer 1995), 185–7; Thompson quoted in Warkentin, *Western Interior of Canada*, 103.

2: Cultures in Contact: 1670–1821

1. James W. St. G. Walker, 'The Indian in Canadian Historical Writing', *Canadian Historical Association Historical Papers* (1971), 21–51.

2. Bruce G. Trigger, *Natives and Newcomers* (Montreal: McGill-Queen's University Press, 1985); James Walker contributed an excellent historiographical essay to Ian A.L. Getty and Antoine S. Lussier, eds, *As Long as the Sun Shines and the Water Flows : A Reader in Canadian Native Studies* (Vancouver: University of British Columbia Press, 1983), which describes this 'new' Indian history.

3. Margaret Conrad, Alvin Finkel, and Cornelius Jaenen, *History of the Canadian Peoples*, vol. 1 (Toronto: Copp Clark Pitman 1993), 24–41.

4. Olive P. Dickason, *Canada's First Nations: A History of Founding Peoples from Earliest Times* (Toronto: McClelland and Stewart, 1992).

5. Laura Peers, *The Ojibwa of Western Canada, 1780–1870* (Winnipeg: University of Manitoba Press, 1994).

6. Catherine Flynn and E. Leigh Syms, 'Manitoba's First Farmers', *Manitoba History* (Spring 1996), 4–11.

7. Duncan McGillivray quoted in A.S. Morton, *A History of the Canadian West to 1870–71*, 2nd edn (Toronto: University of Toronto Press, 1973), 459.

8. John S. Milloy, *The Plains Cree: Trade, Diplomacy, and War, 1790–1870* (Winnipeg: University of Manitoba Press, 1988); J.G. Nelson, *The Last Refuge* (Montreal: Harvest House, 1973).

9. Arthur J. Ray and Donald Freeman, '*Give Us Good Measure': An Economic Analysis of Relations Between the Indians and the Hudson's Bay Company Before 1763* (Toronto: University of Toronto Press, 1978).

10. Daniel Francis and Toby Morantz, *Partners in Furs: A History of the Fur Trade in Eastern James Bay, 1600–1870* (Montreal: McGill-Queen's University Press, 1983); Glyndwer Williams, *The Hudson's Bay Company and the Fur Trade: 1670–1870* (Winnipeg: HBC, 1987).

11. *A History of Manitoba: Rupert's Land to Riel* (Winnipeg, 1993), 72–4.

12. E.E. Rich, *The Fur Trade and the Northwest to 1857* (Toronto: McClelland and Stewart, 1967); Thomas Schilz, 'Brandy and Beaver Pelts: Assiniboine–European Trading Patterns, 1695–1805', *Saskatchewan History* XXXVII, 3 (Autumn 1984), 95–102.

13. Richard I. Ruggles, 'Mapping of the Interior Plains of Rupert's Land by the Hudson's Bay Company', in Frederick C. Luebke et al., eds, *Mapping the North American Plains* (Norman: University of Oklahoma Press, 1987).

14. Williams, *The Hudson's Bay Company and the Fur Trade*, 39–40.

15. Donald Freeman and Frances L. Dungey, 'A Spatial Duopoly: Competition in the Western Canadian Fur Trade, 1770–1835', *Journal of Historical Geography* 7, 3 (1981).

16. Rich, *The Fur Trade and the Northwest*, 194.

17. Arthur J. Ray, *Indians in the Fur Trade: Their Role as Trappers, Hunters and Middlemen in the Lands Southwest of Hudson Bay, 1660–1870* (Toronto: University of Toronto Press, 1974), Ch. 8; Williams, *The HBC and the Fur Trade*.

18. Quoted in Peter C. Newman, *Company of Adventurers*, vol. I (Markham, ON: Viking, 1985), 278–9.

19. Quoted in Williams, *The HBC and the Fur Trade*, 42.

20. W.A. Sloan, 'The Native Response to the Extension of European Traders into the Athabasca and Mackenzie Basin, 1770–1814', *Canadian Historical Review* LX, 3 (September 1979).

21. Ray, *Indians in the Fur Trade*.

22. Dickason, *Canada's First Nations*, 192–201.

23. Ray, *Indians in the Fur Trade*, Ch. 8.

24. Douglas MacKay, *The Honourable Company: A History of the Hudson's Bay Company* (Toronto: McClelland and Stewart, 1949), 132.

25. Sylvia Van Kirk, *Many Tender Ties: Women in Fur-Trade Society, 1670–1870* (Winnipeg: Watson and Dwyer, 1980); Jennifer S.H. Brown, *Strangers in Blood: Fur Trade Company Families in Indian Country* (Vancouver: University of British Columbia Press, 1980).

26. Lyle Dick, 'The Seven Oaks Incident and the Construction of a Historical Tradition, 1816 to 1870', *Journal of the Canadian Historical Association*, new series no. 2 (1991) 91–113.

3: Fur Trade to Settlement: 1821–1870

1. Keith Wilson, 'Napoleon of the West', *Horizon Canada* 5 (1987), 1129–35; Glyndwer Williams, *The Hudson's Bay Company and the Fur Trade: 1670–1870* (Winnipeg: HBC, 1987).

2. Philip Goldring, 'Employment Relations in the Fur Trade, 1821–1892' (unpublished paper delivered to the Canadian Historical Association, Halifax, 1981).

3. Harold A. Innis, *The Fur Trade in Canada* (Toronto: University of Toronto Press, 1956); Dan Francis and Toby Morantz, 'A New Relationship', Chapter 10 of *Partners in Furs: A History of the Fur Trade in Eastern James Bay, 1600–1870* (Montreal: McGill-Queen's University Press, 1983).

4. John Foster, 'The Métis and the End of the Plains Buffalo in Alberta', *Alberta* 3, 1 (1992), 61–77; Arthur J. Ray, *Indians in the Fur Trade: Their Role as Trappers, Hunters, and Middlemen in the Lands Southwest of Hudson Bay, 1660–1870* (Toronto: University of Toronto Press, 1974), Chapter 8.

5. Ray, *Indians in the Fur Trade*; Simpson quoted in Dan Francis, *Battle for the West: Fur Traders and the Birth of Western Canada* (Edmonton: Hurtig, 1982), 143–7.

6. A.J. Ray, 'Smallpox: The Epidemic of 1837–38', *The Beaver* (Autumn 1975).

7. Alvin M. Josephy, Jr, *The Artist Was a Young Man: The Life Story of Peter Rindisbacher* (Fort Worth, TX: Amon Carter Museum, 1970); 'Peter Rindisbacher', in National Archives of Canada, *A Place in History: Twenty Years of Acquiring Paintings, Drawings and Prints at the National Archives of Canada* (Ottawa: NAC, 1991).

8. Jacqueline Peterson and Jennifer S.H. Brown, *The New Peoples: Being and Becoming Métis in North America* (Winnipeg: University of Manitoba Press, 1985); John Foster, 'Origins of the Mixed Bloods' in L.H. Thomas, ed., *Essays in Western Canadian History* (Edmonton: University of Alberta Press, 1976), 71–82; George F. Stanley, *The Birth of Western Canada: A History of the Riel Rebellions* (Toronto: University of Toronto Press, 1936); Gerhard Ens, *Homeland to Hinterland: Changing Worlds of the Red River Métis in the Nineteenth Century* (Toronto: University of Toronto Press, 1996).

9. W.L. Morton, *Manitoba: A History* (Toronto: University of Toronto Press, 1967).

10. J. Russell Harper, *Paul Kane's Frontier* (Toronto: University of Toronto Press, 1971); Ann Davis and Robert Thacker, 'Pictures and Prose: Romantic Sensibility and The Great Plains in Catlin, Kane, and Miller', *Great Plains Quarterly* 6, 1 (Winter 1986); Diane Eaton and Sheila Urbanek, *Paul Kane's Great Nor-West* (Vancouver: University of British Columbia Press, 1995); 'Paul Kane', in National Archives, *A Place in History*.

11. David McNab, 'The Colonial Office and the Prairies in the Mid-Nineteenth Century', *Prairie Forum* 3, 1 (Spring 1978), 21–38.

12. E.E. Rich, *The Fur Trade and the Northwest to 1857* (Toronto: McClelland and Stewart, 1967), Chapter 15; Alexander Morris, *The Hudson's Bay and Pacific Territories* (Montreal, 1859).

13. Suzanne Zeller, *Inventing Canada: Early Victorian Science and the Idea of a Transcontinental Nation* (Toronto: University of Toronto Press, 1987); Hind and Hector quoted in John Warkentin, ed., *The Western Interior of Canada: A Record of Geographical Discovery, 1612–1917* (Toronto:

McClelland and Stewart, 1964); Doug Owram, *Promise of Eden: The Canadian Expansionist Movement and the Idea of the West, 1856–1900* (Toronto: University of Toronto Press, 1980).

14. Lilly Koltun, 'Pre-Confederation Photography in Toronto', *History of Photography* 2, 3 (July 1978), 249–63; Ralph Greenhill, *Early Photography in Canada* (Toronto: University of Toronto Press, 1965); Richard J. Huyda, *Camera in the Interior: H.L. Hime, Photographer* (Toronto: Coach House Press, 1973); Andrea Kunard, 'The Photography of Humphrey Lloyd Hime in the 1858 Red River-Assiniboine Exploratory Expedition' (unpublished paper).

15. Irene Spry, 'The Great Transformation: The Disappearance of the Commons in Western Canada', in Richard Allen, ed., *Man and Nature of the Prairies* (Regina: Canadian Plains Research Center, University of Regina, 1976), 19–45.

16. Frits Pannekoek, *A Snug Little Flock: The Social Origins of the Red River Resistance of 1869–70* (Winnipeg: Watson and Dwyer, 1991).

17. Owram, *Promise of Eden*, Chapter 4.

18. Gerald Friesen, 'Plain People's Country', (unpublished paper delivered to the Canadian Historical Association, Montreal, 1995); Gerhard Ens, 'Prologue to the Red River Resistance: Pre-liminal Politics and the Triumph of Riel', *Journal of the Canadian Historical Association* new series no. 5 (1994), 111–23.

19. J.M. Bumsted, 'Crisis at Red River', *The Beaver* 75, 3 (June–July 1995), 23–34; Thomas Flanagan, *Louis 'David' Riel: Prophet of the New World* (Toronto: University of Toronto Press, 1979).

20. G.F.G. Stanley, *Louis Riel: Patriot or Rebel* (Ottawa: Canadian Historical Association, 1970).

4: Making the Prairie West Canadian: 1870–1900

1. Lewis Herbert Thomas, *The Struggle for Responsible Government in the North-West Territories, 1870–97* (Toronto: University of Toronto Press, 1956, 1978).

2. R.C. Macleod, *The North West Mounted Police and Law Enforcement, 1873–1905* (Toronto: University of Toronto Press, 1976); S.W. Horrall, 'Sir John A. Macdonald and the Mounted Police Force for the Northwest Territories', *Canadian Historical Review* LIII, 2 (June 1972), 179–200.

3. Phillip Goldring, 'The First Contingent: The North-West Mounted Police, 1873–74' and 'Whisky, Horses and Death: The Cypress Hills Massacre and Its Sequel', in *Canadian Historic Sites: Occasional Papers in Archaeology and History* 21 (Ottawa: National Parks and Historic Sites, 1979), 5–70; Dufferin cited in 'The First Contingent'.

4. Gerald Friesen, *The Canadian Prairies: A History* (Toronto: University of Toronto Press, 1984), Chapter 8; Robert Thacker, 'Canada's Mounted: The Evolution of a Legend', *Journal of Popular Culture* 14 (Fall 1980), 300–3; George F.G. Stanley, 'The Man Who Sketched the Great March', in Hugh A. Dempsey, ed., *Men in Scarlet* (Calgary: Historical Society of Alberta, 1974), 27–49; Wallace Stegner, *Wolf Willow: A History, a Story, and a Memory of the Last Plains Frontier* (New York: Viking, 1966), 81–110.

5. John Foster, 'The Métis and the End of the Plains Buffalo in Alberta', *Alberta* 3, 1 (1992), 61–77; William A. Dobak, 'Killing the Canadian Buffalo, 1821–1881', *Western Historical Quarterly* XXVII, 1 (Spring 1996), 33–52; Barry Potyondi, 'Loss and Substitution: The Ecology of Production in Southwestern Saskatchewan, 1860–1930', *Journal of the Canadian Historical Association*, new series no. 5 (1994), 213–35; W.F. Butler, *The Great Lone Land* (London, 1872).

6. Mackenzie quoted in J.R. Miller, *Skyscrapers Hide the Heavens* (Toronto: University of Toronto Press, 1989; 2nd edn 1992), 162.

7. John L. Tobias, 'Canada's Subjugation of the Plains Cree, 1879–1885', *Canadian Historical Review* LXIV, 4 (1983), 519–48.

8. Robert S. Allen, 'The Breaking of Big Bear', *Horizon Canada* 5 (1987), 1190–5.

9. Chester Martin, *'Dominion Lands' Policy*

(Toronto, 1937); James M. Richtik, 'The Policy Framework for Settling the Canadian West, 1870–1880', *Agricultural History* 49, 4 (1975), 613–28.

10. W.A. Waiser, 'A Willing Scapegoat: John Macoun and the Route of the CPR', *Prairie Forum* 10, 1 (1985), 65–82; Pierre Berton, *The National Dream: the Great Railway, 1871–1881* and *The Last Spike* (Toronto: McClelland and Stewart, 1970 and 1974); Michael Bliss, *Northern Enterprise: Five Centuries of Canadian Business* (Toronto: McClelland and Stewart, 1987), Chapter 8.

11. D.N. Sprague, *Canada and the Métis, 1869–1885* (Waterloo, ON: Wilfrid Laurier University Press, 1988); Thomas Flanagan, *Metis Lands in Manitoba* (Calgary: University of Calgary Press, 1991); Brad Milne, 'The Historiography of Métis Land Dispersal, 1870–1890', *Manitoba History* (Autumn 1995), 30–41.

12. Gerhard Ens, 'Dispossession or Adaptation?: Migration and Persistence of the Red River Metis, 1835–1890', *Canadian Historical Association Historical Papers* (1988), 120–44.

13. Don McLean, *1885: Metis Rebellion or Government Conspiracy?* (Winnipeg: Pemmican Publications, 1985); Bob Beal and Rod Macleod, *Prairie Fire: the 1885 North-West Rebellion* (Edmonton: Hurtig, 1984).

14. Walter Hildebrandt, 'The Battle of Batoche', *Prairie Forum* 10, 1 (Spring 1986), 17–64.

15. J.R. Miller, *Skyscrapers Hide the Heavens: A History of Indian-White Relations in Canada* (Toronto: University of Toronto Press, 1989), Chapter 11; Brian Hubner, 'Horse Stealing and the Borderline: the NWMP and the Control of Indian Movement, 1874–1900', *Prairie Forum* 20, 2 (Fall 1995), 281–300; Sarah Carter, *Lost Harvests: Prairie Indian Reserve Farmers and Government Policy* (Montreal and Kingston: McGill-Queen's University Press, 1990).

16. J.R. Miller, J.R., *Shingwauk's Vision : A History of Native Residential Schools* (Toronto: University of Toronto Press, 1996); Katherine Pettipas,

Severing the Ties that Bind: Government Repression of Indigenous Religious Ceremonies on the Prairies (Winnipeg: University of Manitoba Press, 1994).

17. M.K. Lux, 'Beyond the "Biological Invasion" Theory of World History: Disease and Native Peoples on the Canadian Prairies, 1880–1920' (unpublished paper delivered to the Canadian Historical Association, Montreal, 1995).

18. David H. Breen, *The Canadian Prairie West and the Ranching Frontier 1874–1924* (Toronto: University of Toronto Press, 1983).

19. Richard Maxwell Brown, 'Law and Order on the American Frontier: the Western Civil War of Incorporation', in John McLaren et al., eds, *Law for the Elephant, Law for the Beaver: Essays in the Legal History of the North American West* (Regina and Pasadena: Canadian Plains Research Center, 1992), 75–89.

20. Barry Potyondi, *In Palliser's Triangle: Living in the Grasslands, 1850–1930* (Saskatoon: Purich Publishing, 1995), 44–83; Donald Worster, 'Cowboy Ecology', Chapter 3 of *Under Western Skies: Nature and History in the American West* (New York: Oxford University Press, 1992).

21. Lyle Dick, *Farmers 'Making Good': The Development of Abernethy District, Saskatchewan, 1880–1920* (Ottawa: Parks Canada, 1989).

22. Royden K. Loewen, *Family, Church, and Market: A Mennonite Community in the Old and the New Worlds, 1850–1930* (Urbana: University of Illinois Press, 1993); Howard Palmer, *Land of the Second Chance: A History of Ethnic Groups in Southern Alberta* (Lethbridge: Lethbridge Herald, 1972).

23. John C. Lehr and Yossi Katz, 'Crown, Corporation and Church: the Role of Institutions in the Stability of Pioneer Settlements in the Canadian West, 1870–1914', *Journal of Historical Geography* 21, 4 (1995), 413–29.

24. W.L. Morton, *Manitoba: A History* (Toronto: University of Toronto Press, 1967), Chapter 10; R. Douglas Francis, '"Rural Ontario West": Ontarians in Alberta', in Howard and Tamara

Palmer, eds, *Peoples of Alberta: Portraits of Cultural Diversity* (Saskatoon: Western Producer Prairie Books, 1985), 123–42; Robert Craig Brown, 'Canadian Nationalism in Western Newspapers', *Alberta Historical Review* 10, 3 (1962), 1–7; Stegner, *Wolf Willow*, 85.

5: The Twentieth Century Belongs to the Canadian West, 1901–1920

1. D.J. Hall, *Clifford Sifton*, vol. 1, *The Young Napoleon, 1861–1900* and vol. 2, *The Lonely Eminence, 1901–1929* (Vancouver: University of British Columbia Press, 1981 and 1985).

2. Walter Nugent, *Crossings: The Great Transatlantic Migrations, 1870–1914* (Bloomington: University of Indiana Press, 1992); Marvin McInnis, 'Migration' and 'Elements of Population Change', Plates 27 and 28 in Donald Kerr et al., *Addressing the Twentieth Century*, vol. III of *The Historical Atlas of Canada, 1891–1961* (Toronto: University of Toronto Press, 1990).

3. Patricia E. Roy, *A White Man's Province: British Columbia Politicians and Chinese Immigrants, 1858–1914* (Vancouver: University of British Columbia Press, 1989); W. Peter Ward, *White Canada Forever: Popular Attitudes and Public Policies towards Orientals in British Columbia* (Montreal: McGill–Queen's University Press, 1978).

4. John C. Lehr, '"The Peculiar People": Ukrainian Settlement of Marginal Lands in Southeastern Manitoba', in David C. Jones and Ian MacPherson, eds, *Building Beyond the Homestead: Rural History on the Prairies* (Calgary: University of Calgary Press, 1985).

5. Harold Troper, *Only Farmers Need Apply* (Toronto: Griffin House, 1972); Donald Avery, *'Dangerous Foreigners': European Immigrant Workers and Labour Radicalism in Canada, 1896–1932* (Toronto: McClelland and Stewart, 1979).

6. A. Ross McCormack, 'Networks among British Immigrants and Accommodation to Canadian Society: Winnipeg, 1900–1914', *Histoire sociale/Social History* 34 (1984), 357–74.

7. Doug Owram, 'Conclusion' in *Promise of Eden: The Canadian Expansionist Movement and the Idea of the West 1856–1900* (Toronto: University of Toronto Press, 1992).

8. Kenneth Norrie, 'The National Policy and the Rate of Prairie Settlement', *Journal of Canadian Studies* 14, 1 (Fall 1979), 63–76; Norrie, 'Dry Farming and the Economics of Risk Bearing: The Canadian Prairies 1870–1930', *Agricultural History* 51, 1 (1977), 134–48; Trevor J.O. Dick, 'Canadian Wheat Production and Trade, 1896–1930', *Explorations in Economic History* 17 (1980) 275–302.

9. Simon M. Evans, 'The End of the Open Range Era in Western Canada', *Prairie Forum* 8, 1 (1983), 71–87; David H. Breen, *The Canadian Prairie West and the Ranching Frontier, 1874–1924* (Toronto: University of Toronto Press, 1983); Kennedy cited in Frank Carrell, *Canada's West and Farther West: Latest Book on the Land of Golden Opportunities* (Quebec, 1911).

10. Grant MacEwan, *Charles Noble: Guardian of the Soil* (Saskatoon: Western Producer Prairie Books, 1983); Jaroslav Petryshyn, *Peasants in the Promised Land: Canada and the Ukrainians, 1891–1914* (Toronto: James Lorimer, 1985); Donald M. Loveridge, '"The Garden of Manitoba": The Settlement and Agricultural Development of the Rock Lake District and the Municipality of Louise, 1878–1902', (Ph.D. thesis, University of Toronto, 1986); P.L. McCormick, 'Transportation and Settlement: Problems in the Expansion of the Frontier in Saskatchewan and Assiniboia in 1904', *Prairie Forum* 5, 1 (1980), 14–16; Paul Voisey, *Vulcan: The Making of a Prairie Community* (Toronto: University of Toronto Press, 1988).

11. Verda Niddrie, 'The Johnsons of Eagle Valley', *Alberta History* 43, 2 (Spring 1995), 25–7.

12. Cecelia Danysk, *Hired Hands: Labour and the Development of Prairie Agriculture, 1880–1930* (Toronto: McClelland and Stewart, 1995); W.J.C. Cherwinski, 'In Search of Jake Trumper: The Farm Hand and the Prairie Farm Family',

in David C. Jones and Ian MacPherson, eds, *Building Beyond the Homestead* (Calgary: University of Calgary Press, 1985), 111–34.

13. Nellie McClung, *In Times Like These* (Toronto, 1915), quoted in John Herd Thompson, 'Bringing in the Sheaves: The Harvest Excursionists, 1890–1929', *Canadian Historical Review* LXI, 4 (1978), 467–89; Frances Swyripa, *Wedded to the Cause: Ukrainian-Canadian Women and Ethnic Identity, 1891–1991* (Toronto: University of Toronto Press, 1993); Lesley Erickson, 'The Interplay of Ethnicity and Gender: Swedish Women in Southeastern Saskatchewan', in David DeBrou and Aileen Moffatt, eds, *'Other' Voices: Historical Essays on Saskatchewan Women* (Regina: Canadian Plains Research Center, 1985), 94–111; Wsevolod W. Isajiw, 'Occupational and Economic Development', in Manoly R. Lupul, ed., *A Heritage in Transition: Essays in the History of Ukrainians in Canada* (Toronto: McClelland and Stewart, 1982), 59–84.

14. Katherine Harris, 'Homesteading in Northeastern Colorado, 1873–1920: Sex Roles and Women's Experience', in Susan Armitage and Elizabeth Jameson, eds, *The Women's West* (Norman: University of Oklahoma Press, 1987), 165–78; Catherine Cavanaugh, 'The Limitations of the Pioneering Partnership: The Alberta Campaign for Homestead Dower', in Catherine Cavanaugh and Jeremy Mouat, *Making Western Canada: Essays on European Colonization and Settlement* (Toronto: Garamond, 1996), 186–214; Veronica Strong-Boag, 'Pulling in Double Harness or Hauling a Double Load: Women, Work and Feminism on the Canadian Prairie', *Journal of Canadian Studies* 21, 3 (1986), 32–52.

15. T.D. Regehr, *The Canadian Northern Railway: Pioneer Road of the Northern Prairies 1895–1918* (Toronto: University of Toronto Press, 1976).

16. A.A. den Otter, *Civilizing the West: The Galts and the Development of Western Canada* (Edmonton: University of Alberta Press, 1982).

17. G.E. Mills, *Buying Wood and Building Farms:*

Marketing Lumber and Farm Building Designs on the Canadian Prairies (Ottawa: National Historic Sites, 1991).

18. Paul Voisey, 'The Urbanization of the Canadian Prairies, 1871–1916', *Histoire sociale/Social History* 15 (1975), 77–101; Alan Artibise, *Winnipeg: A Social History of Urban Growth* (Montreal and Kingston, McGill-Queen's University Press, 1975); Artibise, 'The Urban West: The Evolution of Prairie Towns and Cities to 1930', *Prairie Forum* 4, 2 (1979), 237–62; J. William Brennan, *Regina: An Illustrated History* (Toronto: James Lorimer, 1989); Max Foran, *Calgary: An Illustrated History* (Toronto: James Lorimer, 1978); Donald G. Wetherall and Irene R.A. Kmet, *Town Life: Main Street and the Evolution of Small Town Alberta, 1880–1947* (Edmonton: University of Alberta Press, 1995).

19. A. Ross McCormack, *Reformers, Rebels, and Revolutionaries: The Western Canadian Radical Movement 1899–1919* (Toronto: University of Toronto Press, 1977). Sifton quoted in J.M. Bliss, *Canadian History in Documents, 1763–1966* (Toronto: Ryerson Press, 1966), 203–5.

20. Gerald Friesen, *The Canadian Prairies: A History* (Toronto: University of Toronto Press, 1984), Chapter 14; J. William Brennan, 'Wooing the Foreign Vote', *Prairie Forum* 3, 1 (1978), 61–78.

21. David E. Smith, *Prairie Liberalism: The Liberal Party in Saskatchewan 1905–71* (Toronto: University of Toronto Press, 1975).

22. Lewis G. Thomas, *The Liberal Party in Alberta: A History of Politics in the Province of Alberta, 1905–1921* (Toronto: University of Toronto Press, 1959); D.R. Babcock, 'Autonomy and Alienation in Alberta: Premier A.C. Rutherford', *Prairie Forum* 6, 2 (1981), 117–28.

23. Richard Allen, 'The Social Gospel as the Religion of the Agrarian Revolt', in Carl Berger and Ramsay Cook, eds, *The West and the Nation: Essays in Honour of W.L. Morton* (Toronto: McClelland and Stewart, 1976), 174–86; Girard Hengen, 'A Case Study in Urban Reform: Regina Before the First World War', *Saskatchewan History* XLI, 1 (1988), 19–34.

24. Elizabeth Kalmakoff, 'Naturally Divided: Women in Saskatchewan Politics, 1916–1919', *Saskatchewan History* 46, 2 (1994), 3–18.

25. John Herd Thompson, *The Harvests of War: The Prairie West, 1914–1918* (Toronto: McClelland and Stewart, 1978), Chapter 5.

26. David Jay Bercuson, *Confrontation at Winnipeg: Labour, Industrial Relations, and the General Strike* (Montreal: McGill-Queen's University Press, 1974); J.M. Bumsted, *The Winnipeg General Strike of 1919: An Illustrated History* (Winnipeg: Watson and Dwyer, 1994); G.S. Kealey, '1919: The Canadian Labour Revolt', *Labour/Le Travail* 13 (1984), 11–44.

6: Harsh Realities of Region, 1921–1939

1. John Sandilands, *Western Canadian Dictionary and Phrase Book* (Winnipeg, 1913, reprinted Edmonton: University of Alberta Press, 1977).

2. *Grain Growers' Guide*, 10 June 1914; 29 July 1914.

3. Russell Hann, *Farmers Confront Industrialism* (Toronto: New Hogtown Press, 1975); Brian R. McCutcheon, 'The Patrons of Industry in Manitoba, 1890–1898', in Donald Swainson, ed., *Historical Essays on the Prairie Provinces* (Toronto: McClelland and Stewart, 1970), 142–65; Ian MacPherson, *The Co-operative Movement on the Prairies, 1900–1955* (Ottawa: Canadian Historical Association, 1979); MacPherson and John Herd Thompson, 'The Business of Agriculture: Prairie Farmers and the Adoption of "Business Methods", 1880–1950', in R. Douglas Francis and Howard Palmer, eds, *The Prairie West: Historical Readings* (Edmonton: University of Alberta Press, 1992), 475–96.

4. W.L. Morton, *The Progressive Party in Canada* (Toronto: University of Toronto Press, 1950).

5. John Herd Thompson with Allen Seager, *Canada 1922–1939: Decades of Discord* (Toronto: McClelland and Stewart, 1985), Chapter 2.

6. Roger Gibbins, *Prairie Politics and Society: Regionalism in Decline* (Toronto: Butterworth, 1980), Chapter 2.

7. C.F. Wilson, *A Century of Canadian Grain* (Saskatoon: Western Producer Prairie Books, 1978); V.C. Fowke, *The National Policy and the Wheat Economy* (Toronto: University of Toronto Press, 1957).

8. Garry Fairbairn, *From Prairie Roots: The Remarkable Story of the Saskatchewan Wheat Pool* (Saskatoon: Western Producer Prairie Books, 1982); Allan Levine, *The Exchange: 100 Years of Trading Grain in Winnipeg* (Winnipeg: Peguis Publishing, 1987).

9. Alan Artibise, *Winnipeg: An Illustrated History* (Toronto: James Lorimer, 1977).

10. Ronald Lappage, 'Sport Between the Wars', in Don Morrow et al., *A Concise History of Sport in Canada* (Toronto: Oxford University Press, 1989), Chapter 5.

11. David C. Jones, *Empire of Dust: Settling and Abandoning the Prairie Dry Belt* (Edmonton: University of Alberta Press, 1987).

12. William Paul Ferguson, *The Snowbird Decades: Western Canada's Pioneer Aviation Companies* (Toronto: Butterworth, 1979); James H. Gray, *The Roar of the Twenties* (Toronto: Macmillan, 1975).

13. Donald Avery, *'Dangerous Foreigners': European Immigrant Workers and Labour Radicalism in Canada, 1896–1932* (Toronto: McClelland and Stewart, 1979), Chapter 4.

14. Rose T. Harasym, 'Ukrainians in Canadian Political Life, 1923–1945', in Manoly R. Lupul, ed., *A Heritage in Transition: Essays in the History of Ukrainians in Canada* (Toronto: McClelland and Stewart, 1982), 108–25; George Hoffman, 'The New Party and the Old Issues: The Saskatchewan Farmer-Labour Party and the Ethnic Vote, 1934', *Canadian Ethnic Studies* XIV, 2 (1982), 1–20.

15. Raymond Huel, 'J.J. Maloney: How the West Was Saved from Rome, Quebec, and the Liberals', in John E. Foster, ed., *The Developing West* (Edmonton: University of Alberta, 1985), 221–41; Howard Palmer, 'Reluctant Hosts: Anglo-Canadian Views of Multiculturalism in the Twentieth Century', in R. Douglas Francis and Donald B. Smith, *Readings in Canadian*

History, vol. 2, *Post-Confederation* (Toronto: Harcourt-Brace, 1994), 142–61.

16. Patricia Roome, 'Amelia Turner and Calgary Labour Women, 1919–1935', in Linda Kealey and Joan Sangster, eds, *Beyond the Vote: Canadian Women and Politics* (Toronto: University of Toronto Press, 1989), 89–117; Thompson with Seager, *Canada 1922–1939,* Chapter 4.

17. Frances Swyripa, *Wedded to the Cause: Ukrainian-Canadian Women and Ethnic Identity, 1891–1991* (Toronto: University of Toronto Press, 1993); Veronica Strong-Boag, 'Pulling in Double Harness or Hauling a Double Load: Women, Work and Feminism on the Canadian Prairie', *Journal of Canadian Studies* 21, 3 (1986), 32–52; Helen Potrebenko, *No Streets of Gold: A Social History of Ukrainians in Alberta* (Vancouver: New Star Books, 1977); Gunn quoted in L.J. Wilson, 'Educational Role of the United Farm Women of Alberta', *Alberta History* 25, 2 (1977), 28–36.

18. James H. Gray, *Men Against the Desert* (Saskatoon: Modern Press, 1967) and *The Winter Years: The Depression on the Prairies* (Toronto: Macmillan, 1966).

19. James Struthers, *No Fault of Their Own: Unemployment and the Canadian Welfare State, 1914–1941* (Toronto: University of Toronto Press, 1983).

20. Aberhart to J.H. Caldwell, 29 March 1933, in W. Norman Smith Papers, Glenbow-Alberta Archives.

21. Alvin Finkel, *The Social Credit Phenomenon in Alberta* (Toronto: University of Toronto Press, 1989); L.H. Thomas, ed., *William Aberhart and Social Credit in Alberta* (Toronto: Copp Clark, 1977).

22. John A. Kendle, *John Bracken: A Political Biography* (Toronto: University of Toronto Press, 1979); Howard R. Lamar, 'Comparing Depressions: The Great Plains and Canadian Prairie Experiences, 1929–1941', in Gerald D. Nash and Richard W. Etulain, *The Twentieth Century West: Historical Interpretations* (Albuquerque: University of New Mexico Press, 1989), 175–206; Harry C. McDean, 'Social Scientists and Farm Poverty on the North American Plains, 1933–1940', *Great Plains Quarterly* 3, 1 (1983), 17–29; W.L. Morton, 'The Bias of Prairie Politics', in Donald Swainson, ed., *Historical Essays on the Prairie Provinces* (Toronto: McClelland and Stewart, 1970), 289–300; David R. Elliott and Iris Miller, *Bible Bill: A Biography of William Aberhart* (Edmonton: Reidmore Press, 1987).

7: Prairie Canada Recast: 1940–1971

1. Reginald H. Roy, 'The 7th (Western) Canadian Infantry Brigade', *Saskatchewan History* XXXIV, 3 (Autumn 1981), 102–12.

2. Fred Hatch, 'Wings of War', *Horizon Canada* 5 (1987), 2396–400; Ken Tingley, ed., *For King and Country: Alberta in the Second World War* (Edmonton: Reidmore Books, 1995).

3. Howard Palmer, 'Ethnic Relations in Wartime: Nationalism and European Minorities in Alberta during the Second World War', *Canadian Ethnic Studies* XIV, 3 (1982), 1–23; John Herd Thompson, *Ethnic Minorities in Two World Wars* (Ottawa: Canadian Historical Association, 1993).

4. Peter Melnycky, 'Alberta's Ukrainians During the Second World War', in Tingley, *For King and Country,* 327–44.

5. James Dempsey, 'Alberta's Indians and the Second World War', in Tingley, *For King and Country,* 39–52; James R. Miller, *Skyscrapers Hide the Heavens: A History of Indian-White Relations in Canada* (Toronto: University of Toronto Press, 1989), Chapter 12.

6. Ian MacPherson and John Herd Thompson, 'An Orderly Reconstruction: Prairie Agriculture in World War Two', *Canadian Papers in Rural History* IV (1984), 11–32.

7. Jake Schulz, *The Rise and Fall of Canadian Farm Organizations* (Winnipeg: n.p., 1955); David Monod, 'The End of Agrarianism: The Fight for Farm Parity in Alberta and Saskatchewan, 1935–48', *Labour/Le Travail,* 16 (1985), 117–43; D'Arcy Hande, 'Parity Prices and the

Farmers' Strike', *Saskatchewan History* XXXVIII, 3 (1985), 81–96; James N. McCrorie, 'The Saskatchewan Farmers' Movement: A Case Study' (Ph.D. thesis, University of Illinois, 1972).

8. Seymour Martin Lipset, *Agrarian Socialism: The Cooperative Commonwealth Federation in Saskatchewan* (Berkeley: University of California Press, 1950); Lewis H. Thomas, 'The CCF Victory in Saskatchewan, 1944', *Saskatchewan History* XXXIV, 1 (1981), 1–16.

9. J. William Brennan, ed., *Building the Co-operative Commonwealth: Essays on the Democratic Socialist Tradition in Canada* (Regina: Canadian Plains Research Center, 1985); John H. Archer, *Saskatchewan: A History* (Saskatoon: Western Producer Prairie Books, 1980), Chapter 14.

10. Nelson Wiseman, *Social Democracy in Manitoba: A History of the CCF-NDP* (Winnipeg: University of Manitoba Press, 1983), Chapter 4.

11. Alvin Finkel, *The Social Credit Phenomenon in Alberta* (Toronto: University of Toronto Press, 1989); David E. Smith, 'A Comparison of Prairie Political Developments in Saskatchewan and Alberta', *Journal of Canadian Studies* 4 (1969), 21–4; Myron Johnson, 'The Failure of the CCF in Alberta: An Accident of History', in Carlos Caldarola, ed., *Society and Politics in Alberta* (Toronto: Methuen, 1979), 87–107.

12. James G. MacGregor, *A History of Alberta* (Edmonton: Hurtig, 1972), Chapter 19; John Richards and Larry Pratt, *Prairie Capitalism: Power and Influence in the New West* (Toronto: McClelland and Stewart, 1979).

13. John Conway, *The West: The History of a Region in Confederation*, 2nd edn (Toronto: James Lorimer, 1994), Chapter 7.

14. Gerald Friesen, 'The Prairie West Since 1945: An Historical Survey', in A.W. Rasporich, ed., *The Making of the Modern West: Western Canada Since 1945* (Calgary: University of Calgary Press, 1984), 1–35; T.R. Weir, 'The Population', in P.J. Smith, ed., *The Prairie Provinces* (Toronto: University of Toronto Press, 1972), 83–98.

15. P.J. Smith, 'Changing Forms and Patterns in the Cities', in Smith, ed., *The Prairie Provinces*, 99–117.

16. Barry Broadfoot, *Next-Year Country: Voices of Prairie People* (Toronto: McClelland and Stewart, 1988), 121–4.

17. W. Peter Ward, 'Population Growth in Western Canada, 1901–1971', in John E. Foster, ed., *The Developing West: Essays in Canadian History in Honour of Lewis H. Thomas* (Edmonton: University of Alberta Press, 1983), 155–77.

18. Roger Gibbins, *Prairie Politics and Society: Regionalism in Decline* (Toronto: Butterworth, 1980), Chapter 3.

19. Denis Smith, *Rogue Tory: The Life and Legend of John G. Diefenbaker* (Toronto: Macfarlane, Walter and Ross, 1995).

20. J.L. Granatstein, 'Medicare: Saskatchewan Moves the Nation', in *Canada 1957–1967: Years of Uncertainty and Innovation* (Toronto: McClelland and Stewart, 1986), 169–97.

21. David E. Smith, *The Regional Decline of a National Party: Liberals on the Prairies* (Toronto: University of Toronto Press, 1981).

22. James M. Pitsula, 'The Saskatchewan CCF Government and Treaty Indians, 1944–1964', *Canadian Historical Review* LXXV, 1 (1994), 21–52; James R. Miller, *Skyscrapers Hide the Heavens: A History of Indian-White Relations in Canada* (Toronto: University of Toronto Press, 1989), Chapter 12; Olive Dickason, *Canada's First Nations: A History of Founding Peoples from the Earliest Times* (Toronto: McClelland and Stewart, 1992), Part V.

23. Brenton M. Barr, 'Reorganization of the Economy since 1945', in Smith, ed., *The Prairie Provinces*, 65–81.

8: The New West and the Nation

1. Peter C. Newman, 'Western Canada's Sense of Isolation Deepens', Kingston *Whig-Standard*, 17 Jan. 1970.

2. Thomas Peterson, 'Manitoba: Ethnic and Class Politics', in Martin Robin, ed., *Canadian Provincial Politics: The Party Systems of the Ten Provinces* (Toronto: Prentice-Hall, 1972); Nelson

Wiseman, *Social Democracy in Manitoba: A History of the CCF-NDP* (Winnipeg: University of Manitoba Press, 1983), Chapter 6.

3. David K. Elton and Arthur M. Goddard, 'The Conservative Takeover, 1971– ,' in Carlos Caldarola, ed., *Society and Politics in Alberta: Research Papers* (Toronto: Methuen, 1979), 49–70.

4. Peter Desbarats, 'West's Diverging Provinces Share Distrust of East', Montreal *Gazette*, 24 Nov. 1971; John Richards and Larry Pratt, *Prairie Capitalism: Power and Influence in the New West* (Toronto: McClelland and Stewart, 1979); Jack Ludwig, 'The Seventies Belong to Lougheed', *Maclean's* (July 1975), 19–23.

5. Nick Hills, 'Western Premiers Hang Tough in Gang-up on Ottawa', Montreal *Gazette*, 4 April 1973.

6. Peter Desbarats, 'Western Independence Drive Quiet, but Discontent Lingers', Montreal *Gazette*, 17 Nov. 1971; Nick Hills, 'Separatist Group May Run Against Alberta's Premier', Montreal *Gazette*, 5 Feb. 1975; Larry Pratt and Garth Stevenson, eds, *Western Separatism: The Myths, Realities, and Dangers* (Edmonton: Hurtig, 1981).

7. 'Alberta: The New Industrial State', *Time* (5 Aug. 1974), 5–11; Suzanne Zwarun, 'Alberta Gold', *Maclean's* (18 April 1977).

8. Harry Bruce, 'After All, We Invented Alberta', *Toronto Star* 11 Dec. 1974; Jon H. Pammett, 'Public Orientation to Regions and Provinces', in David J. Bellamy, Pammett, and Donald C. Rowat, eds, *The Provincial Political Systems: Comparative Essays* (Toronto: Methuen, 1976), 86–99.

9. Jack Ludwig: 'Get an Outfit, Be a Cowboy', *Maclean's* (July 1975).

10. G.S. Basran and D.A. Hay, eds, *The Political Economy of Agriculture in Western Canada* (Toronto: Garamond, 1988); Barry Wilson, *Beyond the Harvest: Canadian Grain at the Crossroads* (Saskatoon: Western Producer Prairie Books, 1981).

11. Garry Fairbairn, *From Prairie Roots: The Remarkable Story of the Saskatchewan Wheat Pool* (Saskatoon: Western Producer Prairie Books, 1982); Grace Skogstad, 'Farmers and Farm Unions in the Society and Politics of Alberta', in Carlos Caldarola, ed., *Society and Politics in Alberta: Research Papers* (Toronto: Methuen, 1979), 223–55.

12. Linda Gerber, 'The Development of Canadian Indian Communities: A Two-dimensional Typology Reflecting Strategies of Adaptation to the Modern World', *Canadian Review of Sociology and Anthropology*, 16 (1979), 404–24; J. Rick Ponting and Roger Gibbins, *Out of Irrelevance: A Socio-Political Introduction to Indian Affairs in Canada* (Toronto: Butterworth, 1980).

13. J. Arthur Lower, *Western Canada: An Outline History* (Vancouver: Douglas and McIntyre, 1982), 263–4.

14. J.D. House, *The Last of the Free Enterprisers: The Oilmen of Calgary* (Toronto: Macmillan, 1980.)

15. J.F. Conway, *The West: The History of a Region in Confederation*, 2nd edn (Toronto: James Lorimer, 1994), Chapter 8.

16. Andrew Nikiforuk, Sheila Pratt, and Don Wanagas, *Running on Empty: Alberta after the Boom* (Edmonton: NeWest, 1987).

17. I.L. McCreary and W.H. Furtan, 'Income Distribution and Agricultural Policies', *Prairie Forum* 13, 2 (1988), 241–50.

18. David Jay Bercuson and Barry Cooper, *Deconfederation: Canada without Quebec* (Toronto: Key Porter, 1991); Thomas Flanagan, *Waiting for the Wave: the Reform Party and Preston Manning* (Toronto: Stoddart, 1995); W.L. Morton, 'The Bias of Prairie Politics', in Donald Swainson, ed., *Historical Essays on the Prairie Provinces* (Toronto: McClelland and Stewart, 1970), 289–300.

19. 'How the West has won the jobs race', *Globe and Mail*, 13 May 1996; Peter C. Newman, 'CP Ltd.: Betting on the West's dominance', *Maclean's* (20 May 1996), 44; 'Old Alberta Moon', quoted by permission of Ian Tyson, Longview, AB.

Selected Bibliography

Other Bibliographies

Artibise, Alan F.J. *Western Canada since 1870: A Select Bibliography and Guide*. Vancouver: University of British Columbia Press, 1978.

Friesen, Gerald. 'Historical Writing on the Prairie West'. Pp. 1–26 in R. Douglas Francis and Howard Palmer, eds. *The Prairie West: Historical Readings*. Edmonton: University of Alberta Press, 1992.

Peel, Bruce Braden. *A Bibliography of the Prairie Provinces to 1953*. 2nd edn. Toronto: University of Toronto Press, 1973.

Thompson, John Herd. 'The West and the North'. Pp. 341–73 in Doug Owram, ed. *Canadian History: A Reader's Guide*. Vol. 2. *Confederation to the Present*. Toronto: University of Toronto Press, 1994.

General Histories

Archer, John H. *Saskatchewan: A History*. Saskatoon: Western Producer Prairie Books, 1980.

Cavanaugh, Catherine, and Jeremy Mouat, eds. *Making Western Canada: Essays on European Colonization and Settlement*. Toronto: Garamond Press, 1996.

Conway, John. *The West: The History of a Region in Confederation*. 2nd edn. Toronto: James Lorimer, 1994.

Friesen, Gerald. *The Canadian Prairies: A History*. Toronto: University of Toronto Press, 1984.

Lower, J. Arthur. *Western Canada: An Outline History*. Vancouver: Douglas and McIntyre, 1982.

Morton, W.L. *Manitoba: A History*. Toronto: University of Toronto Press, 1967.

Palmer, Howard and Tamara. *Alberta: A New History*. Edmonton: Hurtig, 1990.

Swainson, Donald. *Historical Essays on the Prairie Provinces*. Toronto: McClelland and Stewart, 1970.

The Fur Trade

Francis, Dan. *Battle for the West: The Fur Traders and the Birth of Western Canada*. Edmonton: Hurtig, 1983.

Francis, Dan, and Toby Morantz. *Partners in Furs: A History of the Fur Trade in Eastern James Bay, 1600–1870*. Montreal: McGill-Queen's University Press, 1983.

Ray, Arthur J. *Indians in the Fur Trade: Their Role as Trappers, Hunters, and Middlemen in the Lands Southwest of Hudson Bay, 1660–1870*. Toronto: University of Toronto Press, 1974.

Rich, E.E. *The Fur Trade and the Northwest to 1857*. Toronto: McClelland and Stewart, 1967.

Williams, Glyndwer. *The Hudson's Bay Company and the Fur Trade: 1670–1870*. Winnipeg: HBC, 1987. A special issue of the magazine *The Beaver*.

Native Peoples

Carter, Sarah. *Lost Harvests: Prairie Indian Reserve Farmers and Government Policy*. Montreal:

McGill-Queen's University Press, 1990.

Dickason, Olive P. *Canada's First Nations: A History of Founding Peoples from Earliest Times*. Toronto: McClelland and Stewart, 1992.

Elias, Peter. *The Dakota of the Canadian Northwest: Lessons for Survival*. Winnipeg: University of Manitoba Press, 1988.

Miller, J.R. *Skyscrapers Hide the Heavens: A History of Indian-White Relations in Canada*. Toronto: University of Toronto Press,1989; 2nd edn 1993.

Milloy, John S. *The Plains Cree: Trade, Diplomacy, and War, 1790–1870*. Winnipeg: University of Manitoba Press, 1988.

Peers, Laura. *The Ojibwa of Western Canada, 1780–1870*. Winnipeg: University of Manitoba Press, 1994.

Samek, Hana. *The Blackfoot Confederacy 1880–1920: A Comparative Study of Canadian and U.S. Indian Policy*. Albuquerque: University of New Mexico Press, 1987.

The Métis

Beal, Bob, and Rod Macleod. *Prairie Fire: The 1885 North-West Rebellion*. Edmonton: Hurtig, 1984.

Ens, Gerhard. *Homeland to Hinterland: Changing Worlds of the Red River Métis in the Nineteenth Century*. Toronto: University of Toronto, 1996.

Flanagan, Thomas. *Louis 'David' Riel: Prophet of the New World*. Toronto: University of Toronto Press, 1979.

Pannekoek, Frits. *A Snug Little Flock: The Social Origins of the Riel Resistance 1869–70*. Winnipeg: Watson and Dwyer, 1991.

Sprague, D.N. *Canada and the Métis, 1869–1885*. Waterloo, ON: Wilfrid Laurier University Press, 1988.

Stanley, George F. *The Birth of Western Canada: A History of the Riel Rebellions*. Toronto: University of Toronto Press, 1936.

Making the Prairies Canadian

Buckley, Helen. *From Wooden Ploughs to Welfare: Why Indian Policy Failed in the Prairie Provinces*. Montreal: McGill-Queen's University Press, 1992.

den Otter, A.A. *Civilizing the West: The Galts and the Development of Western Canada*. Edmonton: University of Alberta Press, 1982.

Hall, David J. *Clifford Sifton*. Vol. 1. *The Young Napoleon, 1861–1900*. Vol. 2. *The Lonely Eminence, 1901–1929*. Vancouver: University of British Columbia Press, 1981, 1985.

Macleod, R.G. *The North-West Mounted Police and Law Enforcement 1873–1905*. Toronto: University of Toronto Press, 1976.

Martin, Chester. *'Dominion Lands' Policy*. Toronto: Macmillan, 1937. Re-issued with an excellent introduction by L.H. Thomas (McClelland and Stewart, 1973).

Owram, Doug. *Promise of Eden: The Canadian Expansionist Movement and the Idea of the West, 1856–1900*. Toronto: University of Toronto Press, 1980. Reprinted with a new preface, 1992.

Pettipas, Katherine. *Severing the Ties that Bind: Government Repression of Indigenous Religious Ceremonies on the Prairies*. Winnipeg: University of Manitoba Press, 1994.

Thomas, Lewis H. *The Struggle for Responsible Government in the North West Territories, 1870–1897*. Toronto: University of Toronto Press, 1956; 1978.

Tobias, John. 'Canada's Subjugation of the Plains Cree, 1879–1885'. *Canadian Historical Review*, 1983.

Farming, Ranching, and Environmental Change

Bennett, John W., and Seena B. Kohl. *Settling the Canadian-American West: Pioneer Adaptation and Community Building*. Lincoln: University of Nebraska Press, 1996.

Breen, David. *The Canadian Prairie West and the Ranching Frontier 1874–1924*. Toronto: University of Toronto Press, 1982.

Dick, Lyle. *Farmers 'Making Good': The Development of Abernethy District, Saskatchewan, 1880–1920*. Ottawa: Parks Canada, 1989.

Fowke, V.C. *The National Policy and the Wheat Economy*. Toronto: University of Toronto Press 1957, 1973.

Jones, David C., and Ian MacPherson, eds. *Building Beyond the Homestead*. Calgary: University of Calgary Press, 1985.

Nelson, J.G. *Man's Impact on the Western Canadian Landscape*. Toronto: McClelland and Stewart, 1976.

Potyondi, Barry. *In Palliser's Triangle: Living in the Grasslands, 1850–1930*. Saskatoon: Purich Publishing, 1995.

Taylor, Jeffery. *Fashioning Farmers: Ideology, Agricultural Knowledge, and the Manitoba Farm Movement, 1890–1925*. Regina: Canadian Plains Research Center, 1994.

Voisey, Paul. *Vulcan: The Making of A Prairie Community*. Toronto: University of Toronto Press, 1988.

Building Railways and an Urban Network

Artibise, Alan F.J. *Winnipeg: An Illustrated History*. Toronto: James Lorimer, 1977.

Brennan, J.W. *Regina: An Illustrated History*. Toronto: James Lorimer, 1989.

Dempsey, Hugh A. ed. *The CPR West: The Iron Road and the Making of a Nation*. Vancouver: Douglas and McIntyre, 1984.

Eagle, John A. *The Canadian Pacific Railway and the Development of Western Canada, 1896–1914*. Montreal: McGill-Queen's University Press, 1989.

Foran, Max. *Calgary: An Illustrated History*. Toronto: James Lorimer, 1978.

Regehr, T.D. *The Canadian Northern Railway: Pioneer Road of the Northern Prairies 1895–1918*. Toronto: University of Toronto Press, 1976.

Ethnicity, Class, and Gender

Avery, Donald H. *'Dangerous Foreigners': European Immigrant Workers and Labour Radicalism in Canada, 1896–1932*. Toronto: McClelland and Stewart, 1979.

Bercuson, David J. *Confrontation at Winnipeg: Labour, Industrial Relations and the General Strike*. Montreal: McGill–Queen's University Press, 1974. Revised edn, 1990.

Danysk, Cecelia. *Hired Hands: Labour and the Development of Prairie Agriculture, 1880–1930*. Toronto: McClelland and Stewart, 1995.

Fairbanks, Carol, and Sara Brooks Sundberg. *Farm Women on the Prairie Frontier*. New Jersey: Scarecrow Press 1983.

Kinnear, Mary, ed. *First Days, Fighting Days: Women in Manitoba History*. Regina: Canadian Plains Research Center 1987.

Loewen, Royden. *Family, Church and Market: A Mennonite Community in the Old and New Worlds, 1850–1930*. Urbana: University of Illinois Press 1993.

McCormack, A. Ross. *Reformers, Rebels, and Revolutionaries: The Western Canadian Radical Movement 1899–1919*. Toronto: University of Toronto Press, 1977.

Palmer, Howard. *Patterns of Prejudice: A History of Nativism in Alberta*. Toronto: McClelland and Stewart, 1982.

Petryshyn, Jaroslav. *Peasants in the Promised Land: Canada and the Ukrainians, 1891–1914*. Toronto: James Lorimer, 1985.

Swyripa, Frances. *Wedded to the Cause: Ukrainian-Canadian Women and Ethnic Identity, 1891–1991*. Toronto: University of Toronto Press, 1993.

Strong-Boag, Veronica. 'Pulling in Double Harness or Hauling a Double Load: Women, Work and Feminism on the Canadian Prairie'. *Journal of Canadian Studies* 21, 3 (1986), 32–52.

Thompson, John Herd. *The Harvests of War: The Prairie West, 1914–1918*. Toronto: McClelland and Stewart, 1978.

Intellectual History

Davidson, Arnold E. *Coyote Country: Fictions of the Canadian West*. Durham, NC: Duke University Press, 1994.

Fairbanks, Carol. *Prairie Women: Images in American and Canadian Fiction*. New Haven: Yale University Press 1986.

Francis, R. Douglas. *Images of the West: Changing Perceptions of the Canadian Prairies, 1690–1960*. Saskatoon: Western Producer Prairie Books, 1989.

Harrison, Dick. *Unnamed Country: The Struggle for a*

Canadian Prairie Fiction. Edmonton: University of Alberta Press, 1977.

Rees, Ronald. *Land of Earth and Sky: Landscape Painting of Western Canada*. Saskatoon: Western Producer Prairie Books, 1984.

Ricou, Laurie. *Vertical Man/Horizontal World: Man and Landscape in Canadian Prairie Fiction*. Vancouver: University of British Columbia Press, 1973.

Wetherall, Donald G., and Irene Kmet. *Useful Pleasures: The Shaping of Leisure in Alberta, 1896–1945*. Regina: Canadian Plains Research Center, 1990.

Political History

Brennan, J.W. ed. *Building the Co-operative Commonwealth: Essays on the Democratic Socialist Tradition in Canada*. Regina: Canadian Plains Research Center, 1985.

Caldarola, Carlos. ed. *Society and Politics in Alberta*. Toronto: Methuen, 1979.

Elliot, David, and Iris Miller. *Bible Bill: A Biography of William Aberhart*. Edmonton: Reidmore Books, 1987.

Finkel, Alvin. *The Social Credit Phenomenon in Alberta*. Toronto: University of Toronto Press, 1989.

Gibbins, Roger. *Prairie Politics and Society: Regionalism in Decline*. Toronto: Butterworth, 1980.

Kendle, John. *John Bracken: A Political Biography*. Toronto: University of Toronto Press, 1979.

Laycock, David. *Populism and Democratic Thought in the Canadian Prairies, 1910–1945*. Toronto: University of Toronto Press, 1990.

Lipset, S.M. *Agrarian Socialism: The Cooperative Commonwealth Federation in Saskatchewan; A Study in Political Sociology*. Berkeley: University of California Press 1950; 2nd ed. NY: Doubleday Anchor, 1968).

Macpherson, C.B. *Democracy in Alberta: Social Credit and the Party System*. Toronto: University of Toronto Press, 1953.

Morton, W.L. *The Progressive Party in Canada*. Toronto: University of Toronto Press, 1950.

Sharp, Paul F. *The Agrarian Revolt in Western Canada*. Minneapolis: University of Minnesota Press 1948.

Smith, David E. *Prairie Liberalism: The Liberal Party in Saskatchewan 1905–71*. Toronto: University of Toronto Press, 1975.

Thomas, Lewis G. *The Liberal Party in Alberta: A History of Politics in the Province of Alberta 1905–1921*. Toronto: University of Toronto Press, 1959.

Wiseman, Nelson. *Social Democracy in Manitoba: A History of the CCF–NDP*. Winnipeg: University of Manitoba Press, 1983.

Young, Walter D. *Democracy and Discontent: Progressivism, Socialism and Social Credit in the Canadian West*. 1969; 2nd edn. Toronto: McGraw-Hill Ryerson, 1978.

The Prairie West Transformed

Badgley, Robin F., and Samuel Wolfe. *Doctor's Strike: Medical Care and Conflict in Saskatchewan*. Toronto: Macmillan, 1967.

Basran, G.S., and D.A. Hay, eds. *The Political Economy of Agriculture in Western Canada*. Toronto: Garamond Press, 1988.

Eisler, Dale. *Rumours of Glory: Saskatchewan and the Thatcher Years*. Edmonton: Hurtig, 1987.

Richards, John, and Larry Pratt. *Prairie Capitalism: Power and Influence in the New West*. Toronto: McClelland and Stewart, 1979.

Smith, David E. *The Regional Decline of a National Party: Liberals on the Prairies*. Toronto: University of Toronto Press, 1981.

Wilson, Barry. *Politics of Defeat: The Decline of the Liberal Party in Saskatchewan*. Saskatoon: Western Producer Prairie Books, 1980.

——. *Beyond the Harvest: Canadian Grain at the Crossroads*. Saskatoon: Western Producer Prairie Books, 1981.

US Comparisons

Limerick, Patricia Nelson. *The Legacy of Conquest: The Unbroken Past of the American West*. New York: W.W. Norton, 1987.

Nugent, Walter. 'Comparing Wests and Frontiers'. Pp. 803–34 in Clyde A. Milner et al., eds. *The Oxford History of the American West*. New York: Oxford University Press, 1994.

Robbins, William G. *Colony and Empire: the Capitalist Transformation of the American West.* Lawrence: University Press of Kansas, 1994.

White, Richard *'It's Your Misfortune and None of My Own': A History of the American West.* Norman: University of Oklahoma Press, 1991.

INDEX

PLEASE NOTE: Page numbers in italic type refer to illustration captions.